THOMAS DE QUINCEY'S RELUCTANT AUTOBIOGRAPHY

Thomas DeQuincey's *Reluctant* Autobiography

JOHN C. WHALE

CROOM HELM
London & Sydney

BARNES & NOBLE BOOKS
Totowa, New Jersey

Croom Helm Ltd, Provident House, Burrell Row,
Beckenham, Kent BR3 1AT

Croom Helm Australia Pty Ltd, First Floor, 139 King Street,
Sydney, NSW 2001, Australia

British Library Cataloguing in Publication Data

Whale, John C.
Thomas de Quincey's reluctant autobiography.
1. De Quincey, Thomas – Criticism and
interpretation
I. Title
828'.808 PR4537

ISBN 0-7099-3615-X

First published in the USA 1984 by
Barnes & Noble Books
81 Adams Drive,
Totowa, New Jersey, 07512

Library of Congress Cataloging in Publication Data

Whale, John C.
Thomas De Quincey's reluctant autobiography.

Includes bibliographical references.
1. De Quincey, Thomas, 1785-1859. 2. De Quincey,
Thomas, 1785-1859 – Technique. 3. Authors, English – 19th
century – Biography. I. Title.
PR4537.W47 1984 828'.809 83-27511
ISBN 0-389-20461-7

Printed and bound in Great Britain

CONTENTS

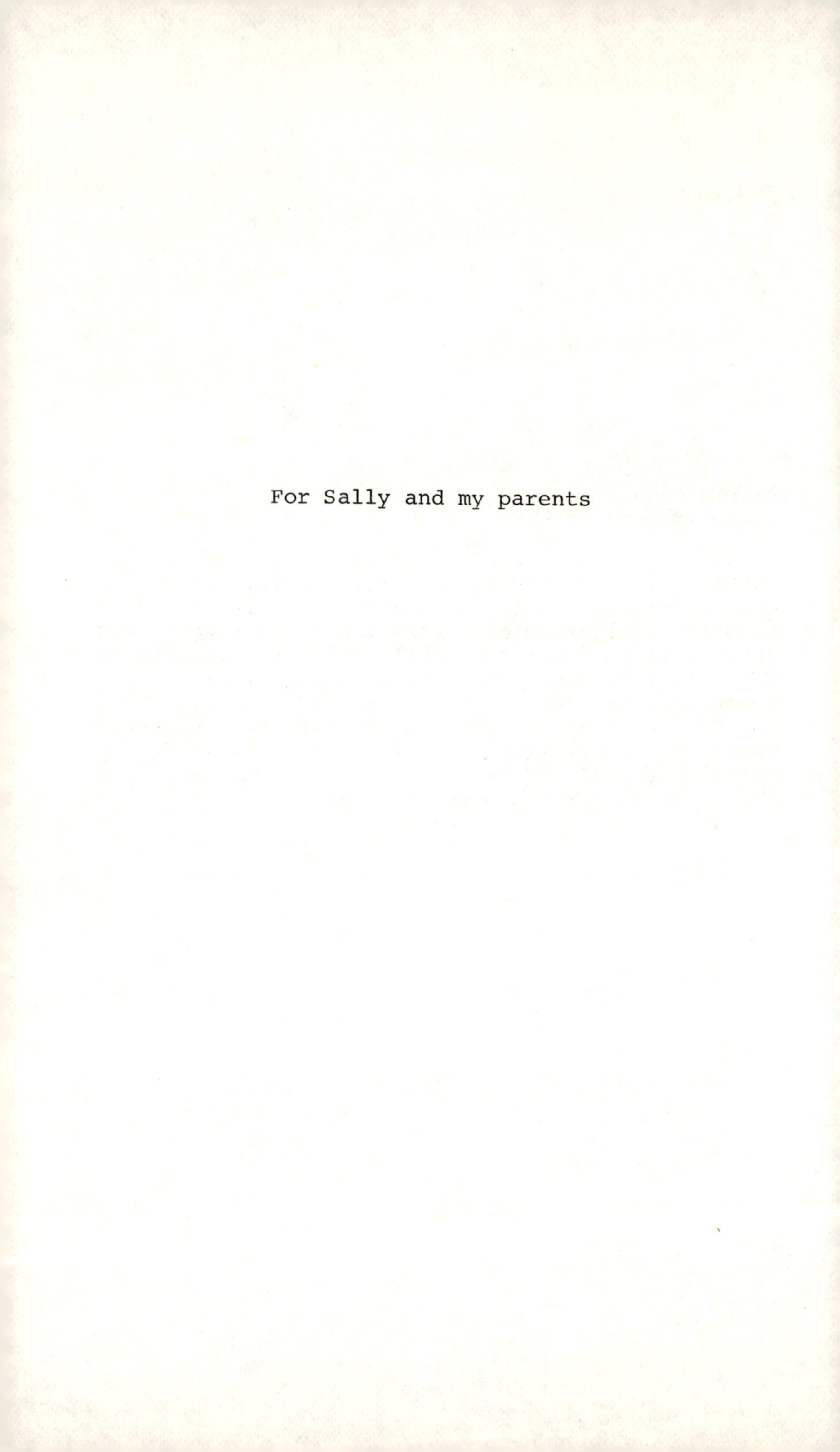
For Sally and my parents

A TEXTUAL NOTE

References to De Quincey's works are usually to David Masson's standard, but incomplete edition of 1889-90. Where the earlier version of *Confessions of an English Opium-Eater* is referred to I have followed the text of Aileen Ward's edition (New York, 1966) based on the 1822 book form. David Wright's edition of *Recollections of the Lakes and the Lake Poets* (Harmondsworth, 1970) has been used because it is the most complete collection. The original Blackwood's texts of *Suspiria de Profundis* and *The English Mail-Coach* have been used in Chapter Three where those works are considered in some detail.

ACKNOWLEDGEMENTS

Special thanks are due to Patricia M. Ball who supervised the original research project: I am grateful for her guidance and her example. Thanks are also due to the friends and colleagues who helped and encouraged me in the Department of English at University College Cardiff and in the School of English at the University of Leeds, especially to Peter Garside who read an earlier draft at a crucial stage. I am grateful to the Editors of _Essays in Criticism_ for permission to reprint a version of 'De Quincey's Anarchic Moments' (vol. XXXIII, 1983, no. 4). Most thanks of all are due to Sally.

INTRODUCTION

De Quincey provides a valuable example of how an imaginative talent, in some respects typical of the isolated Romantic artist, was forced to comply with a more immediate regard for social sanction. Despite his own well-known adverse reaction to his career as a journalist De Quincey's works find many ways to successfully exploit the opportunities afforded by their context. His various autobiographical writings move between the extremes of provocative confession, lyrical introspection, moralistic declaration and polite anecdotage. De Quincey inherited a familiar and specific type of contact with his public which presented him with some difficulties, but which also answered some of his specialist requirements. Even though his work reveals the pressure of its context, the world of the magazines was not entirely antagonistic to the demands of a Romantic autobiographer.

That De Quincey 'could speak of confidentiality as an ability rather than a failure of restraint'[1] points to the specialist nature of the autobiographer's task. Even if the public reception of his work was likely to be sympathetic it did not offset the difficulties involved in literary self-exploration. For De Quincey autobiography was not simply a 'record' or communication of his past life to his readership. The link between the writer and the reader offered a mediatory possibility allowing for a greater degree of indirectness, because the act of autobiography was not solely referential but dramatic and revelatory. As Roy Pascal says:

> The life is represented in autobiography not as something established but as a process; it is not simply the narrative of the voyage, but the voyage itself. There must be in it a sense of

> discovery, and where this is wanting, and the autobiography appears as an exposition of something understood from the beginning, we feel it a failure[2]

Although the original motive might be to register past experiences, since emotional experience now has a special public as well as a private credence, the retrospective judgement and linguistic techniques of the autobiographer encourage the creation of a work which is more than naïvely commemorative. There is a potentially vital friction between a belief in the value of past emotional experience and the techniques used to analyse it. In De Quincey's case, this disparity in autobiography brings him closer to the central Romantic poetic predicament articulated by Robert Langbaum:

> the essential idea of romanticism ... is, I would suggest, the doctrine of experience - the doctrine that the imaginative apprehension gained through immediate experience is primary and certain, whereas the analytic reflection that follows is secondary and problematical. The poetry of the nineteenth and twentieth centuries can thus be seen in connection as a poetry of experience - a poetry constructed upon the deliberate disequilibrium between experience and idea, a poetry which makes its statement not as an idea but as an experience from which one or more ideas can be abstracted as problematical rationalisations.[3]

The importance of De Quincey's autobiographical writings lies in this quality of providing a dramatic enactment of personality which facilitates a further definition of and therefore a development away from the primary experience. Reference to the past self and its experience is the starting-point for new considerations and consequent gains in self-knowledge. The emphasis is on the change effected by the retrospective vision. The fundamental principle of Romantic creativity, as Patricia Ball says,

> is not self-expression, but self-exploration and discovery. The poems are the living substance of this inquiry, the one method of scrutinizing experience without loss of its subjective immediacy. The self is indeed the starting point of such poetry, but it is also its goal, only to be known by being

> imaginatively grasped as it weaves the complex web of its own experience ... The poets are alert to the complexity of the experiencing self, they regard identity not as an evident fact but as an ultimate achievement, its realised possession both the motive and the reward for creative exertion.[4]

The complications that immediately arise upon adopting the retrospective position of the autobiographer are, in short, the disparity between the writer's sense of being a private individual and a member of the public, and the related fact that self-consciousness might lead to self-alienation. Stephen Spender considers the former as, perhaps, the initial difficulty which faces an autobiographer:

> Yet unless one is to oneself entirely public, it seems that the problem of an autobiographer, when he considers the material of his own past, is that he is confronted not by one life - which he sees from the outside - but by two.[5]

As Spender's essay continues this fairly simple idea develops to accommodate his belief that 'in literature the autobiographical is transformed'.[6] A sense of surprise or a recognition of discovery is often present as a result of these two basic reasons for transformation. Ruskin states quite simply in Praeterita: 'For as I look deeper into the mirror, I find myself a more curious person than I had thought'.[7] Even in this work, which professes to operate upon a 'fixed resolve to set down the facts continuously',[8] the autobiography offers an unexpected portrait of personality, so that Ruskin finds it necessary (which is uncharacteristic) to interrupt his continuous statement by making a direct appeal to the reader: 'it becomes at this point desirable that I should know, or at least try to guess, something of what the reader's reflections *are*! and whether in the main he is getting at the sense of the facts I tell him'.[9]

Such a need to define the relationship between the autobiographer and his reader may be seen as a form of mediation in some ways characteristic of a 'confessional' technique. It allows for greater control at the same time as promoting the specific purpose of the autobiographer. As Frank D. McConnell has said of this aspect of the confessional imagination - 'The audience ... is simultaneously, a projection of the confessor's personality and a strict limit to that personality's expansion'.[10] Similarly, 'the drive of *The Prelude* toward mediation is not an evasion or refusal of visionary power but a means to that power'.[11] De Quincey's ability to anticipate the response of his readership, and to carefully pre-determine it, rather than being considered a belittling concession, can be seen to be a necessary preparation for an extreme autobiographical vision.

An awareness of this particular link with the public makes it possible to explore Mario Praz's claim that, 'From humble, commonplace starting-points, De Quincey escapes at once into a magic universe'[12] and to develop his depiction of a bourgeois opium-eater with a Victorian morality. The problem before the autobiographer is to find an audience and win its sympathy as well as being true to a vision of himself. For this reason De Quincey's autobiography partially refutes Georges Poulet's statement that: 'De Quincey and Baudelaire were inclined to escape from the narrow track of ordinary time, and to try to create for themselves and maintain as long as possible, the illusion of an artificial eternity'.[13] De Quincey would have realised how such an 'escape' could endanger the sympathy of his audience. The claim of veracity which is one of the distinguishing characteristics of an autobiography is dependent upon an ability to 'convince' the reader:

> All that is required of the autobiographer - it is a very large "all" - is that his language and his design answer to the truth of his experience. We cannot ascertain whether it in fact does, for obviously we have no independent check on how it felt to live his life. But he must convince us that the book is living up to the truth.[14]

The presentation of experience that we are given is inevitably susceptible to the needs of this relationship. When it manifests itself in forms of apology and justification the autobiographical statement is necessarily and desirably indirect.

Not because it provided a straightforward reception for a purely descriptive autobiographical vision, but because it was distanced from a direct introspection, the periodical context allowed De Quincey to approach his own intimate experience from an angle which opened up new possibilities - both for himself and for his audience. Of course, as in the case of opium, he also had extraordinary experiential events to reveal to his public so that he performed a double function. In the very act of delivery he could find new possibilities and changed conclusions. Due to his context the public commentator might work simultaneously, or in alternation with the isolated, privately lyrical autobiographer.

In this respect the periodical setting most probably exaggerated the polarities in De Quincey's work already present as a result of the transitional era in which he lived. The public platform operating alongside the earnest autobiographical statement means that he has much in common with the Victorian sage as described by John Holloway.[15] Like Carlyle he 'constantly invites the reader to meditate humbly and carefully on some assertion that he admits is essentially simple. The kind of understanding that he has at heart is a kind which supervenes upon dutiful attentiveness'.[16] In De Quincey's case this is because he makes general declarations from experiential knowledge. His autobiographical concerns converge with those of the Victorians not only in such preoccupations as the pariah figure and the London landscape, but also in the techniques of delivery which are available in such a context.

De Quincey had to attune himself to a fairly large and demanding public and managed to do so with some success, especially in the case of the <u>Confessions</u>. His journalistic context provided a pressure which informs his insights into and sensitivity towards language, so that his work transcends any claims that it is simply the production of a pioneer literary psychologist. Just as Albert Goldman's study of De Quincey's scholarly, often pretentious journalism reveals 'fresh evidence of his capacity as an imaginative writer',[17] so in examining the more important autobiographical works a wider and more specific significance can be claimed for them, not by emphasising their extreme nature, but by analysing their tactical presentation of experience.

This presentation is partly determined by the type and the variety of techniques available in such magazine writing. De Quincey's extensive work in the field of autobiography reveals a consistent process of interaction between the dictates of the magazines and a Romantic exploration of experience. An examination of this relationship as it manifests itself in the two versions of <u>Confessions of an English Opium-Eater</u>, <u>Suspiria de Profundis</u>, <u>Autobiographic Sketches</u>, <u>The English Mail-Coach</u> and

Recollections of the Lakes and the Lake Poets, need not travesty the individuality of the different texts. There is a recognisable method uniting these separate though related works. De Quincey's reluctant autobiography displays a method which uses the tactics of a difficult context to represent and interpret the significance of his past experience.

NOTES

1. Elizabeth Bruss, *Autobiographical Acts* (Baltimore and London, 1976), p. 93.
2. Roy Pascal, *Design and Truth in Autobiography* (London, 1960), p. 82.
3. Robert Langbaum, *The Poetry of Experience* (London, 1957), p. 28.
4. Patricia M. Ball, *The Central Self* (London, 1968), p. 64.
5. Stephen Spender, 'Confessions and Autobiography' in *The Making of a Poem* (London, 1955), p. 64.
6. Ibid., p. 65.
7. John Ruskin, *Praeterita*, *The Works of John Ruskin*, E.T. Cook and Alexander Wedderburn (eds.) (London, 1908), vol. XXXV, p. 243.
8. Ibid., p. 279.
9. Ibid.
10. Frank D. McConnell, *The Confessional Imagination: A Reading of Wordsworth's Prelude* (Baltimore and London, 1974), p. 44.
11. Ibid., p. 35.
12. Mario Praz, *The Hero in Eclipse in Victorian Fiction* (Oxford, 1956), p. 86.
13. Georges Poulet, 'Timelessness and Romanticism', *Journal of the History of Ideas*, vol. XV, no. 1 (1954), p. 19.
14. John M. Morris, *Versions of the Self* (London/New York, 1966), p. 213.
15. John Holloway, *The Victorian Sage* (New York, 1965, first published 1953).
16. Ibid., pp. 4-5.
17. Albert Goldman, *The Mine and the Mint* (Carbondale and Edwardsville, 1965), p. 10.

Chapter 1

THE PUBLISHER'S DEVIL

At the age of seventeen De Quincey anticipated both in spirit and subject one of the main-springs of his literary activity when he wrote in his diary:

> The intimate connection which exists between the body and the mind, has never (to my knowledge) been sufficiently enlarged on in theory or insisted on in practice. To show the ultimate cause of this ... would be very difficult, though not I think impossible.[1]

This statement provides an early indication of the area which he was to explore through autobiography - his willingness to describe and theorise upon his own bodily and mental conditions. The most important difficulties he faced in undertaking that exploration are recorded throughout his career as a journalist, and are to form the basis of our analysis. De Quincey carried out his self-examinations in a disruptive, unsympathetic context. Although he did not set out directly to analyse his difficulties wholly in the spirit of objective, psychological inquiry, his account of the physical and mental sufferings attendant upon his experience as a periodical writer allows us to appreciate more fully the nature of his autobiographical works.

Assessing initially the isolation and restrictions of his private situation (in the midst of composition, financial difficulties, opium addiction and a complex tangle of personal relationships) we may arrive at a wider understanding of De Quincey's translation of private experience into public statement. The extent of that translation may be measured by the curious, elusive quality characteristic of his autobiographical writings - his reluctance to define the reality of his experience simply by revealing the particularities of this intimate context. Appreciation of De Quincey as a critic of experience in such statements as 'He indeed knew how to analyse the human heart through all its deep windings, but he offers no key of access to his own'[2] and 'along with his self-revelation ran the strictest reticence'[3] at least testifies to the completeness of the translation. The autobiography is both the statement and the process of struggle against the problem of deciphering and transforming experience into words, of constructing a literary personality.

It is in the nature of the resistance, the struggle necessary in first of all experiencing, and later writing about a form of personal revelation which determines the dynamic conflict and therefore the significance of De Quincey's autobiographical writings. To agree with his daughter that 'something must ... be allowed for his great power of expounding his sufferings' because it is 'a power which of itself ... removes him from that extreme of loneliness which has no such outlet' and in which she saw 'the inevitable loneliness of the human spirit' rather than 'a complaint of personal isolation',[4] would be to accept too readily the movement towards a wider significance. The reluctance or struggle manifest in that movement justifies our concern by revealing the process through which the private context leads to the published magazine article.

Out of a situation of personal isolation, distanced through illness and debt from his publishers and his family, De Quincey became aware of the double responsibility he bore to himself as an individual, and to himself as a member of society. The difficulties of reconciling these two facets of identity in his actual situation leads to a problematic relationship between self-assertive, specific statements, and general or abstract statements. The so-called truth of his autobiographical works manifests itself not in one or the other, but in a reciprocal movement between public and private.

The isolation which De Quincey witnessed as a translator and recorder of his own experience was paralleled in his social role of journalist or public commentator. We can see in his autobiographical writings the combined responsibilities of fidelity to personal experience and belief in the value of presenting such experience to his readership. The earnestness with which he faced such responsibilities and gauged their difficulty is revealed in the following extract from a letter:

> The literature of an infant, its preferences and memorable experiences, and above all, a circumstantial account of those passages in its reading which were awakening enough to shock, to startle, and awe-strike, or profound enough to become life-long remembrances, would unquestionably (if recorded with the sincerity of self-attesting truth which I have made it a point of religion to observe) most profitably enlarge the drowsy realms of psychology ... as soon as ever any the most positive experience does not quadrate with popular ideas, as in mesmeric phenomena, everybody treats the experience with laughter and scorn, showing thus the most obstinate hostility ... The passages which I have recorded as so durably affecting myself are not gathered from books; the reader sees that they report real and not counterfeit experiences.[5]

In order to evaluate De Quincey's mission as a reporter or recorder of experience, to understand his privileged position which enabled him to handle 'a *very, very* little incident - one of those which pass so fugitively that they are gone whizzing away into Lethe almost before your attention can have arrested them'[6] it is necessary to assess the environment in which he composed.

The history of De Quincey's relationship with his publishers is exceptional, not characteristic. His lack of tact with Blackwood determined his move to The London Magazine where the Confessions (intended originally for Blackwood's Edinburgh Magazine) was published in 1821. He was, apparently, 'never popular with the Londoners' and 'was a thorn in the flesh'.[7] Although there was generally more friction between writers and editors at the London, especially under Taylor's command, De Quincey's long association with Blackwood's after his return to Edinburgh reveals how difficult he was to manage. Only Joseph Conrad's correspondence with Blackwood rivals De Quincey's with its commentary of illness and suffering.[8] His 'endless record of plans for articles, small payments made, irregularities, sorrows, misunderstandings, explanations, apologies, entreaties, and thanksgivings'[9] proved too much for the courteous and seemingly generous John Blackwood. Mrs Oliphant's detailed history of Blackwood's is not quite free of the lasting resentment which

De Quincey's career produced,[10] while the more recent account of F.D. Tredrey even reveals that his portrait was never allowed to be hung.[11] To examine De Quincey's experience as a periodical writer is to see the problems of such writing in an extreme form.

According to one of his more comprehensive biographers, De Quincey 'became a man of letters, a figure in English prose, almost in spite of himself';[12] for his entry into the journalistic profession was made under the duress of financial hardship and resulted in a separation from his family which was deeply felt:

> I have something really important to tell the world on some very important subjects: and if I had been happier in my pecuniary affairs, I should have told part of it before this: but grief of mind for so long a period on account of my fatal embarrassments - and latterly the overwhelming suffering of separation from my wife's society, has made it impossible for me to write generally or at all except on transient topics or upon fugitive impulse.[13]

This sense of isolation and urgency was exacerbated by his handling of his relationship with the publishers, whether it was Hessey of the London Magazine or his Scottish counterparts William Blackwood, Tait or James Hogg. His fastidiousness about revision which first became obvious to Wordsworth as early as 1810 (when De Quincey prepared his Convention of Cintra pamphlet for the press)[14] gradually developed into a habit which tried the patience of the various publishers, especially since his means of communicating with them for submission of articles and corrections of proof was by messenger-carried notes which were necessarily brief. De Quincey's sense of isolation was strengthened as he found such a form of communication inadequate to express quickly the complexity and the subtlety of the difficulties which he faced. Conversely, he was led into equal anguish when having thought he had been successful in his communication, he found by the nature of the reply that he had been completely misunderstood:

> I am at a loss to understand your wishes or your movements. You cannot surely have misread my explanatory note. What I then wished to point out was - the self-counteracting policies of the Press. Two powers at work - centrifugal and centripetal; one thwarting the

> growth of the "copy" by calling for proof; one thwarting the proofs by calling for "copy".[15]

When in 1831 events with Blackwood reached breaking-point over such a misunderstanding De Quincey could only reply, 'Your misapprehend me in what I said of notes. I never could have any reason to complain of any neglect on your part'.[16] Again, in 1856, although he brings the problem out into the open, the tell-tale capitals and underlinings show that even in his last great effort for the first British edition of his works, the same problem had not really been resolved,

> I am much afraid - that in consequence of the very imperfect means for communicating with the Press which I now possess or ever have possessed (being at all times reduced to the single resource of writing - which, to evade misinterpretation and constant ambiguity, requires a redundancy of words - and, after all that is done on my part, requires in addition a Reader that is not only singularly attentive, but also that has a surplus of leisure time - Premising all this, I am and have been at all stages of this nominal reprint (but virtually rifacimento) of the Confessions, in terror of mutual understandings - consequently of each party unintentionally thwarting or embarrassing the other by movements at cross purposes.[17]

The trauma produced by these mere practicalities of business (the need to speak rather than write, the plea for a sympathetic reader) points to the lack of mediatory possibilities available to De Quincey in his position as a journalist. Watching him 'in hourly contact with his printer, racing to keep ahead of the press and to keep up with the proofs, two demons menacing him from opposite directions'[18] it is possible to see this steady sense of individual isolation, constant behind the hurly-burly of the magazines, complementing and sustaining a power of self-exploration and definition. As a result his works can express a sense of the enclosure and apartness of identity with either anguish or resignation. In the case of the following description it is fictionalised:

> one feels one's self sleeping alone, utterly divided from all call or hearing of friends, doors open that should be shut, or unlocked

> that should be triply secured, the very walls gone, barriers swallowed up by unknown abysses, nothing around one but frail curtains, and a world of illimitable night, whisperings at a distance, correspondence going on between darkness and darkness, like one deep calling to another, and the dreamer's own heart the centre from which the whole network of this unimaginable chaos radiates, by means of which the blank *privations* of silence and darkness become powers the most *positive* and awful.[19]

More characteristically, De Quincey expresses a similar sense of identity, with greater formality and generalisation, in his introduction to the intriguingly titled 'Letters from a Modern Author to his Daughters on the Useful Limits of Literature Considered as a Study for Females':

> You have been in some measure a witness to the fortitude with which I have borne these later calamities. True it is that we, who see most of each other, nearest relations united in the same household, see but little of that inner world, that world of secret self-consciousness, in which each of us lives a second life apart and with himself alone, collateral to his other life, or life which he lives in common with others.[20]

In both these instances, although the first is obviously more threatening, there is a slightly suppressed realisation of the benefits pertaining to an isolated position and its attendant sufferings. De Quincey might well be speaking of the achievement of the isolated consciousness when he describes its ability to make of 'blank *privations*' 'powers the most *positive* and awful'. Similarly, his description of the 'world of secret self-consciousness' follows a self-congratulatory statement which makes lack of communication appear to be a source of strength. Having experienced such adverse conditions De Quincey seems to have been aware that 'agitation' had made possible a creative expansion of his intellectual faculties.

De Quincey was well aware even of the obvious benefits that can arise from writing as a journalist, though he goes beyond the obvious by linking self-observation to a 'consciousness of creative energies', so that 'improvisation' is potentially a revelatory and not simply a combining process:

> a score of practised writers for the press will have been self-observing enough to notice a phenomenon which I have many times noticed - viz., that hurry and severe compression from an instant summons that brooks no delay, have often a tendency to furnish the flint and steel for eliciting sudden scintillations of originality; sometimes in what regards the picturesque felicity of the phrase, sometimes in what regards the thought itself, or its illustrations. To *autoschediaze*, or improvise, is sometimes in effect to be forced into a consciousness of creative energies, that would else have slumbered through life. The same stimulation to the creative faculty occurs even more notoriously in musical improvisations.[21]

Under this kind of pressure De Quincey found that actions of the mind normally associated with creativity, such as memory, actually became a constituent part of the suffering. The very prodigality of his mind menaces him in a situation where he is passive and incapable of action. Retrospectively he could feel compensated for his long struggle at the press, though at the time the revelatory power of his mind, when under intense pressure, was one of the reasons for his inability to finish articles or to deliver them on time. Even in the early 1820s at the London Magazine he became 'a by-word - indeed a positive joke'[22] for failures of this sort.

It seems as if the combination of evils which exerted itself upon him, even once he had decided upon the subject for an article - the need to clothe and feed his family, to avoid imprisonment for debt, to overcome illnesses and the effects of opium - produced an environment tending to make the creative and intellectual faculties of the mind powers in themselves, as if they had become dissociated from De Quincey himself. In such a way a crisis of identity took place at the same time as a unique opporwas afforded for distinguishing and defining the individual actions and faculties of the mind. In particular, De Quincey was threatened by the arbitrary action of his memory:

> Rarely do things perish from my memory that are worth remembering ... Still it is a fact that this pertinaceous life of memory for things that simply touch the ear does, in fact, beset me. Said but once, said softly, not marked at all, words revive before me in darkness and

> solitude; and they arrange themselves gradually into sentences, but through an effort of a distressing kind, to which I am in a manner forced to become a party.[23]

In a series of articles about Coleridge, which appeared in Tait's Magazine from September 1834 to January 1835, De Quincey again considers this passive role at the hands of an active memory, even though he now presents it as a shared generalised truth and not as a personal revelation:

> Phantoms of lost power, sudden intuitions, and shadowy restorations of forgotten feelings, sometimes dim and perplexing, sometimes by bright and furtive glimpses, sometimes by a full and steady revelation, overcharged with light - throw us back in a moment upon scenes and remembrances that we have left full thirty years behind.[24]

Part of the suffering which is occasioned by experience of this kind, as is suggested by the repetition of 'sometimes' and the way in which the verb is delayed, is the consciousness the sufferer has of its disconnected and arbitrary nature. Although at the time it may appear to have no rationale, no organisation, over the long-term, just as words 'arrange themselves gradually into sentences',[25] this fragmentary mere process becomes a unified whole. A major part in this act of assimilation would appear to be played by embodying abstractions of thought and feeling, so that process becomes a product, an achievement. De Quincey appears to have no doubt that such an attainment is both valuable and necessary in certain special cases:

> Pain driven to agony, or grief driven to frenzy is essential to the ventilation of profound natures ... a nature which is profound in excess, so as to be in peril of wasting itself in interminable reverie, cannot be awakened sometimes without afflictions that go to the very foundations, heaving, stirring, yet finally harmonising[26]

A testimony to this belief is to be found in the critical distinction he makes between 'genius' and 'talent':

> *Talent* is intellectual power of every kind,

> which acts and manifests itself by and through the *will* and the *active* forces. *Genius*, as the verbal origin implies, is that much rarer species of intellectual power which is derived from the *genial* nature - from the spirit of suffering and enjoying - from the spirit of pleasure and pain, as organised more or less perfectly; and this is independent of the will. It is a function of the *passive* nature.[27]

Not without the knowledge of this agitated experience could De Quincey have been aware of the vital metamorphic capacity of his own consciousness, its ability to reconstruct its own past life in association with apparently external objects and situations:

> A chorus of elaborate harmony, displayed before me as in a piece of arras work, the whole of my past life - not as if recalled by an act of memory, but as if present, and incarnated in the music: no longer painful to dwell upon.[28]

De Quincey's task as an autobiographer was in part to mimic verbally this act of incarnation, to arrest the ever-changing, fast-moving phenomena of his experience, and to link them to intelligible forms. Of course, as we have seen, this verbal task must have been active and have proceeded a good deal along the way, even before he consciously decided to compose. Indeed, words themselves may represent or stand alone as 'external objects' in the process forming the very substance of experience.

As well as owing its depth to his traumatic experiences brought on by his attempts to compose for the magazines De Quincey's autobiography may be said to have gained from an insight into the creative process itself, precisely because these very experiences heightened the difficulties and the various faculties involved in the act of composition. While suffering opened up his 'genial nature' it also made him self-conscious of the revelation, so that the autobiography was born out of a dual combination of experience and analysis, of extreme insularity and critical objectivity. This combination was far from being entirely conducive to the production of literary works, while it was certainly confusing, often painful, to De Quincey himself. Occasionally these two sides of his nature acted in opposition to each other even when he felt he had material to communicate: 'I laboured like a sibyl instinct with the burden of prophetic woe, as often as I found myself dealing with a topic in which the understanding combined with deep feeling to suggest mixed and tangled thoughts'.[29] Very often De Quincey found himself in this position - unable to write, even though he was convinced that he had the most original material to put before his audience. Indeed, it would appear that the strength of his compulsion to write acted detrimentally; in proportion to its strength was its efficacy to deny him any result. Coleridge seems to have experienced a similar dissociation of the energies that usually combine in the interests of creativity:

> Illness never in the smallest degree affects my intellectual powers. I can *think* with all my ordinary vigour in the midst of pain; but I am beset with the most wretched and unmanning reluctance and shrinking from action. I could not upon such occasions take the pen in hand to write down my thoughts for all the wide world.[30]

It might well be expected, considering the central nature of the sufferings outlined so far, that autobiographical compositions struck De Quincey as too serious, of too profound a cost in experience, regardless of other considerations (such as privacy, the sanctity of his own intimate life) to meet the immediate, seemingly gratuitous demands of the press. An imbalance of this sort, between the importance he placed on certain subjects, not least his own experience, and the day by day whimsicality of the context in which they were to be published, made the act of composition distasteful as well as painful to him. De Quincey did not consider such a magazine as Blackwood's a degrading place in which to exhibit his works, but he found uncongenial the demands which such a journal necessarily exercised; its constant calls for copy and proof, the speed at which it made deadlines and alterations. Partly for these reasons, and partly because these reasons had been exaggerated by the effects of opium,[31] De Quincey found that,

> I, like Mr. Coleridge, could not endure what I had written for sometime after I had written it. I also shrunk from treating any subject which I had much considered; but more, I believe, as recoiling from the intricacy and the elaborateness which had been made known to me in the course of considering it, and on

> account of the difficulty or the toilsomeness which might be fairly presumed from the mere fact that I *had* long considered it, or could have found it necessary to do so, than from any blind mechanical feeling inevitably associated (as in Coleridge it was) with a second survey of the same subject.[32]

When in 1825 this difficulty with composition reached a crisis, and was combined, as so often in De Quincey's case, with physical illness that blended imperceptibly into mental anxiety or depression, he reacted bitterly to his forced labours at the press. In a letter to his close friend John Wilson ('Christopher North' of the Noctes Ambrosianae) he revealed the strength of his dissatisfaction:

> though I have written not as one who labours under much depression of mind, - the fact is, I *do* so. At this time calamity presses upon me with a heavy hand:- I am quite free of opium - but it has left the liver, which is the Achilles heel of almost every human fabric, subject to affections which are tremendous for the weight of wretchedness attached to them. To fence with these on the one hand, and with the other to maintain the war with the wretched business of hack author, with all its horrible degradations - is more than I am able to bear.[33]

At this stage in his career the possibility that he might yet be able to remove himself from the mercy of his publishers was one he still contemplated with some hope - 'with a good publisher and leisure to premeditate what I write, I might yet liberate myself ... and show my face in the world no more'.[34] Later on in his career De Quincey might not have wholly endorsed the sentiment of this statement, even though he could claim that:

> In 1821 ... I went up to London avowedly for the purpose of exercising my pen, as the one sole source then open to me for extricating myself from a special embarrassment (failing which case of dire necessity I believe that I should never have written a line for the press)[35]

That De Quincey could react so violently against his profession at a moment of crisis shows that he did not consider the urgent climate of the periodical press entirely beneficial to his creative talents. Although, as we have seen, the need to write quickly might reveal new thoughts and illustrations which otherwise would not have been considered, it was also capable of burdening him with too many ideas, and on occasion might even promote his feelings of disgust and dissatisfaction so that they simply formed another barrier in the apparently insuperable task of composition. Instead of fostering creativity, his anguish in the process of composition, at least in the short-term, appeared to be a negative power. He once described it as 'the anxious and corroding thoughts and suffering state of mind under which I have written'.[36]

Because of this, De Quincey's various theoretical, critical comments upon the creative process include numerous statements and suggestions of its negative, degenerate nature, anticipating decadent Romantic statements. Similarly, his idea of the unity of personality and its connection with the past is qualified by a recognition of the 'blank mementos of powers extinct',[37] the dead-ends and illusions of experience. These run counter to his well-known and perhaps more to be expected appreciation of organic unity and continuity.

A further instance of the interpenetration of physical illness and his intellectual faculties, which is reported by one of his acquaintances, again points to a distinction between the positive revelations of memory, those of significance, and those which are tantalising, startling distractions:

> "I must explain to you", he said, "that I have suffered for the last ten years and more from a most dreadful ailment, to an extent of which I never heard in any other instance" - a stagnation of blood in the legs, resulting in an effect upon the system of "intense, intolerable torpor", during which it was impossible to hold or at any rate to guide, a pen; the torpor being, however, compatible with a "frightful recurrence of long-ago imagery and trifles of the past".[38]

This curious mixture, amongst the misery of composition, of startling intellectual energies, some that are productive, others that merely baulk progress and lead to no result, might be said to explain in part De Quincey's constant duality of response to his own works, his seemingly contradictory statements as to what constitutes the starting-point or the subject of his art. Similarly, his choice of subjects which may not appear to be morally circumspect (such as his preoccupation with murder and secret societies) might be thought to have originated in the stark duality we can see in this experience of composition. At its best De Quincey's imagination was able to make use of this duality by successfully reconstructing and analysing those moments when a subconscious succession of negative and positive impulses is suddenly interrupted and brought to consciousness. The relationship which has been examined[39] between his essay 'On the Knocking at the Gate in Macbeth' and his 'Postscript' to On Murder Considered as One of the Fine Arts reveals an exploration of this sudden interruption or suspension. It can be seen to be directly related to those troubled times at the press, and under the influence of opium, when, as he describes it near the end of the Confessions, 'I had the torments of a man passing out of one mode of existence into another, and liable to the mixed or alternate pains of birth and death'.[40]

Through suffering De Quincey gained an imaginative insight into the way in which the creative faculty was sometimes in a perilously close proximity to mental activities of a chaotic and anarchic nature. In retrospect it appeared:

> as if ivory carvings and elaborate fretwork and fair enamelling should be found with worms and ashes amongst coffins and the wrecks of some forgotten life or some abolished nature. In parts and fractions eternal creations are carried on, but the nexus is wanting, and life and the central principle which should bind together all the parts at the centre, with all its radiations to the circumference, are wanting. Infinite incoherence, ropes of sand, gloomy incapacity of vital pervasion by some one plastic principle, that is the hideous incubus upon my mind always.[41]

When he came to revise his more important works he needed to familiarise himself again with this state of mind, and he found that the effort necessary to do so was disproportionate to the slight benefits that it seemed to afford. During his 'solitary labour'[42] of revision on the Confessions in 1856 he wrote to James Hogg his publisher:

> My dear Sir, if you were to overhaul the Proofs

> of the last week, you would see that there is really an enormity of work that altogether disappears in the final result, like masonry buried out of sight in the foundations of a temple.[43]

Again, De Quincey appears to be considering the insularity of his position. This appeal to Hogg, the very sense of disproportion, seems to have arisen from his compulsion to view his own case from the outside, to consider the altered manuscript from Hogg's point of view, and then to sense the ridiculous appearance of his own commentary.

De Quincey's extraordinarily eloquent descriptions of his problems, mostly in the private context of letters to publishers and friends, are in themselves acts of mediation, attempts at clarifying or rationalising the confusions and contradictions of private experience. In this sporadic but consistent commentary there is a wilful attempt to justify and consolidate his role as a social being by sympathising with a view of himself taken from that outside world. The extent to which both his mental and physical sufferings as well as the results of his efforts on that revision of 1856 could be observed by others, appeared to be uppermost in his mind when he wrote:

> this improvement has been won at the price of labour and suffering, that, if they could be truly stated, would seem incredible. A malady of a very peculiar character, which has attacked me intermittingly for the last eleven years, came on in May last, almost concurrently with the commencement of this revision: and so obstinately has this malady pursued its noiseless, and what I may call subterraneous siege, since none of the symptoms are externally manifested[44]

De Quincey did not wish to present this kind of commentary - this mere catalogue of his illnesses - before the public. He believed that there was 'a mysterious sensibility connected with real suffering which recoils from circumstantial rehearsal or delineation, as from violation offered to something sacred, and which is, or should be dedicated to privacy'.[45] He also feared that accusations of obscurity and eccentricity might be linked directly or immediately to his experience and not to the agent of that experience. His own experience was worthy of publication if it could provide an example or an illustration of some more general, universal principle, which normally meant that many modifications were necessary. He did not desire a pure or simple correspondence. Indeed, at the end of the Confessions some readers might have been puzzled to find him making the following declaration: 'To fight up against the wearing siege of an abiding sickness imposes a fiery combat - I attempt no description of this combat, knowing the unintelligibility and the repulsiveness of all attempts to communicate the incommunicable'.[46] De Quincey's reference here to his personal knowledge of the difficulty of communicating to others the extent and characteristics of his internal sufferings is substantiated in a letter he wrote in 1844.[47] It would appear that he found he could not make even his own daughters aware of the most powerful forces which dictated the strange timetable of his life. His frustrated attempts at communication, which must have reinforced his perception of the 'world of secret self-consciousness'[48] led to feelings of disgust and horror when he realised in the midst of composition that he had failed to convey an adequate correspondence to real experience. The isolation of De Quincey's situation is for the moment mediated by the expectation of sympathy from a close friend:

> No purpose could be answered by my vainly endeavouring to make intelligible for my daughters, what I cannot make intelligible for myself, the undecipherable horror that night and day broods over my nervous system. One effect of this is - to cause at uncertain intervals such whirlwinds of impatience as precipitate me violently whether I will or not, into acts that would seem insanities, but are not such in fact, as my understanding is never under any delusion. Whatever I may be writing becomes suddenly overspread with a dark frenzy of horror. I am using words perhaps, that are tautologic. But it is because no language can give expression to the sudden storms of frightful revelations opening upon me from some abyss of an eternity, an eternity not coming but past and irrevocable. Whatever I may have been writing is suddenly wrapt as it were in one sheet of consuming fire: the very paper is poisoned to my eyes: I cannot endure to look at it: and I sweep it away into vast piles of unfinished letters or inchoate pages begun and interrupted

> under circumstances the same in kind, though differing unaccountably in degree.[49]

The passage ends with De Quincey seeking to explain the contained nature of his suffering and the consequent misunderstanding which took place in his own household:

> I am always alone in my study so nobody witnesses these paroxysms: nor if they did would my outward appearance testify to the dreadful transports within. They interpret the case so far as it is made known to them by any practical result of my delay or my neglect, as indolence or caprice or distracting occupations. At the worst they put it down amongst my foibles, for which I am sure they find filial excuses. Why should I ... attempt to explain the inexplicable.[50]

In a letter written in the spring of 1844 he concludes a searching description of his situation with something of an apology:

> This long story I have told you, because nothing short of this could explain my conduct, past, present, and future. And thus far there is an interest for all the world - that I am certain of this, viz., that misery is the talisman by which man communicates with the world outside our fleshy world.[51]

This conclusion to the letter is significant because it shows how an emphatic general statement based on personal conviction arises out of the details of the private experience. It also reveals that the compulsion to make such a pronouncement accords with a desire to explain his deviations from the norms of social behaviour. The movement is a daring one since it defers to social acceptability, seeks to claim its affinity with it, and then preaches to it; ending as it had begun, from an outside position. The person who makes such a statement is likely to uphold the values of society while remaining an outsider.

De Quincey's fear of being misunderstood in his sufferings led him to make exhaustive analyses and fine distinctions where even he thought they might not have been warranted. The necessity to explain his behaviour, even though there were not obvious manifestations of his terrible condition, was so great that it forced him to embark upon the difficult task of communication no matter how reluctant he might have been to do so. Once he had begun the elaborate nature of the experience precluded any direct or short explanation, so that his attempts to justify himself socially were difficult to realise and not easily understood. His sense of being an outsider must have been strengthened by the amount of explanation necessary even to convince his family and close friends. His journals for the year 1844 reveal that the feeling of social isolation had become so menacing that he considered himself to be persecuted by the seemingly separate wilful actions of his mind:

> This night, Wednesday, December 25, about 7 p.m., has first solemnly revealed itself to me that I am and have long been under a curse, all the greater for being physically and by effort endurable, and for hiding itself, i.e., playing in and out from all offices of life at every turn of every moment. Oh, dreadful! by degrees infinitely worse than leprosy - than - But oh, what signifies the rhetoric of a case so sad![52]

Even in this most private context it would seem that De Quincey felt as if all his attempts at expressing and explaining his complex experience failed altogether to make any significant representation of the real case; if he cannot find words, the words that he has are the 'rhetoric of a case' and not conveyors of his urgent immediate predicament. His comparison with leprosy, though it may be felt to be disturbing because disproportionate, nevertheless suggests the social isolation attendant upon his situation, and emphasises most poignantly the very fact that his own sufferings are unseen, inexplicable, even though in such close proximity to the everyday workings of society.

Not simply the misery itself but the inability to express it, to make others aware of it, constitutes the full effect of De Quincey's suffering. Where his inner turmoil did manifest itself in his day-to-day routine - his procrastination, his tardiness and confusion in journalistic affairs, his reluctance to attend social gatherings - it was again as if he were persecuted, not in, but by the very intimacy of his situation. A more open and profoundly public setting, such as he once experienced as an anonymous periodical writer, might have provided a more congenial platform upon which to have fulfilled the courtesies and responsibilities of a member of society:

> Did you ever read of leprosy as it existed in Judea or - and that was worse - as it existed in Europe during the dark ages? Did you ever read of that tremendous visitation in the early days of Judaism, when, if the poor patient would have hushed up his misery in silence, the walls of his house whispered of his whereabouts. Horrible! that a man's own chamber - the place of his refuge and retreat - should betray him! ... Not fear or terror, but inexpressible misery is the last portion of the opium-eater.[53]

There is also a sense here of De Quincey's reluctance to be forced out on to that wider social platform, an intimation of his preference for the comfortable confinement and insularity of family life, the anonymity provided by the smaller private groupings in society. This statement suggests an ambivalence in De Quincey's view of public and private identity: he recognises the safety of private life and the threat of public life at the same time as he is capable of reversing the equation. Both public and private alternate between being beneficial and negative forces, each capable of threatening or protecting identity. Such a contradiction might lead to the conclusion that De Quincey needed to move between the two extremes of his public and private worlds, attempting to define himself in a movement consisting of the contraction and expansion of varying social sympathies. In the examples of suffering presented so far it can be seen how the fluctuation of De Quincey's intellectual and imaginative faculties, themselves giving the appearance of being alternately productive and threatening, leads to a sense of isolation in both professional and personal spheres. According to De Quincey's own retrospective judgements such a painful fluctuation corresponded to an expansion of personality and promoted genius. Just as his experience, at a certain period of opium addiction, meant that he was constantly 'passing out of one state of existence into another'[54] so the pain caused in the act of composition by operating on a most private and public level at the same time produced both personal and public benefits. Having been isolated by the experiences we have noticed De Quincey also felt himself to have witnessed operations of the human mind from a privileged vantage-point. Part of his burden, he thought, lay in the personal necessity and public responsibility of communicating his findings. To remedy his isolation and to continue the process of self-definition were in accordance with the function of a public-commentator and 'moralist'. In such a way might anonymity be reconciled with a confessional utterance.

In the midst of these difficult circumstances De Quincey needed to produce articles for his publishers if he was to remedy his financial position. The natural urgency of the magazines was intensified by his own immediate problems. As a father and supporter of a household he felt the full force of his responsibilities pressing upon him in the act of composition. When he reviewed The Life and Adventures of Goldsmith: A Biography in 1848 he could sympathise with the poet's poverty, yet realise the added burden of family responsibilities which Goldsmith did not have to face:

> Suppose the case of a man who has helpless dependants upon himself summoned to face some sudden failure of his resources: how shattering to the power of exertion, and, above all, of exertion by an organ so delicate as the creative intellect, dealing with subjects so coy as those of imaginative sensibility, to know that instant ruin attends his failure ... but success is impossible, with any powers whatever, unless in a genial state of these powers; and this geniality is to be sustained, in the case supposed whilst the eyes are fixed upon the most frightful of abysses yawning beneath his feet.[55]

It is clear that in the heat of the moment De Quincey found this alignment of public and private responsibilities painful because it was so direct. The two were here brought together with a threatening intensity. After the event, when it could be 'recollected in tranquillity' this productive connection might be made to bear the fruit of the pressure exercised upon the 'genial' faculties of the writer. Similarly, if De Quincey were to have attempted to present the vision of his experience directly through his autobiographical writings he might have experienced the same sort of pressure. He knew well that, 'Grief does not parade its pangs nor the anguish of despairing hunger willingly count again its groans or its humiliations'[56] at the same time as he realised that such documentation did not constitute an article of any serious merit. To present the minutiae or raw material of his autobiography might satisfy a morbid curiosity but it travestied his self-esteem and the responsibility he willingly bore to his readership.

In the presentation of material to the magazines De Quincey found that the necessary corrections of proof and copy, and his dealings with the messenger boys instead of the editors themselves, cut him off from any direct access to the vehicle of his publications. In that situation he was denied the chance of reconciling public and private responsibility. He was isolated because he could not break through the barriers upon which 'publicity' functioned. His dilemma was the fact that the machinations of the press - its corrections, omissions and refusals - formed a barrier between him and the public, without acting in a mediatory capacity. Even though sub-editors might alter the text of his manuscript, De Quincey still appeared as its author and suffered the consequences of his responsibility:

> Who is answerable for the beauty, for the grandeur, for the effect of my papers? Can he pretend to say I will be so? He cannot. He might as well say: You shall act as I think morally right, and I become answerable for the result. He cuts away one-half from Michael Angelo's Sistine Chapel, and says I will be responsible. He sends for a house-painter to coat with paint the Transfiguration of Raphael, and holds that if he bears the blame no harm is done ... But where or how does he bear the blame? My name is there: *his* is not.[57]

At least once, towards the end of his career, De Quincey's ability to exercise the authority of his conscientious concern for his publications was threatened by illness, and he implored Blackwood himself to come to his home so that the problem could be remedied directly and not through any middle parties:

> I am ashamed to request the favour of your coming down to his place ... throughout the day I have been falling out of dream into dream from pain and want of sleep, so as to have <u>lost from my memory all the course of what I have sent to the press</u> - Without some <u>personal</u> explanations I fear that I shall be unable to extricate

myself.[58]

It can be seen from this instance that the difficulty of enforcing an earnest moral commitment in a series of articles for a journal lay in the terrible finality of each successive instalment, even before the series was complete, or there had been time to revise and check the copy. And for De Quincey, autobiography represented a special case, for it contained in its very nature a special claim of veracity and had to make good that claim on both public and private levels. Once the autobiographical material had been ascertained, defined over the years, De Quincey seems to have felt an obligation to honour his own retrospective vision, which had then to accord with the further responsibilities of communicating with the reader, and in deference to his family and friends. It was no easy matter reconciling these often conflicting considerations, even in a tranquil frame of mind. The speed expected by his publishers caused De Quincey much anguish when combined with the difficult responsibility he bore over this claim of veracity. When he revised his Autobiographic Sketches for the collected edition of his works entitled Selections Grave and Gay he reminded his readers in the preface of the disparity between the more leisurely climate under which they had been revised, and the climate in which they had originally been published:

> Now that mode of publication is unavoidably disadvantageous to a writer, except under unusual conditions. By its harsh peremptory punctuality, it drives a man into saying the thing that is not. They won't wait an hour for you in a Magazine or a Review; they won't wait for the truth ... Here is one evil of journal-writing - viz., its overmastering precipitation.[59]

In order to minimise the possibility of 'saying the thing that is not' De Quincey seems to claim that in his Confessions he partly resolved the conflict between public and private responsibility by deliberately imagining for himself a 'false' intimate context; though this was after he had calculated the distortions which could arise from the dominance of an insulated personal vision, no matter how sincere:

> In cases which touch too closely upon their own

> rights and interests, all men should hesitate to trust their judgement: thus far I imposed a restraint upon myself, as all just and conscientious men would do: in everything else I spoke fearlessly and as if writing private memoirs for my own dearest friends.60

To be conscientious in this case is to recognise a moral commitment to the public world. Such a commitment need not, however, coincide with, or satisfy the expectations of a magazine audience. As far as De Quincey saw the readers of newspapers and journals mirroring in their response the arbitrary disconnections and sensationalism of the new journalistic productions it most certainly did not. Seen from this point of view, De Quincey's responsibility to his public might be expected to have more than a note of paternalism about it. His advocation of restraint to preserve an objective truth probably did not quadrate with expectations surrounding his most famous literary production, especially since it seemed to claim in its title an affinity with a tradition of confessional writings openly revelatory and sensational. De Quincey's immediate denial of these expectations reveals how his avowed public responsibility attempts to stabilise and make more durable his own literary context by reaching beyond its temporary publicity to a principle adumbrating personal and public veracity.

In the same way that this concern had to be presented in an ephemeral context De Quincey's act of composition itself found its long-considered material cast in an immediate experience. It has already been seen how the revelatory potential of journalistic writing might act in opposition to De Quincey's creativity: when he desired to proceed directly to his autobiographical commentary new ideas confronted him, often impeding his progress. While De Quincey's autobiography may be considered as a product of long-term development, born out of a conflict at the press, it received a further dimension by coming into contact again with this immediate situation, so that what had been long considered was made to contend with startling new forces. Not least among these, of course, was De Quincey's anticipation of the response from his readership. In a sense, this anticipation probably constituted the most important direct confrontation between author and reader. It manifests itself throughout his writings being, perhaps, most obvious in the _Confessions_, where it takes a rhetorical form of address and response, question and answer. In that autobiographical framework the author's own anticipation is made to enact the mediatory function which could take place in a dialogue, at the same time as giving the work a dramatic sense of the present moment.

In professional rather than artistic terms De Quincey's articles also needed to possess a relatively obvious relationship with the buyers of the magazines if they were to be accepted by the editors. To this extent the link between the author and his reader was pre-determined: in order that an article be published and realise the artistic dialogue we have noticed, it must correspond at least in some small part to the market exploited by the particular magazine. De Quincey was well aware of this situation; another disadvantage of writing for journals he recognised was 'its effect at times in narrowing your publicity'.[61] Because of this financial market impulse his own expectation of that confrontation with the reader could not be really direct. Sometimes it was denied altogether. Even Blackwood turned down De Quincey's articles because they were occasionally unsuitable. After such an occasion in 1844 a letter to Wilson reveals how Blackwood's refusal obscured De Quincey's understanding of this relationship between audience, magazine and article:

> You may or may not be aware that about 3 months ago an art. of mine was thrown back upon my hands by Mr. Blackwood upon which more than upon any I ever wrote, I had relied for money. Immense distress followed. This same art., upon my belief that Mr. B. had misconceived its nature, was sent again: and again returned ... Am I unable to write? Far from it! I was never so able in my whole life. But to what end should I write? ... Never was I in so much force for writing: but as respects Maga, I am thoroughly disheartened; for I do not perceive the law or principle on which Bl. rejects or receives.[62]

Even if on occasion he could overcome these difficulties De Quincey might then have to contend with (although he could equally exploit) the uneven composition of _Blackwood's_ readership and the conventions under which it operated. He also inherited from _Blackwood's_ and the _London Magazine_ a readership which was used to accepting literature as fact. In his case, however, 'the same convention working in reverse gave the impression that De Quincey's 'Confessions' was fiction, the Opium-Eater a fictional character'.[63]

While the approaches to publicity were fraught with misunderstanding and obstructions, so once inside, the dilemma was that there seemed to be no middle way: only after the event, when the finality of an article, or even an instalment in a series had been realised, could De Quincey attempt to assess his public response from the reviews and letters which followed. The act of publication appeared to possess no centre: it moved from expectation straight through to verdict, making his compositions seem vulnerable and isolated because they were irretrievable and exempt from immediate qualification. It was partly because of this that De Quincey was forced to create his own mediatory devices: they were capable of being agents of his responsibility. His sense of the printed word as a testimony to the author's full acceptance of that responsibility explains his hesitance in embarking on a large project which, while it made large promises to the reader, was subject to the capricious turns of the publishing world. In order to make clear the extent of his obligation to the reader De Quincey suggested to Blackwood that he be anonymous at the beginning of a new series:

> I should wish, if it were possible, to be anonymous for this first *debut* - that is, anonymous on the title page; for otherwise it would be easy for you, with your command of all avenues to the public ear, to make the authorship effectually known, though not so formally as by this distinct acknowledgement on the title.[64]

In this awareness of 'formality', in the willingness to recognise the authority of the public pact, De Quincey does not draw an over-fine distinction but confirms his belief in the viability of manners and conventions. This is implicit in his defence of anonymity which follows:

> Do not suppose that I am underwriting myself. I neither ever did, nor do I think I could underwrite myself on any subject whatever; for in order to write at all, I find it necessary to create for myself a real interest in my theme. Neither, again, have I any nervous tremors connected with the act of appearing before

> the public. But simply on politic considerations, looking forward to the possibility that I might not realise the whole of what was expected from me, it seems prudent[65]

This contradictory mixture of necessity and sincerity, of 'prudence' and 'real interest' is one which appears to have allowed De Quincey to function between personal and public commitment. For example he found some satisfaction in answering the response to the Confessions in 1821 by making use of the traditional 'letter to the editor', at the end of which he signed himself 'XYZ', thus continuing the half-hearted anonymity of the work itself. Even while correcting another journalist's suggestion that the 'Opium-Eater' might be a fictitious character De Quincey continues to play the role. This is in accordance with the way in which he accepts the spirit of the suggestion: he makes his earnest claim to veracity by moving through a mannerly social decorum:

> this scruple on the question of authenticity comes in the shape which might have been anticipated from his own courteous and honourable nature ... Thus shaped, I cannot have any right to quarrel with this scruple. But on many accounts I should be sorry that such a view were taken of the narrative by those who may have happened to read it. And therefore I assure Mr. Montgomery, in this public way, that the entire Confessions were designed to convey a narrative of my own experience as an Opium-Eater, drawn up with entire simplicity and fidelity to the facts[66]

If this was the kind of response which could be accepted graciously there was another kind which De Quincey found more difficult to cope with. In 1824 an article appeared in a newspaper libellously parodying the Confessions and referring to the fact that his first child was born before marriage.[67] But it was not until 1841 that he referred to the article publicly, saying it 'trespassed on decency, not only by its slander, but, in some instances, by downright obscenity; and, worse than that, by prurient solicitations to the libidinous imagination, through blanks, seasonably interspersed'.[68]

In his sensitivity to such attacks De Quincey realised how the power of publicity itself could sponsor the 'libidinous imagination' yet defy his own 'delicate creative intellect'[69] and 'coy ... imaginative sensibility'[70] if it were not checked by the counter forces of convention such as courtesy and reticence. In order to encourage his creative powers a delicate balance had to be maintained so that the pressure of the public context stimulated but did not crush the action of his imagination. Working not against the pressure of this context but through his resistance to it, De Quincey managed to benefit from his belief in both his private experience and the conventions of the social world. It was a twin response which contained a potentially creative antagonism. De Quincey expressed the nature of this response when describing his suffering in a letter of 1845:

> No man can have descended more profoundly than myself into the consolations of utter solitude, no man can ever have weaned himself more entirely from *dependence* upon sympathy; but, at the same time, perhaps, no man has ever felt it more keenly.[71]

Because of this duality in the circumstances of composition and publication De Quincey's works are delicately poised; particularly in his most 'impassioned' autobiographical works there is a provocative alternation between independent self-assertion and the sympathy or authority of accepted truths. When De Quincey described the effect which Cathy Wordsworth's death had on him he was pleased to find the psychological experience authenticated by current medical knowledge.[72] In the same way, the actual description of his attachment to the child points quite openly to the combination of the two extremes: 'Over and above my excess of love for her, I had always viewed her as an impersonation of the dawn and the spirit of infancy; and *this abstraction seated in her person*'[73] (my italics). Here the congeniality to De Quincey's mind of the relationship between the individual and the general, concrete and abstract, is analogous to his acceptance of both public formality and isolated personal experience. There is a satisfying concurrence of internal and external forces.

De Quincey's ability to recognise the importance of the simultaneous action of internal and external forces, such as we have been considering in his experience of the process of publication, extended beyond his own immediate circumstances. He refers to it in a philosophical terminology in a letter to his daughter, when he anticipated his grand-daughter's childhood:

> In April next, when dear little Eva will have completed her sixth month, when, first of all, she will be capable of enjoying, there will be something *extra* to enjoy. That is, speaking Germanically, and therefore pedantically, as the *subjective* (viz., the power of spectating) will then be in the very meridian of its development in Eva, so correspondingly will the *objective* (viz., the thing to be spectated, or in base vulgar the spectacle), be travelling for three months - April, May, June - through all the stages of its revelation.[74]

As De Quincey continues the letter, the relevance to his own position as a journalist deepens, especially if we remember his starting-point of isolation and his need of a sympathetic reader or listener to act in a mediatory capacity:

> therefore it follows that taking Eva as the centre of a secret and insulated world, the contemplating and the thing contemplated, the beholding and the thing beheld, the subject and the object, will blossom concurrently. Neither will outrun the other. No pulse of Eva's sensibilities will perish for want of an object, no day of loveliness will perish for want of an observer.[75]

A process of definition is able to take place because of the alignment of the public and the private worlds: each reacts against the other so that each becomes mutually intelligible:

> Eva, therefore, is invoked by the coming spring as the reader of the silent legend - Spring is invoked by the tutelary genius of Eva as the lock whose secret wards made known to itself the powers of the key which deciphers them; ... and very seriously it is true, that with the earliest of her self-revealing faculties will coincide a great physical revolution outside. And this I have always regarded as a signal privilege of a child.[76]

De Quincey sought to make out of the threatening stark duality of the act of publication this kind of comforting 'coincidence'. He could fabricate a position which seemed to by-pass the self-conscious act of publication, or he could appear to rest easy within its established conventions. In order to present his reader with his autobiographical record he needed a common ground upon which to work, and these two alternatives both provided viable artistic techniques of illusion which would allow that record to be transmitted under cover of a temporary alignment of author and reader. In a sense, this temporary and artificial relationship was a means of arriving at a more profound link between the two. In the last quotation, for example, the ending 'And this I have always regarded as a signal privilege of a child' is as significant for De Quincey's ability to see the 'signal privilege' as it is for its confirmation of a universal human principle. Both the affirmative 'I' and the general 'a child' join together to make good the conclusion to the observation.

As De Quincey's autobiography delivers psychological observations based on personal discovery, and being therefore necessarily engaged in a reciprocal action which validates the general truth at the same time as the personal, the privileged position of the observer himself cannot be discounted. When De Quincey makes his famous statement regarding 'involutes' in 'The Affliction of Childhood' it is as much an explanation of his experience as it is a pronouncement derived from it. His declaration of it as a truth is inseparable from its effect upon him as a truth:

> And, recollecting it, I am struck with the truth, that far more of our deepest thoughts and feelings pass to us ... as *involutes* (if I may coin that word) in compound experiences incapable of being disentangled, than ever reach us *directly*, and in their own abstract shapes.77

Here the interdependence of De Quincey's act of recollection and his claim of wider significance mirrors the actual statement which is made: both the mode of communication and the thought share a recognition of the mutual dependence of concrete and abstract, internal and external, a willingness to operate a principle of truth from a combination of the two sides. He is defined in front of the reader in that movement between personal and public relevance.

Certainly, maintaining this combination in

balanced proportion is not without its difficulties. The earnestness with which De Quincey prided himself on claims of veracity and defended them (especially since that truth was not simply factual, but was to a large degree experiential) could lead to claims of sentimentality. In a letter to a close friend in 1837 De Quincey realises that the general statement he has just made is open to such a claim: 'That which is *remembered* only suddenly puts on the blossoming of *hope*, and wears the vernal dress of happiness that has vanished'.[78] His reaction is to steadfastly maintain his autobiographical position of correspondence to his own experience: 'Is this sentimental? Be it so; but then also it is intensely true; and sentimentality cannot avail to vitiate the truth; on the contrary truth avails to dignify and exalt the sentimental'.[79] Because it has developed from and still promotes this personal correspondence the general statement may on occasion have to bear considerable strain. Sometimes it deliberately communicates that strain, making the reader realise the nature of the autobiographer's dilemma. So too, it is a means of appealing to the reader by making the general statement betray its own urgency. In other words De Quincey heightens the immediacy of the past event at the same time as he makes his claim for both personal and general truth. In the publication of such statements personal anguish has to accord with public responsibility and convention.

To view De Quincey as a journalist, while considering his most important autobiographical works, need not be incompatible with a high estimate of his achievement. Albert Goldman suggested that his study of De Quincey as a journalist,

> cannot help but cause present-day scholars to reform rather drastically their notion of De Quincey when they learn ... that his many works of a scholarly or intellectual nature are almost all derived in the most direct way from printed sources ... In every article of this kind, De Quincey has produced a clever piece of hack work - translating, abstracting, and abridging, piecing together inadequate notes preserved for such purposes, and in general worked like some hard-pressed inhabitant of Grub Street.[80]

The 'reformed notion' of the journalist can consolidate the importance of the autobiographical works. Appreciating the problems of De Quincey's position as a journalist leads to an understanding of the intimate connection which exists between his internal world of illness, composition and responsibility, and his professional roles of autobiographer, learned scholar and public commentator. It is not in the nature of this connection simply to remedy private isolation by engaging in one of these roles. Nor is it simply to remedy the split identity apparently caused by opium, or more particularly by the duality resident in the act of publication. De Quincey's autobiographical writings reveal a confrontation between the interests of an act of confession and the authoritative role of a scholarly journalist. This is evident in what might wrongly be considered as De Quincey's simple paraphrase of Wordsworth's idea of the 'spontaneous overflow of powerful feelings ... recollected in tranquillity'. De Quincey's version refers to the 'spontaneous overflow of real unaffected passion, deep, and at the same time original, and also *forced into public manifestation of itself*, from the necessity which cleaves to all passion alike of seeking external sympathy'[81] (my italics). Although the terms used here are, as is frequently the case, those belonging to the realm of expression and communication they have to contend with a process of 'public manifestation' which highlights the problems of deciphering and constructing experience.

De Quincey's letters to publishers and friends on the subject of his difficult situation as a journalist form a commentary which shares the fundamental concerns of his autobiographical writings. They too focus on the problematical relationship between language and experience. De Quincey is not simply the victim or the accurate recorder of experience, but also its interpreter. Experience, especially the kind with which he deals, is conceived of as being obscure, complex and symbolic. As he delivers his specialised account of certain crucial aspects of his life in his role of interpreter De Quincey also encounters a frightening split between the public and the private facets of his situation. The very fact of publication represents an abrupt transition from isolated personal experience to the conventions of magazine journalism.

NOTES

1. Thomas De Quincey, <u>A Diary of Thomas De Quincey</u>, Horace A. Eaton (ed.) (New York, 1927),

p. 141.

2. H.A. Page, *Thomas De Quincey: His Life and Writings* (London, 1897), Second Edition, vol. I, p. 160.

3. Ibid., vol. II, p. 66.

4. James Hogg (ed.), *De Quincey and His Friends* (Edinburgh, 1895), p. 218.

5. Page, *Life and Writings*, vol. I, p. 284.

6. Ibid.

7. Josephine Bauer, 'The London Magazine 1820-29', *Anglistica* (Copenhagen, 1953), p. 87.

8. F.D. Tredrey, *The House of Blackwood 1804-1954* (Edinburgh and London, 1954), p. 191.

9. Ibid., p. 45.

10. Mrs Oliphant, *Annals of a Publishing House: William Blackwood and His Sons* (Edinburgh and London, 1897), Second Edition, vol. I, pp. 422-444.

11. Tredrey, *House of Blackwood*, p. 236.

12. Horace A. Eaton, *Thomas De Quincey: a Biography* (New York, Oxford, 1936), p. 256.

13. Ibid., p. 293.

14. See John E. Jordan, *De Quincey to Wordsworth: The Biography of a Relationship* (Berkeley and Los Angeles, 1962), pp. 110-111, 123-124, 134-136, 163, 198.

15. Willard Hallam Bonner, 'De Quincey at Work', *The University of Buffalo Studies*, vol. XI (1936), pp. 78-79.

16. Eaton, *Thomas De Quincey: A Biography*, p. 353.

17. Bonner, 'De Quincey at Work', p. 69.

18. Ibid., p. 56.

19. Thomas De Quincey, *The Collected Writings of Thomas De Quincey*, David Masson (ed.) (14 vols., Edinburgh, 1889-90), vol. XII , p. 236.

20. Page, *Life and Writings*, vol. I, p. 304.

21. Ibid., vol. II, pp. 173-174.

22. Edward Sackville-West, *A Flame in Sunlight* (London, 1936), p. 228.

23. Page, *Life and Writings*, vol. II, pp. 247 f.

24. Masson, vol. II, p. 204.

25. Page, *Life and Writings*, vol. II, p. 247.

26. Thomas De Quincey, *The Posthumous Works of Thomas De Quincey*, Alexander H. Japp (ed.) (London, 1893), vol. II, p. 12.

27. Masson, vol. I, p. 194 n.

28. Page, *Life and Writings*, vol. II, p. 246.

29. Ibid., p. 256.

30. S.T. Coleridge, *Table Talk*, *Coleridge's Works*, T. Ashe (ed.) (London, 1909), p. 140

31. I refer here to the authority of De Quincey himself, immediately preceding my next quotation.

32. Masson, vol. III, p. 76.

33. Eaton, Thomas De Quincey: A Biography, pp. 304 f.

34. Ibid.

35. Masson, vol. III, p. 127.

36. Oliphant, Annals of a Publishing House, vol. I, p. 436.

37. Masson, vol. II, pp. 204 ff:

> In the presence of *enduring* features of nature it is that such evanescent hauntings of our past and forgotten selves are most apt to startle and waylay us. These are *positive* torments from which the agitated mind shrinks in fear; but there are others *negative* in their nature - that is, blank mementos of powers extinct, and faculties burnt out within us.

38. Hogg (ed.), De Quincey and His Friends, p. 222.

39. See Geoffrey Carnall, 'De Quincey on "The Knocking at the Gate"', Review of English Literature, vol. II, no. 1 (1960); Vincent A. De Luca, 'De Quincey's "Knocking at the Gate in Macbeth": Dream and Prose Art', ELN, 13 (1976), pp. 273-278; John E. Jordan, 'De Quincey's Dramaturgic Criticism', ELH (1951).

40. Masson, vol. III, p. 448.

41. Page, Life and Writings, vol. I, p. 325.

42. Bonner, 'De Quincey at Work', pp. 67-68.

43. Ibid.

44. Page, Life and Writings, vol. II, p. 48.

45. Thomas De Quincey, 'A Letter to William Wordsworth', Recollections of the Lakes and the Lake Poets, David Wright (ed.) (Harmondsworth, 1970), p. 112.

46. Masson, vol. III, p. 221.

47. Eaton, Thomas De Quincey: A Biography, pp. 417-418.

48. Page, Life and Writings, vol. I, p. 304.

49. Eaton, Thomas De Quincey: A Biography, p. 418.

50. Ibid.

51. Page, Life and Writings, vol. I, p. 329.

52 Ibid.

53. Ibid., pp. 329-330.

54. Masson, vol. III, p. 448.

55. Ibid., vol. IV, p. 292.

56. Ibid., vol. II, p. 55.

57. Thomas De Quincey, De Quincey Memorials, A.H. Japp (ed.) (New York, 1891), vol. II, pp. 180-181.

58. Bonner, 'De Quincey at Work', pp. 91-92.

59. Thomas De Quincey, Selections Grave and Gay From Writings Published and Unpublished, of Thomas De Quincey, Revised and Arranged by Himself (14 vols., Edinburgh, 1853-60), vol. I, pp. vi f.

60. Masson, vol. II, p. 464.

61. De Quincey, Selections Grave and Gay, vol. I, p. vi ff.

62. Eaton, Thomas De Quincey: A Biography, pp. 379-381.

63. Michael Allen, Poe and the British Magazine Tradition (New York, 1969), pp. 68 f.

64. Oliphant, Annals of a Publishing House, p. 432.

65. Ibid.

66. Masson, vol. III, p. 464.

67. See Jordan, De Quincey to Wordsworth, p. 230.

68. Masson, vol. III, p. 176.

69. Ibid., vol. IV, p. 292.

70. Ibid.

71. Sackville-West, A Flame in Sunlight, p. 270.

72. Wright (ed.), Recollections of the Lakes and the Lake Poets, p. 370.

73. Ibid., p. 372.

74. Page, Life and Writings, vol. II, pp. 87-88.

75. Ibid.

76. Ibid.

77. Masson, vol. I, p. 39.

78. Page, Life and Writings, vol. I, p. 307.

79. Ibid.

80. Albert Goldman, The Mine and the Mint (Carbondale and Edwardsville, 1965), p. 9.

81. Masson, vol. I, p. 194.

Chapter 2

LITERATURE AS RESISTANCE AND POWER

RESISTANCE

In De Quincey's difficult situation as a journalist his progress in the act of composition could be both thwarted and encouraged by the varying degrees of intimacy and publicity connected with his context. An alignment of public and private responsibilities created a dichotomy in his appraisal of his own imaginative powers. This dichotomy is also present in his critical writings on other authors. De Quincey's work as a literary critic reveals how imaginative 'power' is in his view related to difficulty and suffering. The apparently negative experience of composition could eventually turn out to have been creative.

One of De Quincey's fundamental concerns as an autobiographer - his notion of fidelity to past experience - could be threatened by capricious acts of memory or consolidated by affirmative acts of memory. The experience of composition constituted a revelatory context because the medium of language could radically compromise directness of communication, at the very least by providing the possibility of ambiguities. In the same way that De Quincey managed to operate as a magazine writer in the formal compromise of the public pact so, too, a fruitful compromise could arise out of this opposition from language itself. De Quincey's critical statements are informed by his experience of composition and they show how, ultimately, a source of power lay in this opposition: the resistance provided De Quincey with a dynamic foundation on which to structure his reluctant autobiography.

De Quincey's conception of a work of literature rests, to a large extent, on his belief that the act of composition is a revelatory context, and that at their best certain types of literature (those most congenial to his own interests) convey the writer's own sense of this to the reader. It is for this reason that he celebrates Burke's prose as opposed to Johnson's:

> For one moment, reader, pause upon the spectacle of two contrasted intellects, Burke's and Johnson's: one an intellect essentially going forward, governed by the very necessity of growth, by the law of motion in advance; the latter essentially an intellect retrogressive, retrospective, and throwing itself back on its own steps ... The result from these original differences of intellectual constitution ... is, that Dr. Johnson never, in any instance, GROWS a truth before your eyes whilst in the act of delivering it or moving towards it. All that he offers up to the end of the chapter he had when he began. But to Burke, such was the prodigious elasticity of his thinking, ... the mere act of movement became the principle or cause of movement. Motion propagated motion, and life threw off life. The very violence of a projectile as thrown by *him* caused it to rebound in fresh forms, fresh angles, splintering, coruscating, which gave out thoughts as new (and as startling) to himself as they are to his reader.[1]

It might seem strange to find De Quincey opposed to a retrospective vision, but the characteristic nature of his experience of autobiographical writing would seem to lie in that ambivalent and seemingly contradictory phrase 'necessity of growth'. While Burke's elasticity of thinking implies an openness, it also involves a potentially hazardous submission. In such a phrase De Quincey combines an organic with a mechanical appreciation of the creative process.

This kind of combined response from De Quincey derives from his experience as a periodical and newspaper writer. The distinction between Burke and Johnson appears in the context of a debate on style as it is governed by oratory and conversation. De Quincey's evaluation of Burke's apparently spontaneous movement is imbued with the past experience of his own career, and a realisation of a particular type of literature and a particular type of effect. Using an analogy which stresses the mechanical side of his appreciation De Quincey explains the principle governing his own context:

> Like boys who are throwing the sun's rays into the eyes of a mob by means of a mirror, you must shift your lights and vibrate your reflections at every possible angle, if you would agitate the popular mind extensively. Every mode of intellectual communication has its separate strength and separate weakness, - its peculiar embarrassments, compensated by peculiar resources.[2]

The extent to which De Quincey writes of a mechanical part being played in literary production qualifies, but does not necessarily contradict, his promotion of the organic concept. The mechanical opposition provided by language is, in fact, conducive to revelatory acts of imagination. It is the combination of these two aspects which is crucial in De Quincey's critical thinking:

> Style may be viewed as an *organic* thing and as a *mechanic* thing. By organic, we mean that which, being acted upon, reacts, and which propagates the communicated power without loss. By mechanic, that which, being impressed with motion, cannot throw it back without loss, and therefore soon comes to an end. The human body is an elaborate system of organs; it is sustained by organs. But the human body is exercised as a machine, and as such may be viewed ... Now, the use of words is an organic thing, in so far as language is connected with thoughts, and modified by thoughts. It is a mechanic thing in so far as words in combination determine or modify each other.[3]

This combination of organic and mechanic leads De Quincey to an understanding of how spontaneity and self-consciousness in art can happily co-exist. It is particularly from his insistence on the mechanic side, however, that De Quincey comes to a full appreciation of self-consciousness. In an autobiographical work it can provide a further means of self-definition. As we saw earlier, a text can convey this self-consciousness of the writer in opposition to his craft. In an autobiographical work the act of composition could lead to another reassessment of the original past experience. This would seem to constitute an analogous situation to that described by Wordsworth in a famous statement from his Preface to the Lyrical Ballads, 1802:

> I have said that Poetry is the spontanous overflow of powerful feelings: it takes its origin from emotion recollected in tranquillity: the emotion is contemplated till by a species of reaction the tranquillity gradually disappears, and an emotion, similar to that which was before the subject of contemplation, is gradually produced, and does itself actually exist in the mind.[4]

Considering De Quincey's case we may say that this secondary emotion rather than being conducive to and present in composition, as Wordsworth argues for himself, is actually produced by the writer's recognition of resistance in composition. Because this recognition is of resistance, and often of difficulty, it tends to obscure its affinity with Coleridge's fine perception of creativity in his attempt to define the distinguishing characteristic of poetry: 'What is this? It is that pleasurable emotion, that peculiar state and degree of excitement, which arises in the poet himself in the act of composition'.[5] Geoffrey Hill has written that, 'Readers of the Biographia Literaria may note that Coleridge's concern is not so much with thought as with "the mind's self-experience in the act of thinking"',[6] and that this 'self-experience' is most clearly realised by the process of '"win[ning one's] way up against the stream"'.[7] De Quincey possessed a kindred sort of concern especially as regards the peculiar difficulties of autobiographical writing. Contemplating the popular style of his own age he felt that he was denied this kind of 'self-experience':

> Direct objective qualities it is always by comparison easy to measure; but the difficulty commences when we have to combine with this outer measurement of the object another corresponding measurement of the subjective or inner qualities by which we apply the measure; that is, when besides the objects projected to a distance from the spectator, we have to allow for variations or disturbances in the very eye which surveys them. The eye cannot see itself; we cannot project from ourselves, and contemplate as an object, our own contemplating faculty, or appreciate our own appreciating power.[8]

The possibility which De Quincey considers here, of

being confined within his own subjective viewpoint, is one to which he was not always willing to accede. It was precisely this power of self-projection which solaced his subjective literary explorations, and which he was eager to recognise in other writers. Indeed, he frequently argues that an appreciation of 'our appreciating power' is the life-force of subjective literature. Again, he emphasises the extent to which this is a necessary, inevitable result, pre-determined by the writer's situation, rather than a sought-after and self-inspired achievement:

> To hang upon one's thoughts as an object of conscious interest, to play with them, to watch and pursue them through a maze of inversions, evolutions, and harlequin changes, implies a condition of society ... like that in the monastic ages, forced to introvert its energies from mere defect of books[9]

This kind of situation, where external realities which could aid the writer in his aim of self-definition are denied, led De Quincey to an awareness of the important part which could be played in the act of self-definition by the resistance offered by language itself. It appeared to be a closed circuit where the writer was forced to find all the material within himself, though he was aided by the discrepancy between the thought or feeling and the adequacy of the particular word or words to describe it. His own knowledge of this experience made him draw a firm distinction between subjective and objective literature. But far from lamenting the nature of the former, he was ready to assert its peculiarity and praise its benefits. Again, writing of his own age he states:

> The excess of external materials has sometimes oppressed their creative power, and sometimes their meditative power. The exuberance of *objective* knowledge - that knowledge which carries the mind to materials existing *out* of itself, such as natural philosophy, chemistry, physiology, astronomy, geology, where the mind of the student goes for little and the external object for much - has had the effect of weaning men from subjective speculation, where the mind is all in all and the alien object next to nothing, and in that degree has weaned them from the culture of style.[10]

It is De Quincey's own knowledge of an insulated position which makes him aware of the extent to which form and content cannot be dissociated. Although, in that last quotation, he appears to refer to style as if it can be considered separately, he does so to correct an audience which is dependent on such separations.

It is in his emphasis on this resistance offered in the particular context of almost completely subjective writing that De Quincey offers his most valuable commentaries on the workings of the imagination. When this debate between form and content necessarily converges on autobiographical writing the urgency of De Quincey's address to his audience highlights the importance of that type of writing for him as a manifestation of his own identity:

> There arises a case entirely different, where style cannot be regarded as a *dress* or alien covering, but where style becomes the *incarnation* of the thoughts. The human body is not the dress or apparel of the human spirit: far more mysterious is the mode of their union. Call the two elements A and B; then it is impossible to point out A as existing aloof from B, or *vice versa*. A exists in and through B; B exists in and through A ... Imagery is sometimes not the mere alien apparelling of a thought, and of a nature to be detached from the thought, but it is the coefficient that, being superadded to something else, absolutely *makes* the thought as a *third* and separate existence.
>
> In this third case, our English tendency to undervalue style goes more deeply into error than in the other two. In those two we simply underrate the enormous services that are or might be rendered by style to the interests of truth and human thinking; but in the third case we go near to abolish a mode of existence ... There are many ideas ... which are only to be arrested and realized by a signal *effort* - by a struggle and *nisus* both of reflection and of large combination.[11]

The importance placed on 'signal *effort*' here, and the depth of sympathy in the repetition of 'existence' should intensify concern for De Quincey's achievement of popularising the Romantic theory of the organic conception of language. In his recognition that such an incarnation 'absolutely *makes* the thought as a *third* and separate existence', De Quincey intimates the extent to which he associates this organic concept with the revelatory capacity of the act of composition. It is a recognition of the vital but necessarily separate entity of a work of art. It is separate because of the resistance offered by language to the pre-conceived idea. It is vital because the resistance demands an amalgam which is not simply a compromise, but a union which creates a new statement. The autobiographical implications of this are that the autobiographical statement is seen to exist in its own right, not simply as an extension or a reference back to the non-literary life of the writer: and that this recognition is accompanied by a further act of self-definition precisely because of this separation.

The process of writing is also revelatory because it articulates experiences which have not been linked together and drawn out into coherency. In the very mechanics of composition, in the demand for unity and the desire for continuity, De Quincey realises that subjective material is brought to a stage where it is recognisably different from the experience in its pre-literary form. This discovery is intimately linked to his appreciation of the organic capacity of language. Using an analogy of refracted light which is significantly similar to the one he used to describe the requisite tactics of a popular writer, and which captures well an appreciation of the mechanical in physical alignment with the organic, De Quincey again seeks to affirm his knowledge of the peculiarity of subjective writing:

> he who has to treat a vague question, such as Cicero calls a *quaestio infinita*, where everything is to be furnished out of his own peculiar feelings, or his own way of viewing things ... soon finds that the manner of treating it not only transcends the matter, but very often, and in a very great proportion, *is* the matter. In very many subjective exercises of the mind, - as, for instance, in that class of poetry which has been formally designated by this epithet (meditative poetry, we mean ...), the problem before the writer is to project his own inner mind; to bring out consciously what yet lurks by involution in many unanalysed feelings; in short, to pass through a prism and radiate into distinct elements what previously had been even to himself but dim and confused ideas intermixed with each other. Now, in such cases, the skill with

> which detention or conscious arrest is given to the evanescent, external projection to what is internal, outline to what is fluxionary, and body to what is vague, - all this depends entirely on the command over language as the one sole means of embodying ideas; and in such cases the style, or, in the largest sense, *manner*, is confluent with the matter.[12]

De Quincey acknowledges, when making a similar statement, his indebtedness to Wordsworth for enunciating the idea that language is 'the *incarnation* of thoughts'. But it is in his deviation from this mainstream Romantic doctrine, promulgated by his close associates Wordsworth and Coleridge, that De Quincey has dissatisfied his critics. He continued to make distinctions between rhetoric and eloquence, between 'the literature of knowledge and the literature of power', which are thought to exclude too extensively from the organic concept.

By viewing language as resistance, because of its ability to transform in the process of clarifying preconceived experiences, De Quincey seems to have viewed it as an intermediary agent to which the literary statement or effect was the necessary consequence. Language is in many respects an outside agent reacting against the assimilation of personal experience. De Quincey's considerations of 'style' as opposed to 'content' do not simply represent a naïve contradiction of the organic doctrine mentioned above, but contain the evidence of his autobiographical experience. It is as a means, as an intermediary which is capable of affecting the mind of the reader (who can also be the author) that language reveals its revelatory capacity, its 'external projection' which creates, orders and clarifies. This is especially true of feelings, as De Quincey well knew:

> But to feel is not to feel consciously. Many a man is charmed by one cause who ascribes the effect to another. Many a man is fascinated by the artifices of composition who fancies that it is the subject which has operated so potently.[13]

The inference to be drawn from De Quincey's appreciation of the revelatory nature of the act of composition is that it involved both an organic re-creation and a mechanical, external resistance.

De Quincey's numerous comments upon rhetoric

and didactic poetry testify to his belief in language as an indirect means of communicating literary content. The very strengths of these types of literature, as he understands them, rely upon a profound comprehension of this indirectness. De Quincey's descriptions of the seventeenth century prose writers Sir Thomas Browne and Jeremy Taylor show that he valued their works particularly for their quality of capturing that same self-consciousness in the act of writing evident in Burke and Coleridge. His descriptions of their work illustrate his discussions on rhetoric and eloquence. Significantly, he praises Browne and Taylor for their ability to move between both 'rhetoric' and 'eloquence', and stresses how the imaginative life of their work is achieved through the alternating opposition of these two 'types': 'in them only, are the two opposite forces of eloquent passion and rhetorical fancy brought into an exquisite equilibrium, - approaching, receding, - attracting, repelling, - blending, separating, - chasing and chased as in a fugue'.[14] Referring to Jeremy Taylor alone he observes:

> that one remarkable characteristic of his style which we have already noticed, viz. the everlasting strife and fluctuation between his rhetoric and his eloquence, which maintain their alternations with force and inevitable recurrence, like the systole and diastole, the contraction and expansion, of some living organ.[15]

Again we have an example of opposition which results in a mechanical exercise of an organic medium. 'Rhetoric' for De Quincey usually means an intellectual mind-play with a given subject, whereas 'eloquence' refers to an urgency of emotion which contains the same evidence of a dramatic enactment of the mind of the writer. His definition of these two is saturated with Wordsworthian overtones:

> By Eloquence we understand the overflow of powerful feelings upon occasions fitted to excite them. But Rhetoric is the art of aggrandizing and bringing out into strong relief, by means of various and striking thoughts, some aspect of truth which of itself is supported by no spontaneous feelings, and therefore rests upon artificial aids.[16]

Although De Quincey often uses these two terms

separately and exclusively his preference was for an interrelation between them. Where one is lacking he is apt to censure. He labels Florian and Chateaubriand as 'elegant sentimentalists' precisely because they are eloquent, but never rhetorical. As a result, and most important of all, in them there is 'no flux and reflux of thought, half-meditative, half capricious'.[17] There is no doubt, in De Quincey's mind, that this motion, as evidence of imaginative life, is the most important factor in assessing a work of art. But it is in the combination of an element which 'overflows' and necessitates communication, and an element which simply brings out 'into relief ... aspects of truth' that De Quincey contemplates a more profound dichotomy of thought about the imagination which brings him closer to Wordsworth. The terms in which Wordsworth describes the Lyrical Ballads closely resemble De Quincey's statements:

> I have said that each of these poems has a purpose. I have also informed my Reader what this purpose will be found principally to be: namely to illustrate the manner in which our feelings and ideas are associated in a state of excitement. But speaking in less general language, it is to follow the fluxes and refluxes of the mind when agitated by the great and simple affections of our nature.[18]

The dichotomy is evident here in Wordsworth's drawing together of a 'purpose' and the passive action of 'following'. He is claiming both a referential veracity and a deliberate construction. These two qualities are by no means mutually exclusive, but they might present some difficulty by requiring the imagination to perform a double function of creating a new truth at the same time as illuminating an old one. De Quincey's formulation of the terms 'rhetoric' and 'eloquence' seems to have been at least partly inspired by a need to satisfy his recognition of this double action of the imagination; its combined process involving a mechanical as well as an organic aspect. His reference to rhetoric's ability of 'bringing out into strong relief ... some aspects of truth', constitutes a reliance upon the idea of mechanical combination which conforms to an eighteenth century conception of the imagination, represented by Burke's statement that: 'the power of the imagination is incapable of producing anything absolutely new; it can only vary the disposition of those ideas which it has received from the senses'.[19] De Quincey's reference to eloquence as 'the overflow of powerful feelings' confirms his belief in the imagination as a vital force, and thereby reveals his allegiance to the Romantic attitude. In his demand for both sides he was, of course, attempting to formulate for himself a satisfactory explanation of the double action of the imagination analogous to that which Coleridge stated in his Biographia Literaria, and which has been described by M.H. Abrams in the following terms:

> despite Coleridge's intoxication with the alchemical change wrought in the universe by his discovery of the organic analogy, he did not hesitate to save, and to incorporate into his own theory, the mechanical philosophy he so violently opposed. Mechanism is false, not because it does not tell the truth, but because it does not tell the whole truth.[20]

De Quincey's terms remain distinct and individual from Coleridge's, however, tending to be more appropriate to the imaginative compromise of his career as a periodical journalist, and to his specialist needs as an autobiographer, as much as to his professed mistrust of Coleridge's distinctions with their metaphysical implications.

Granted that the creative process could for him both create and illuminate according to this double action, De Quincey's comments on didactic poetry and rhetoric, with their emphasis on indirectness might be found to be disconcerting. Here the imaginative effect or 'power' is elicited from the resistance or opposition provided by the subject matter, and not a direct consequence of it. It is as if the subject exercises its difficulty in order to promote the real imaginative concern of the writer. In the act of overcoming this difficulty the imaginative powers are stimulated. This suggests the nature of De Quincey's career as a newspaper and a periodical writer where he was forced into composition, often reluctantly, and where his translations and plunderings from other works, in the best instances, show how he overcame such tedious labours by imaginatively re-creating them in a process of 'rifacimento'. It is this background which partly accounts for the following pronouncement upon the 'true idea of didactic poetry':

> Either the poet selects an art which furnishes

> the *occasion* for a series of picturesque exhibitions ... and in that case it is true that he derives part of his power from the art which he delivers, - not, however, from what is essential to the art, but from its accidents and adjuncts: either he does this, or else ... so far from seeking in his subject for any part of his *power*, he seeks in *that* only for the *resistance* with which he contends by means of the power derived from the verse and the artifices of style.[21]

By '*resistance*' here De Quincey has more in mind than the mere consolation afforded by a difficult intellectual exercise; and this would seem to be substantiated by his discussion of the justification of Virgil's Eclogues. The first possible justification he considers is: 'As a *difficult* and intractable subject, by way of a *bravura*, or passage of execution'.[22] But this is followed by the serious qualification that: 'This is not a very elevated form of poetic art, and too much like rope-dancing'.[23] Clearly, resistance alone, and especially for its own sake, is not to be considered of high merit: it is to be a means to an end. According to De Quincey then, art is to be achieved as an indirect effect of difficulty and, as we have seen before, must contain a form of revelation, which in an autobiographer's situation may be equated with a further level of self-awareness. It is this act of indirect revelation which dictates his appreciation of didactic poetry. The power of this type of work still depends upon its ability to communicate the 'flux and reflux' of a mind agitated upon the subject. To this extent it 'follows', as Wordsworth says, and is therefore an act of imagination. An ultimate directness or full explicitness would travesty this power of imitation, and so De Quincey states quite categorically:

> No poetry can have the function of teaching. It is impossible that a variety of species should contradict the very purpose which contradistinguishes its *genus* ... Poetry, or any one of the fine arts (all of which alike speak through the genial nature of man and his agitated sensibilities), can teach only as nature teaches, as forests teach, as the sea teaches, as infancy teaches - viz., by deep impulse, by hieroglyphic suggestion. Their teaching is not direct or explicit, but

> lurking, implicit, masked in deep incarnations. To teach formally and professedly is to abandon the very differential character and principle of poetry. If poetry could condescend to teach anything it would be truths moral or religious. But even these it can utter only through symbols and actions.[24]

De Quincey's idea of imaginative power as a by-product of resistance overcome conforms to the nature of his enforced periodical writings. It can be seen that it is also in keeping with an appreciation of art as imitation, which first began with Aristotle's notion of *mimesis*. But it is through De Quincey's emphasis upon the impure or difficult medium of language that this idea of imitation is articulated by him in the term '*idem in alio*', which again finds a close parallel in Wordsworth's 'similitude in dissimilitude'.[25] With De Quincey our attention is focused first of all on this difference and so our appreciation of his work as an autobiographer should begin with a denial of any expectation of his autobiography being simply a directly revelatory statement. On the contrary, the revelatory capacity of his autobiography is understood to operate upon a profound recognition that the very disparity between the written word and the experience to which it refers, is conducive to a sharper, conscious appreciation of that experience. In De Quincey's autobiography acts of self-discovery, far from being inconsistent with a highly-wrought, elaborate prose, are thought to be the necessary consequences of artifice. In this sense, too, the autobiographical statement is neither single nor direct. It is with these complexities that De Quincey's autobiography can enact its important function of defining and analysing thoughts and feelings which do not usually come within the range of such conscious scrutiny:

> The unevolved thoughts which pass through the youngest - the rudest - the most inexperienced brain, are innumerable; not detached - voluntary thoughts, but thoughts inherent in what is seen, talked of, experienced, or read of. To evolve these, to make them apprehensible by others, and often even to bring them within their own consciousness, is very difficult to most people; ... and the power, by which this difficulty is conquered, admits of endless culture: and, amongst the modes of culture, is

> that of written composition. ... the direct purpose is to exercise the mind in unravelling its own thoughts, which else lie huddled and tangled together in a state unfit for use, and but dimly developed to the possessor's own consciousness.[26]

Although autobiographical writing undertakes this important action of 'unravelling' fleeting and complexly combined experiences, De Quincey forthrightly denies that it is an easy task. On the contrary, he considers it to be the province of a specialist involved in a delicate and refined activity. At least, this seems to be the implication of his word 'culture', and his reaction against the normal state of unanalysed experiences. He appears to be advocating that such an ability is to be acquired only after numerous attempts: it is a skill which requires a concerted effort if it is to be perfected.

It is by realising the possibilities of artistic elaboration that the sharpest, the most important references can be made to real experience. The benefit of a mature literary autobiography is not simply that its artistic quality therapeutically distances or harmonises the original experiences, but that its sophistication provides an ordered and sensitive counter which can more accurately define those experiences. De Quincey's fastidious concern for rhythm in his prose, which has traditionally supported his literary reputation, and his demand for a musical continuity in the most 'impassioned' passages of his autobiographical writings, are founded upon his realisation that the very distancing ornamentation of art is more conducive to the assessment of 'real' feelings. This would explain both his dislike of an English tradition of naïve confession, which he voices in the opening to his own *Confessions of an English Opium-Eater*, and his contempt for the various forms of realism which were popular in his time. He reacted strongly against the contemporary delight, and faith, in circumstantial details: he objected to the current practice in biographical and autobiographical writing of giving 'the inevitable roll-call of a man's life'. The reasons for this point of view, as we have seen, lie in De Quincey's faith in the viability of art as an indirect form of imitation. It is a point of view which he seems to have shared with Coleridge. Both men used the same analogy of waxwork figures to illustrate their point; De Quincey when describing the distanced, abstracted nature of Greek drama,[27]

Coleridge when attempting to define the nature of imitation itself: 'If there be likeness to nature without any check of difference, the result is disgusting, and the more complete the delusion, the more loathsome the effect'.[28] The more artistically achieved the representation the greater the possibility it provides for viewing the experience. There is no disgust to obstruct the view; the distance acts cathartically and allows the reader, after the immediate recognition of difference, to return all the more eagerly to consider the correspondence to the experience in view.

It is for this reason that De Quincey reacts against a directly confessional utterance: he realises that such a method might obtrude upon the sensibility of his reader and thereby cut him off from the possibility of acting in a sympathetic or mediatory capacity. De Quincey's carefully constructed prose (especially that in The English Mail-Coach) which deliberately declares its own elaborateness, thus performs for him a double function, of registering the earnestness and 'impassioned' feeling of the writer at the same time as invoking the sympathetic attention of the reader. In such a way this very elaborateness is argued to be a 'natural' technique: 'Metre is naturally and necessarily adopted in cases of impassioned themes, for the very obvious reason that rhythmus is both a cause of impassioned feeling, an ally of such feeling, and a natural effect of it';[29] De Quincey's attention to style in the special province of subjective literature is in keeping with the requirements of his task as an autobiographer. The very literary complexity of his work, according to the critical statements we have examined, furthered his aim of a mediated vision which could be both objective and yet demand sympathy from the reader. By saying that 'rhythmus is both a cause of impassioned feeling, an ally of such feeling, and a natural effect of it', De Quincey is also taking into account the idea of self-awareness in the act of composition. The rhythmic aspect of style, as he described it in Burke, contains its own principle of motion, and in that sense it is an ally to De Quincey in offsetting the more resistant difficulties of composition. The continuity afforded by rhythm allows for, even dictates, the progression of the autobiographical statement. It is exactly this kind of continuity which De Quincey fails to find in Hazlitt and Lamb. Of the latter's prose he says: 'It does not prolong itself - it does not repeat itself - it does not propagate itself'.[30] It is this self-propagating style which De Quincey seems to find most congenial to that type of writing which seeks to communicate the very movement of the mind of the writer upon the subject:

> No man can be eloquent whose thoughts are abrupt, insulated, capricious, and (to borrow an impressive word from Coleridge) non-sequacious. Eloquence resides not in separate or fractional ideas, but in the relations of manifold ideas, and in the mode of their evolution from each other. It is not indeed enough that the ideas should be many, and their relations coherent; the main condition lies in the *key* of the evolution, in the *law* of the succession. The elements are nothing without the atmosphere that moulds, and the dynamic forces that combine.[31]

Again, he refers to the process of combination as 'dynamic', a term which can be thought to signify its importance in the creation of something not simply combined but new. It is in the difficulty of achieving such a modulation (which involves a submission to that '*law* of succession') that a further level of self-consciousness is added to the act of autobiography.

Even though such a harmonised and continuous effect often successfully carries the varied fluctuations of the autobiographer's act of exploration, and his attempt to convey that very continuity, De Quincey occasionally seems to deliberately interrupt it. He intrudes with a further level of commentary which makes direct appeals to the reader and which makes explicit the reference to the nature of the text and its aims. As we shall see in Chapter Four, this further level of commentary performs a number of functions for De Quincey, not least being a mediatory agent which offers an opportunity for apology, justification and explanation. But for our present purpose of '*resistance*', it is also a register of difficulty and a concession to the compromise of the periodical context; it can mediate the autobiographical vision but it is also inherent in De Quincey's literary situation.

De Quincey compared the function of the chorus in Greek drama to the Dark Interpreter of his dreams; an analogy could be drawn between his idea of the chorus and the function he performs in making these direct appeals and explanations to the reader.

He refutes the moral function of the chorus in order to place the emphasis on sympathy:

> One great error which remains to be removed is the notion that the chorus either did support, or was meant to support, the office of a moral teacher. The chorus simply stood on the level of a sympathizing spectator, detached from the business and the crash of catastrophe; and its office was to guide or interpret the sympathies of the audience.[32]

While De Quincey's direct interruptions to the reader are often detached from the narrative chronology or the rhythmical progression mentioned above, they often draw attention to the immediate predicament of the act of composition. Frequently they show De Quincey's recognition of his context - the necessity to cater for the readership of the various magazines. To this extent this further level of commentary was enforced; but it also provided a mediating alternative to the rhythmical continuum of the autobiographical statement. It could thus aid De Quincey and the reader, as well as providing a shared experience located in the technique. De Quincey could turn this to his advantage, both subtly manipulating and openly challenging his reader. His description of the characteristic style of Demosthenes recognises this kind of situation (the periodical compromise), is aware of some of the possibilities, but does not speculate on how they can be turned to his advantage:

> It is one which grew naturally ... from the composition of his audience. His audience ... being, in fact, always on the fret, - kept the orator always on the fret. Hence arose short sentences; hence the impossibility of the long, voluminous sweeps of beautiful rhythmus which we find in Cicero; hence the animated form of apostrophe and crowded interrogations to the audience. This robs him of a large variety of structure applied to the logic, or the embellishment, or the music of his composition. His style is full of life, but not ... full of pomp and continuous grandeur. On the contrary, as the necessity of rousing attention, or of sustaining it, obliged the Attic orator to rely too much on the *personality* of direct question to the audience ... In all things, the *immediate* - the instant - the *praesaens praesentissimum*, was

> kept steadily before ... [him] ... by the mere coercion of self-interest.[33]

That phrase 'the *personality* of direct question to the audience' illuminates De Quincey's own role and technique of creating a literary personality. He recognised, especially in Lamb, a new form of contemporary writing which made a special demand upon the reader by requiring him to recognise such a personality. In his essay 'Charles Lamb' De Quincey wrote:

> There is in modern literature a whole class of writers ... standing within the same category: some marked originality of character in the writer becomes a co-efficient with what he says to a common result; you must sympathise with this *personality* in the author before you can appreciate the most significant parts of his views.[34]

The sympathy demanded by the familiar essayist seems to have been born out of a compromise operating against the dictates of the writer, but eventually acknowledged as a source of comfort, and a possible new tactic with which to manipulate the reader.

The significance De Quincey places on the idea of 'resistance' may be viewed as a search for a viable means of communication; not simply overcoming the compromise we have noticed, but being born out of it and successfully exploiting it as a means of power. The difficulties of composition are not, for De Quincey, one of the peripheral effects which linger in the finished product, but an integral and important part of his material. As we shall see later, in an analysis of his Suspiria de Profundis, a good deal of his autobiography concerns itself with the problems of its own genesis. Similarly, De Quincey finds in his appreciation of the mechanical or aggregating part played in creativity, a correspondent power of revelation and creation to the acknowledged organic factor. The resonances of this are most pertinent to his aim of defining his past self: clarification and accurate reconstructions of subjective experiences lead to a new sense of identity; but they are also felt as a fruitful alternative or an extra specific illustration in the formulation of the mainstream Romantic aesthetic. De Quincey's critical statements are central not as theoretical speculations, but as informants of his own practice as an autobiographer. Granted that his compromised situation could be a source of strength, it now remains to analyse its effects, or in De Quincey's words, to assess its 'power'.

POWER

The revelatory aspect of De Quincey's autobiographical writings, their ability to deliver new 'truths' to their audience - 'to bring out consciously what yet lurks by involution in many unanalyzed feelings'[35] works in conjunction with a plea for the reader to imagine the difficulties involved in this task. In De Quincey's case the psychological or analytic aspect of subjective writing joins with an equally strong principle to make the reader not simply understand, but sympathise. The 'power' of De Quincey's autobiographical writings is the product of a rare combination of two types of literature which are more usually separate according to his own most famous critical distinction:

> In that great social organ which, collectively, we call literature, there may be distinguished two separate offices that may blend and often *do* so, but capable, severally, of a severe insulation, and naturally fitted for reciprocal replusion. There is first, the literature of *knowledge*; and secondly, the literature of *power*. The function of the first is - to teach; the function of the second is - to *move*: the first is a rudder; the second, an oar or sail. The first speaks to the mere discursive understanding; the second speaks ultimately ... to the higher understanding or reason, but always *through* affections of pleasure and sympathy.[36]

Although this statement concentrates on the separation of the two types the initial admission at least allows for the possibility of creating an autobiography which is analytic yet demands the imaginative sympathy which may be equated with 'power'.

The revelatory capacity of De Quincey's autobiographical writings would seem to depend on that skill of the autobiographer which deciphers, discovers, rather than that which creates. This seems to be confirmed in another instance where De Quincey concerns himself with the same distinction between the effects of his two types of literature:

> The true antithesis to knowledge, in this case,

> is not *pleasure*, but *power*. All that is literature seeks to communicate power; all that is not literature, to communicate knowledge. Now, if it be asked what is meant by communicating power, I, in my turn, would ask by what name a man would designate the case in which I should be made to feel vividly, and with a vital consciousness, emotions which ordinary life rarely or never supplies occasions for exciting, and which had previously lain unwakened, and hardly within the dawn of consciousness - as myriads of modes of feeling are at this moment in every human mind for want of a poet to organize them? I say, when these inert and sleeping forms *are* organized, when these possibilities *are* actualized, is this conscious and living possession of mine *power*, or what is it?[37]

The emphasis here is on illumination rather than creation, and in De Quincey's use of the word 'organize', we might again consider him to be referring to the dynamic capacity of combination which is capable of 'realizing' or throwing into relief new possibilities because of the effect of juxtaposition. The revelatory capacity of autobiography might be considered to exist in this opportunity it allows for conscious scrutiny. Its extraordinary quality resides not so much in the experiences it discovers as in the potency of its aspect which makes such scrutiny possible. The autobiography is thus democratic as regards its material, but specialist in its technique. Sigmund K. Procter recognised in his study of De Quincey's literary 'theory' that:

> His definition is in psychological terms and carries virtually no suggestion of the supernatural. High as he conceives the poet's function to be, he engages in no worship of the power. He tends to exalt the effect achieved by poetry, not the poet as an individual. Above all, he does not look upon the poet as one charged with the expression of the ego.[38]

By using the word 'organize' De Quincey is again exhibiting this tendency; it is a question of degree rather than an essential difference. It is this emphasis on degree which is most pertinent to his task as an autobiographer, in articulating subconscious or fleeting experiences:

> It is astonishing how large a harvest of new

> truths would be reaped simply through the accident of a man's feeling, or being made to feel, more *deeply* than other men. He sees the same objects, neither more nor fewer, but he sees them engraved in lines far stronger and more determinate: and the difference in the strength makes the whole difference between consciousness and subconsciousness.[39]

For De Quincey, it was Wordsworth who exemplified this quality in a writer; he was thus responsible for bringing 'many a truth into life, both for the eye and for the understanding'.[40] Although De Quincey refers to 'the eye ... and the understanding' here, it is not to those two that his attentions are usually directed. He is more interested in the emotive force attendant upon the discovery, and the conviction which supports it as a truth. The 'great distinction of Wordsworth', he wrote, 'is the extent of his sympathy with what is *really* permanent in human feelings, and also the depth of his sympathy'.[41] It is the insistence first of all on feelings, and a reaction against the 'mere understanding' which characterises the nature of De Quincey's communication of personal discoveries. Feeling is both the cause of the discovery and the means by which it is conveyed through sympathy. When De Quincey writes of 'power' in this context of psychological discovery he seems to be describing the effect on his own feelings as much as the value of the discovery either to himself or to others. Of course, the discovery, by drawing experiences out to be observed by the conscious mind, allows an individual to locate and distinguish the forces which are operating within, and so to that extent allows for greater control. De Quincey senses the degree to which people are governed by unconscious impulses, the existence of which may not always be known. 'Power' in this sense might refer to the secret springs of action upon which conscious behaviour depends:

> And of this let everyone be assured - that he owes to the impassioned books which he has read many a thousand more of emotions than we can consciously trace back to them. Dim by their origination, these emotions yet arise in him, and mould him through life, like forgotten incidents of his childhood.[42]

When De Quincey relates his experience of discovering

one of these 'moulding emotions' he is concerned to register the excitement of the discovery rather than to document it scientifically. Although an analytic skill is required to locate and define the discovery in question, it is secondary to the purpose of communicating the imaginative impact that has occurred.

This impact is primarily one of excitement because the discovery has opened up new possibilities. De Quincey's use of the word 'power' relates to the fact that the range of experience has been expanded by the act of discovery. This explains his enthusiasm and his delight at Wordsworth's example. Autobiography, as we have seen, as well as being a vehicle to convey these new possibilities, also adds to them because of the revelatory nature of the act of composition. In this double sense it explores the possibilities of subjective contemplation and is pleased to find new sources of action, new types of feeling and new evidence of vital processes operating within an individual. Autobiography is a means of constantly expanding the depths of personality rather than simply a means of fixing to allow for rational investigation. It is this felt depth of personality which excites De Quincey rather than the external space of the world of nature. His reaction to King Lear shows how literary 'power' is connected to the expansion of subjective horizons:

> when I am thus suddenly startled into a feeling of the infinity of the world within me, is this power, or what may I call it? Space, again, what is it in most men's minds? The lifeless form of the world without us, a postulate of the geometrician, with no more vitality or real existence to their feelings than the square root of two ... Henceforth, therefore, I shall use the antithesis power and knowledge as the most philosophical expression for literature (that is, Literae Humaniores) and anti-literature (that is, Literae didacticae[43]

This insistence on feelings and the reaction against 'knowledge' has been noted by the two main critics of De Quincey's own critical abilities - Sigmund K. Procter and John E. Jordan. The latter declares that 'the *primum mobile* ... as generally in [his] criticism, was that something "produced to my feelings an effect"',[44] while Procter asserts that, 'he chose an anti-intellectualistic solution to the problem of knowledge, thus turning what was a defeat for the pretensions of reason into a victory for the claims of the feelings'.[45] Though De Quincey's distinction above is obviously extreme, he is reacting more against the non-vital aspect of the world as it manifested itself in his time, than absolutely decrying the possibilities of the geometrician or the external world in general. He speaks to the English public from a specific angle - stimulating the new literature-seeking public in one of his 'Letters to a Young Man Whose Education Has Been Neglected'. He was well aware of the importance of the natural world to Wordsworth, though his references to its importance for himself are very limited. Nevertheless, there is one which satisfies his relation to the natural world which at the same time stresses the nature of the society to which he belongs: on one occasion he contemplates living in isolation in the forests of Canada; the reason is that:

> in England, and in all moderate climates, we are too slightly reminded of nature or the focus of nature. Great heats, or great colds ... or great hurricanes, as in the West Indian latitudes, recall us continually to the sense of a powerful presence, investing our paths on every side; whereas, in England, it is possible to forget that we live amongst greater agencies than those of men and human institutions. Man, in fact, "too much man", as Timon complained most reasonably in Athens, was then, and is now, our greatest grievance in England.[46]

In his Suspiria de Profundis De Quincey similarly reacts against what he calls 'the vortex of the merely human',[47] that is the morbid, demoralising influence of contemporary city life. The 'merely human' refers to a potential grandeur which has not been realised. In its revelatory capacity autobiography reaches beyond the everyday world of habit and dull routine and makes known new possibilities. It is claimed that by making people feel vividly as opposed to an appeal 'to the mere discursive understanding'[48] life or literature effects an expansion of personality:

> Were it not that human sensibilities are ventilated and continually called out into exercise by the great phenomenon of infancy, or of real life as it moves through chance and change, or of literature as it recombines these elements in the mimicries of poetry ... it is

> certain that, like any animal power or muscular energy falling into disuse, all such sensibilities would gradually droop and dwindle. It is in these great *moral* capacities of man that the literature of power, as contradistinguished from that of knowledge, lives and has its field of action.[49]

De Quincey's emphasis on feelings as the essential constituents of his notion of '*power*' need not detract from the moral responsibility of his work. This was no casual or vague belief on his part; as we have already seen, his distinction between genius and talent (which is a product of his experience as a periodical journalist) also rests on this belief in the morally invigorating effect of deep feeling:

> genius is that mode of intellectual power which moves in alliance with the *genial* nature - i.e. with the capacities of pleasure and pain, - whereas talent has no vestige of such an alliance, and is perfectly independent of all human sensibilities. Consequently, genius is a voice of breathing that represents the *total* nature as well as his knowing and distinguishing nature ... Genius is the language which interprets the synthesis of the human spirit with the human intellect, each acting through the other; whilst talent speaks only from the insulated intellect. And hence also it is that, besides its relation to suffering and enjoying, genius always implies a deeper relation to virtue and vice; whereas talent has no shadow of a relation to *moral* qualities.[50]

While true to De Quincey's experience of the act of composition, due to its attention to 'suffering and enjoying', this statement is not confined to his own insular position. By placing it against its mature intellectual background we can see again how the periodical compromise provides an alternative context in which to culture the imagination rather than simply 'compromising' it. This background gives us the material for a sharper assessment of the type of 'power' which could be produced in that compromise as a result of a fruitful kind of resistance.

The important moral function De Quincey assigns to the feelings in artistic production and effect finds some authority and justification in Kant's Critique of Aesthetic Judgement and his pre-Critical work Observations on the Feeling of the Beautiful and Sublime. A section of the latter was translated by De Quincey and appeared in The London Magazine in 1824. As T. Goldthwait has written in the introduction to his translation of Kant's earlier work,[51] the importance of the Sublime lies in its function of 'uniting ... aesthetic with moral experiences'[52] and it 'emerges as an important moral component of the person'.[53] Kant also provides a subjective viewpoint for this moral/aesthetic union: '*The various feelings of enjoyment* or of displeasure rest not so much upon the nature of the external things that arouse them as upon each person's own description to be moved by these to pleasure or pain'.[54] The starting-point of Kant's analysis is to investigate the response of the beholder, the capacity to feel either the effects of the sublime or the beautiful. According to Kant, 'the sublime *moves*', and 'the mien of a man who is undergoing the full feeling of the sublime is earnest, sometimes rigid and astonished'.[55]

This emphasis on the beholder, and the central concern with the effects of the sublime (that is to say, how it registers itself) help to explain Procter's assertion that 'One principal difference between De Quincey's literary theory and that of Wordsworth and Coleridge is that De Quincey occupies himself almost exclusively with an analysis of final effects'.[56] As a result, Procter concludes, De Quincey 'ignores for the most part the process and the agencies by which power is communicated', and therefore he tends 'to value literature ... as communication rather than expression'.[57] Although this, as we have seen, is not strictly true, both the response of the beholder and direct communication would seem to be the natural emphases of De Quincey the autobiographer. The former may be equated in a special sense with the autobiographer's ability to behold his past self and to be conscious of himself in the very act of composition. The latter coincides with his concern for fidelity to past experience.

In Kant, therefore, De Quincey inherited an example of how his own moral sense could be reconciled to a subjective vision which relied on feelings, and feelings which were compatible with a principle of revelation and expansion. By arguing for the sublime as a moral force, Kant may have allowed De Quincey to see how feelings of awe and astonishment could accord with an exploration of his own personality which was not restricted to the 'merely human'.

De Quincey's own ideas of the sublime (which are first evident in the diary he wrote as a seventeen year old)[58] show that he was also aware and perhaps dissatisfied with the native tradition of aesthetic theory which concerned itself with the distinction between the sublime and the beautiful. The peculiarly modern relevance of the sublime for him reveals itself in his reaction against the classical notion propounded by Longinus:

> Let it be remembered that, of all powers which act upon man through his intellectual nature, the very rarest is that which we moderns call the *sublime*. The Grecians had apparently no word for it, unless it were that which they meant by **το σεμνον** : for **υψος** was a comprehensive expression for all qualities which gave a character of life or animation to the composition[59]

Dissatisfied with most of the eighteenth century attempts on this subject, and seeking an aesthetic distinction which would accord with the revelatory nature of his autobiographical vision, and the mixture of mechanical combination and organic incarnation which occurred in its composition, De Quincey may have found congenial examples in Burke and Wordsworth. As John E. Jordan has briefly noted,[60] there is an affinity between one of De Quincey's descriptions of the '*dark* sublime' and Burke's idea of terror as one of the causes of the sublime. There are, however, more similarities, and more significant ones for our purpose of defining De Quincey's autobiographical concerns. When considering terror as a cause of the sublime Burke hints at its moral force by drawing attention to the religious nature of the experience:

> not pleasure, but a sort of delightful horror, a sort of tranquillity tinged with terror; which, as it belongs to self-preservation, is one of the strongest of all the passions. Its object is the sublime. Its highest degree I call *astonishment*; the subordinate degrees are awe, reverence, and respect, which by the very etymology of the words, shew from what source they are derived.[61]

De Quincey would have sympathised not simply with Burke's notion of terror, but his belief in the greater power of emotions involving pain and suffering:

> The passions which belong to self-preservation, turn on pain and danger; they are delightful when we have an idea of pain and danger, without being actually in such circumstances; this delight I have not called pleasure, because it turns on pain, and because it is different enough from any idea of positive pleasure. Whatever excites this delight, I call *sublime*. The passions belonging to self-preservation are the strongest of all the passions.[62]

In De Quincey's autobiography, as we shall see, 'sublime' events in his past experience can be viewed in retrospect with this kind of 'delight' which Burke describes. This delight is heightened because such events may be able to locate and explain the power motivating his subsequent life. In attempting to describe these 'sublime' events of his past life, surprising or astonishing links of continuity may be revealed. The autobiography is both a statement about the nature of his past (how it is considered by the writer at that point) and a further means of redefinition. The element of revelation or discovery which promotes the feelings of astonishment and surprise thus exists on more than one level. Alongside these the autobiography also attempts to operate on a more analytic or rational basis, but this usually follows as a consequence to the experience of discovery. These two elements are to some extent separate because the nature of the revelatory element is of a sort which possesses the whole attention of the writer. It is the power of this irrational or rather non-rational kind which 'possesses' the writer, which accords with the idea of the sublime as described by both Burke and Wordsworth.

When Burke describes the effect of the sublime produced by nature, he declares that one of the distinguishing features of 'astonishment' is its exclusive, prepossessing quality:

> The passion caused by the great and sublime in *nature*, when those causes operate most powerfully, is astonishment; and astonishment is that state of the soul, in which all its motions are suspended, with some degree of horror. In this case the mind is so entirely filled with its object, that it cannot entertain any other, nor by consequence, reason on that object which employs it. Hence arises the great power of the sublime, that, far from being produced by

> them, it anticipates our reasonings, and hurries us on by an irresistable force.[63]

Wordsworth in his uncompleted The Sublime and the Beautiful echoes Burke's description of 'astonishment' and carries further the implications of the exclusion of the rational faculty which takes place in an experience of the sublime: 'For whatever suspends the comparing power of the mind and possesses it with a feeling or image of intense unity, without a conscious contemplation of the parts, has produced that state of mind which is the consummation of the sublime'.[64] Characteristically Wordsworth sees the necessity for this suspended effect to be of temporary duration, allowing then for the action of rational and moral considerations. He seems to sense the danger of the power of the sublime:

> But if the Power contemplated be of that kind which neither admits of the notion of resistance or participation, then it may be confidently said that, unless the apprehension which it excites terminate in repose, there can be no sublimity, and that this sense of repose is the result of reason and the moral law.[65]

Both these statements about the 'suspending' effect of the sublime seem, to the two writers concerned, more appropriate to the awe-inspiring effects of the external natural world, though, of course, in The Prelude Wordsworth traces the growth of this in an intimate involvement with his imaginative and moral life. In De Quincey's case revealed depths of personality correspond to these heights and depths of the natural world. In Burke's discussion of the sublime he would have found an alternative sort of sublime effect which concerned itself with the expanding dimensions of minutiae - which looked as if inwards rather than to the outside world. This introspective aspect of sublime astonishment which Burke delineates would be compatible with De Quincey's own subjectively-defined, autobiographical exploration, especially in the sense in which it describes an expanding depth:

> Greatness of dimension is a powerful cause of the sublime. This is too evident, and the observation too common, to need any illustration; it is not so common to consider in what ways greatness of dimension, vastness of extent or quantity has the most striking effect

> ... we are more struck at looking down from a precipice, than looking up at an object of equal height ... when we attend to the infinite divisibility of matter, when we pursue animal life into these excessively small, and yet organised beings, that escape the nicest inquisition of the sense, when we push our discoveries yet downward, and consider those creatures so many degrees yet smaller, and the still diminishing scale of existence, in tracing which the imagination is lost as well as the sense, we become amazed and confounded at the wonders of minuteness; nor can we distinguish in its effect this extreme of littleness from the vast itself.[66]

Burke's interest in 'the infinite divisibility of matter' parallels De Quincey's fascination with the divisibility not of tangible realities but emotional and intellectual ones. And it is firmly linked to his experience of composition and the stress which he places on 'combination'. In his later life he could write: 'It is not, it has not been, perhaps it never will be, understood - how vast a thing is combination'.[67] It is precisely this 'vast' quality which characterises 'combination' and which is dependent upon his awareness of 'divisibility'. Combination is such a potent force with De Quincey because it makes him all the more conscious of new depths and possibilities in his own past experience and his means of communicating it. As he says 'all words cover ideas, and many a word covers a choice of ideas, and very many ideas split into a variety of modifications'.[68]

Naturally De Quincey could find such a knowledge to be both comforting and frightening. The sublime experience in representing a suspension of the rational or comparing, quantifying faculty of the mind, constituted a release from the 'merely human'. As far as it dissolved the firm boundaries and clear outlines of his past experience and occasionally offered no prospect of conclusion or final assessment it was a threat to his own identity. In the former aspect it triumphed not only over the dull routine or 'morbid stimulation' of London life, but also over his awareness of the false promises, the delusive openings of creative experience. As we saw in the last chapter, his comments about the workings of his own imagination show how perilously close he thought it to powers of a disruptive and anarchic kind. The 'power' of the sublime as it truly registers itself is thus doubly important to him because of his knowledge of the false nature of such experiences: the power of introspection could be wasted by counterfeit attractions of the imagination.

Likewise, the expansion provided by a sublime moment forms part of De Quincey's reaction against the strong impression he has of mundane, habitual experience amounting to no more than a shadow or an illusion. His central concern as an autobiographer is to provide a continuity of experience; to be self-conscious and aware of the passage of time, feeling vividly the various levels and intensities of his life. How strongly he valued the expansive nature of a 'sublime' moment can be estimated from his consideration of this other side of his experience:

> Generally, that is, for a million against a unit, the awful mystery by which the fearful powers of death, and sorrow, and pain, and sin are locked into parts of a whole; so as, in fact, to be repetitions, reaffirmations of each other under a different phase - this is nothing, does not exist. Death sinks to a mere collective term - a category - a word of convenience for purposes of arrangement. You depress your hands, and behold, the system disappears; you raise them, it appears. This is nothing - a cipher, a shadow. Clap your hands like an Arabian girl, and all comes back. Unstop your ears, and it is muffled. To and fro; it is and is not - is not and is. And mighty heaven that such a mockery should cover the whole vision of life! It is and is not; and on to the day of your death you will still have to learn what is the truth.
>
> The eternal now through the dreadful loom is the overflowing future poured back into the capacious reservoir of the past. All the active element lies in that infinitesimal *now*. The future is not except by relation; the past is not at all, and the present but a sign of the nexus between the two.[69]

In this fragment from his Posthumous Works De Quincey might seem to verge on the ludicrous or melodramatic because he is dealing emotively with an idea which is usually considered as a logical platitude. Like Burke's effect of the 'sublime' De Quincey's sense of imaginative power is closely linked to a logical, investigatory ability. He may start out with analytic intentions and then be pleasantly rewarded when the powers of such a method are found to be inadequate. In the extract above it is the normal acceptance of time which appears as a mockery, an inadequate correlative to imaginative experiences - unable to register depth of feeling. When he refers to 'a mere collective term' and 'but a sign' he challenges a tacit acceptance or general understanding which does not convey the sense of dimension, the prospect which brings it alive in the mind.

De Quincey claimed that opium produced, even more dramatically, a sense of time which operated beyond the normal categories. While space and time are both altered by the effect of the drug, and it is this effect which constitutes the 'power', De Quincey's apprehension of that power seems to have been intimately associated with his logical or quantifying faculty. He seems thrilled to find the power overriding his understanding and, to some extent, relies upon this to define and communicate it:

> In the *Opium Confessions* I touched a little upon the extraordinary power connected with opium (after long use) of amplifying the dimensions of time. Space, also, it amplifies by degrees that are sometimes terrific ... Time becomes infinitely elastic, stretching out to such immeasurable and vanishing termini that it seems ridiculous to compute the sense of it[70]

Although he claims here that 'it seems ridiculous to compute the sense of it', it would appear that just such an attempt at computation is, for De Quincey, both a natural response and a means of experiencing the full extent of the 'amplification'. As Burke recognised, the greatness of dimension which is a cause of the sublime and can result from attention to the minute details of the natural world confounds both the imagination and the 'sense'. In De Quincey's case the distinction between these two often seems to be sharply maintained, though, of course, they do work in combination with each other. In Suspiria de Profundis, for example, it is De Quincey's alter ego - the so-called 'Dark Interpreter' of his dreams - who suggests to him the following computation of time:

> Put into a Roman clepsydra one hundred drops of

> water; let these run out as the sand in an hour-glass, every drop measuring the hundredth part of a second, so that each shall represent but the three-hundred-and-sixty-thousandth part of an hour. Now, count the drops as they race along; and, when the fiftieth of the hundred is passing, behold! forty-nine are not, because already they have perished, and fifty are not, because they are yet to come. You see, therefore, how narrow, how incalculably narrow, is the true and actual present.[71]

This apparent narrowness is analogous to his previous 'mere category': both cases show how the mind cannot respond to the notion of time simply by using the standard process of logic. The intellectual or analytic intention of the mind resists and fails to accommodate the depth which is felt in the imaginative experience. The sublime moment informs the 'mere category' by expanding the narrowness of the present, and thus transcends the traditional linear progression.

It is in retrospect that De Quincey manipulates an analytic skill in order to imaginatively recreate sublime moments from his past. Even though it was precisely this part of his mind which was confounded in the original experience, it is now the use of this skill which dramatically recaptures the effect for the reader, and which is a necessary factor in controlling literary communication of complex, simutaneous, though brief psychological processes. The sublime moment is thus contained within a logical framework which accepts the usual methods of chronology and investigation. In this way 'power' is often given a greater credibility and authority, as well as being more easily understood. This is as much a concession to the reader as it is a necessary preliminary to conscious scrutiny. The logical framework mediates the primarily emotive force of the sublime moment, both for the autobiographer and for the reader.

Apart from these considerations, however, the analytic framework, though consequent to the original experience, now provides a valuable check upon it, often balancing, even correcting its extreme nature. This is especially so when as in Suspiria de Profundis De Quincey considers the involuntary acts of his own consciousness - the effects of opium and sudden intrusions of memory. Although such 'moments' provide an expansion which accords with the sublime idea we have been following, they also possess something of an arbitrary and separate nature. When De Quincey describes such an experience: 'and yet suddenly, at a silent command, at the signal of a blazing rocket sent up from the brain, the pall draws up, and the whole depths of the theatre are exposed',[72] he is aware of the degree to which 'at a silent command' contains a threat to his ability to impose his own self-conscious identity upon his experience by an act of will.

Similarly, De Quincey realises the dangers attendant upon the very process of bringing subconscious intrusions under a conscious scrutiny; of analysing sublime moments which would otherwise have been temporary, and confined to imaginative experience. His recognition of this danger was probably emphasised by his public context. The seriousness of his task, and the responsibility which it necessitated, can be gauged from his comments upon 'confession':

> the practice of confession is undoubtedly the most demoralising practice known to any Christian society. Innocent young persons, whose thoughts would never have wandered out upon any impure images or suggestions, have their ... curiosity sent roving upon unlawful quests: they are instructed to watch what else would pass undetained in the mind, and would pass unblameably, on the Miltonic principle ... Nay, which is worse of all, unconscious or semi-conscious thoughts and feelings or natural impulses, rising, like a breath of wind ... are now brought powerfully under the focal light of the consciousness: and whatsoever is once made the subject of consciousness, can never again have the privilege of gay, careless thoughtlessness - the privilege by which the mind, like the lamps of a mail-coach, moving rapidly through the midnight woods, illuminate, for one instant ... This happy privilege is forfeited for ever[73]

With this in mind De Quincey seems to carry out his self-explorations with a good deal of caution, carefully limiting the extent of any logical investigation. Just as the 'power' of the sublime moment must be mediated and, at times, regarded with suspicion, so the objective, rationalising function of his autobiography should be kept in check by being subordinated to the aims of imaginative recreation and correspondence to past experience. Accuracy of objective categorisation is thus balanced by an attempt at experiential veracity. The movement of the autobiography is between these two; modulating and redefining these two extremes of the autobiographer's previous vision and present technique.

This close association of analytic introspection and imaginative expansion provides the limits in which De Quincey's own literature of 'power' functions. Analysis defines and mediates important imaginative events from the past, and provides an instrument for further revelations which may take place in the present act of composition. Most importantly of all, perhaps, it is able to give definition to, and render accessible to a magazine audience the nature and the intensity of imaginative 'power'. When the analytic basis to the autobiographical statement is cut short or seen to be inadequate, it secures the emphasis placed on that 'power', and does not appear as a failure.

In 1836 De Quincey spoke of German philosophy as owing its popularity, and to some extent its usefulness, to the barriers which it seemed to put in the way of rational inquiry. It is against the context of strict logic that he can see the possibilities of imaginative expansion:

> In [its] dark places lies, indeed, the secret of its attraction. Were light poured into them, it would be seen that they are *culs-de-sac*, passages that lead to nothing; but, so long as they continue dark, it is not known whither they lead ... Were it known that upon every path a barrier faces you insurmountable to human steps ... the popularity of this philosophy would expire at once; for no popular interest can long be sustained by speculations which ... are known to be essentially negative and essentially finite. Man's nature has something of infinity within itself, which requires a corresponding infinity in its objects.[74]

In De Quincey's autobiography the logical sense restrains and disciplines, but does not act in opposition to a sense of imaginative power. De Quincey seems to believe that there is a necessary compromise which allows the imagination to flourish alongside the discursive understanding: the two interact to the ultimate benefit of the former. In exploring the subjective infinity to which he refers above, De Quincey realises that a mediated vision promotes a stronger sense of that infinity. The full power of his own 'visionary' experiences can most profitably be communicated to his magazine audience by using a recognisably familiar context. The sublime moments can then be sympathetically (and therefore imaginatively) appreciated, at the same time as they are authenticated and credibilised.

The autobiography thus carries out its revelatory purpose within very specific confines. The limitations imposed upon this purpose are a joint product of the periodical context and the specialist requirements of De Quincey the autobiographer. An interaction with a fairly well defined audience was sometimes conducive to the promotion of imaginative sympathy. The periodical compromise could thus cultivate the autobiographical vision at the same time as particularising it, offering a familiar though potentially dramatic relationship between writer and reader. De Quincey could turn this situation to his advantage, finding it in some ways analogous to the fruitful nature of conversation:

> I felt (and in this I could not be mistaken, as too certainly it was a fact of my own experience) that in the electric kindling of life between two minds, - and far less from the kindling natural to conflict ... than from the kindling through sympathy with the object discussed in its momentary coruscation of shifting phases, - there sometimes arise glimpses and shy revelations of affinity, suggestion, relation, analogy, that could not have been approached through any avenues of methodical study. Great organists find the same effect of inspiration, the same result of power creative and revealing, in the mere movement and velocity of their own voluntaries. ... these *impromptu* torrents of music create rapturous *fioriture*, beyond all capacity in the artist to register, or afterwards to imitate. The reader must be well aware that many philosophic instances exist where a change in the degree makes a change in the kind.[75]

Again, a 'power creative and revealing' is found where it might not have been expected, suddenly presenting itself to the writer, whose task it now becomes to articulate the imaginative effect of its presentation. The difficulty of imitation arises because, as we have seen, it is the extent, the strength of that effect which distinguishes it. De Quincey makes this clear, not only in his statement that 'a change in the degree makes a change in the kind', but in his continued use of that word 'power'.

De Quincey's various critical statements show how much the periodical context exerted its pressures on his own subjective writings. From the resistance which it offered he was able to find both a source of autobiographical revelation and a means of stabilising the most imaginatively invigorating moments from his past. De Quincey's famous distinction between 'the literature of knowledge and the literature of power', which has serious limitations as a useful theoretical terminology, can be examined positively with regard to his autobiographical explorations. His use of the term 'power' might be located in the larger aesthetic debate between the sublime and the beautiful, in which he took a sizeable interest. The singularity of his achievement, however, rests not in the extremities of that debate, but in the viability of presenting the sublime alongside familiarity, in order to support an autobiographical purpose. The methods and techniques De Quincey used in such a presentation form the subject of the next chapter.

NOTES

1. Thomas De Quincey, The Collected Writings of Thomas De Quincey, David Masson (ed.) (14 vols., Edinburgh, 1889-90), vol. X, pp. 269-270.
2. Ibid., p. 139.
3. Ibid., pp. 163-164.
4. William Wordsworth, Preface to the Lyrical Ballads, 1802, R.L. Brett and A.R. Jones (eds.) (London, 1963), p. 266.
5. S.T. Coleridge, Coleridge's Shakespearean Criticism, Thomas Middleton Raysor (ed.) (London, 1930), vol. 1, pp. 163-164.
6. Geoffrey Hill, 'Poetry as Menace and Atonement', The University of Leeds Review, vol. 21 (1978), p. 70.
7. Ibid.
8. Masson, vol. X, p. 153.
9. Ibid., p. 97.
10. Ibid., p. 220.
11. Ibid., p. 262.
12. Ibid., pp. 226-227.
13. Ibid., p. 139.
14. Ibid., pp. 104-105.
15. Ibid., p. 108.
16. Ibid., p. 92.

17. Ibid., p. 121.
18. Wordsworth, Preface to the Lyrical Ballads, p. 247.
19. Edmund Burke, 'On Taste', The Works of The Right Honourable Edmund Burke (London, 1801), vol. I, p. 96.
20. M.H. Abrams, The Mirror and the Lamp (New York, 1953), p. 175.
21. Masson, vol. X, p. 27.
22. Ibid., vol. XI, p. 220.
23. Ibid.
24. Ibid., pp. 88-89.
25. Wordsworth, Preface to the Lyrical Ballads, p. 265.
26. Thomas De Quincey, The Uncollected Writings of Thomas De Quincey, James Hogg (ed.) (London, 1890), vol. I, pp. 193-194.
27. Masson, vol. X, p. 369.
28. S.T. Coleridge, 'On Poesy or Art', in Biographia Literaria, J. Shawcross (ed.) (Oxford, 1967), vol. II, p. 256.
29. Masson, vol. X, p. 172.
30. Ibid., vol. V, p. 234.
31. Ibid., p. 231.
32. Ibid., vol. X, p. 359.
33. Ibid., pp. 329-330.
34. Ibid., vol. V, p. 217.
35. Ibid., vol. X, p. 226.
36. Ibid., vol. XI, p. 54.
37. Ibid., vol. X, p. 48.
38. Sigmund K. Procter, Thomas De Quincey's Theory of Literature (London, 1943), p. 154.
39. Masson, vol. XI, p. 315.
40. Ibid.
41. Ibid., p. 321.
42. Ibid., pp. 59-60.
43. Ibid., vol. X, p. 49.
44. John E. Jordan, Thomas De Quincey, Literary Critic (Berkeley and Los Angeles, 1952), p. 263.
45. Procter, Thomas De Quincey's Theory of Literature, p. 43.
46. Hogg (ed.), Uncollected Writings, vol. 1, p. 128.
47. Masson, vol. XIII, p. 334.
48. Ibid., vol. XI, p. 56.
49. Ibid.
50. Ibid., pp. 382-383.
51. Immanuel Kant, Observations on the Feeling of the Beautiful and Sublime, translated by John T. Goldthwait (Berkeley and Los Angeles, 1965).

52. Ibid., pp. 36-37.
53. Ibid., p. 18.
54. Ibid., p. 45.
55. Ibid., p. 47.
56. Procter, Thomas De Quincey's Theory of Literature, pp. 143-144.
57. Ibid.
58. Horace A. Eaton (ed.), A Diary of Thomas De Quincey, 1803 (New York, 1927), p. 163.
59. Masson, vol. X, p. 400.
60. Jordan, Thomas De Quincey, Literary Critic, p. 60.
61. Edmund Burke, 'On the Sublime and Beautiful', The Works of the Right Honourable Edmund Burke, vol. 1, p. 262.
62. Ibid., pp. 142-143.
63. Ibid., pp. 149-150.
64. William Wordsworth, 'The Sublime and the Beautiful', The Prose Works of William Wordsworth, W.J.B. Owen and Jane Worthington Smyser (eds.) (Oxford, 1974), vol. II, pp. 353-354.
65. Ibid., p. 355.
66. Burke, 'On the Sublime and Beautiful', pp. 171-172.
67. Thomas De Quincey, The Posthumous Works of Thomas De Quincey, A.H. Japp (ed.) (London, 1893), vol. II, p. 62.
68. Masson, vol. VIII, p. 274.
69. Japp (ed.), Posthumous Works, vol. I, p. 228.
70. Masson, vol. XIII, p. 338.
71. Ibid., p. 360.
72. Ibid., p. 348.
73. Hogg (ed.), Uncollected Writings, vol. II, pp. 67-68.
74. Ibid., vol. I, p. 99.
75. Masson, vol. X, pp. 268-269.

Chapter 3

TRANSLATING EXPERIENCE

DIFFICULTY OF COMMUNICATION

The recalcitrant nature of language, its resistance to an autobiographical concern for correspondence to past experience, led to certain difficulties in De Quincey's task of translating experience into words. An assessment of his use of viable methods and techniques makes it difficult to accept a straightforward substitution between literature and experience. De Quincey's artistic status as an autobiographer would seem to rest on the extent of the change taking place in such translations.

De Quincey prided himself on his observation that: 'far more of our deepest thoughts and feelings pass to us ... as *involutes* (if I may coin that word) in compound experiences incapable of being disentangled, than ever reach us *directly* and in their own abstract shapes'.[1] Such a metamorphic action of the consciousness is only partly mirrored in De Quincey's translation of experience into words because his autobiographical work is a mixture of vision and analysis. This latter analytical aspect can appear to be in direct opposition to the invigorating process of combination which has taken place in his own consciousness. At least part of the motivation behind De Quincey's autobiographical achievement resists the very process of unification which it periodically celebrates. While De Quincey often presents incidents from his past assured of their significance and value, his assurance is often gained through his belief that,

> It is because a man cannot see and measure these mystical forces which palsy him, that he cannot deal with them effectually. If he were able really to pierce the haze which so often

> envelops, even to himself, his own secret springs of action and reserve, there cannot be a life moving at all under intellectual impulses that would not, through that single force of absolute frankness, fall within the reach of a deep, solemn, and sometimes even of a thrilling interest.[2]

Here 'absolute frankness' accords with a documentary concern which is thought to be inevitably revealing: simply the fact of an accurate record, it is suggested, will be enough to furnish explanations and therefore defeat the power of combination which has created the 'haze' and made the 'springs of action' secret.

This twin impulse of De Quincey's autobiography - his wish to analyse and separate, and his need to construct a reconciled version of his past is complicated by the revelatory nature of the process. This double-edged characteristic of his work becomes separated in his description of the writings of his two former idols Wordsworth and Coleridge. 'Wordsworth', he wrote, 'is always recording phenomena as they are enjoyed; Coleridge as they reconcile themselves with opposing or conflicting phenomena'.[3] This last statement suggests the extent to which De Quincey's own autobiography is dependent on his sensitive reception of delicate, subtle influxes of thought and feeling. He noticed this characteristic himself, claiming he had a propensity for 'feeling in a moment the secret analogies or parallelisms that connected things else apparently remote'.[4] In De Quincey's case such an acumen for receiving the impressions of fine and varied mental activity recognises a composite of intellectual and emotional forces. As a result, its relationship with words is double-edged; although words cannot do justice to the composite nature of experience they can, nevertheless, granted a viable compromise, provide in their very resistive nature an ally to this sort of contemplation.

Hazlitt, who was qualified to speak of this kind of activity, both from his work on associationist philosophy and from his experience of composition as a journalist, described the 'writer's associations' as:

> habitually intense, not vague or shallow, and words occur to him only as *tallies* to certain modifications of feeling. They are links in the chain of thought ... Again, the student

> finds a stimulus to literary exertion, not in the immediate *eclat* of his undertaking, but in the difficulty of his subject, and the progressive nature of his task. He is not wound up to a sudden and extraordinary effort of presence of mind; but is forever awake to the silent influxes of things.[5]

Hazlitt, like De Quincey, is aware of the creative possibilities present in the difficulty of composition. He depicts in this instance how the approximate correspondence provided by language is conducive to a more open reception of the various alternatives offered to a writer in the very act of writing. In his case such an openness is in accordance with his idea of genius which corresponds to Keats' notion of 'negative capability'. For De Quincey as an autobiographer openness of this sort adds a necessary further dimension to introspection so that self-awareness is not simply imposed, but achieved by viewing experience almost as a thing apart. With this added dimension the act of autobiography increases its revelatory capacity, the autobiographer receiving new discoveries in the role of a passive observer.

Because words may have once been accepted as 'tallies' in the process of feeling the 'secret analogies' and 'parallelisms', the task of either recreatively suggesting or documenting this complex activity is necessarily more difficult. So too, simply to abstract the relevant terminology is to deny the very nature of process which is operating. These are the two main problems in making a literary use out of this special ability to observe experiential phenomena: to invest the language with the emotional realities to which they refer, and to adequately account for the movement of the experience involved. In particular it is the various emotional depths and intensities belonging to the 'analogies' and 'parallelisms' which resist literary communication.

In De Quincey's case, as in Hazlitt's, the affective bias present in his assessment of experience makes great demands upon his linguistic resources. This is evident in his commonplace statement that: 'the flight of our human hours, not really more rapid at any one moment than another, yet oftentimes to our feelings *seems* more rapid'.[6] Hazlitt expressed the extremity of the problem in his dictum: 'there is nothing like feeling *but* feeling'.[7] Similarly, his revolt against abstraction and his plea for openness led him to an equally extreme refusal to deviate from the never-ending possibilities provided by experiential combinations:

> We know the meaning of certain looks, and we feel how they modify one another in conjunction. But we cannot have a separate rule to judge of all their combinations in different degrees and circumstances, without foreseeing all those combinations, which is impossible.[8]

De Quincey, in his turn, found that the amount of abstraction and dislocation necessary to communicate his dilemma as a periodical writer to publishers and friends only succeeded in removing the alarming intensities of his predicament. Musing on the memory of this experience in the Confessions in 1856 he writes:

> I, predisposed to subtleties of all sorts and degrees, had naturally become acquainted with cases that could not unrobe their apparellings down to that degree of simplicity. If in this world there is one misery having no relief, it is the pressure on the heart from the *Incommunicable*. And, if another Sphinx should arise to propose another enigma to man - saying: What burden is that which only is insupportable by human fortitude? I should answer at once - *It is the burden of the Incommunicable*.[9]

While De Quincey was thus conscious that there were prominent and intense areas of his personal life which refused to be artistically portrayed in autobiography, he differed quite significantly from Hazlitt in the extent to which he differentiated between art and experience, and in his continued belief in the value of attempting to describe and analyse complex patterns of his own past experience. From these two points of view he would have been at odds with Hazlitt's assertion in his essay 'On Genius and Common Sense' that:

> In art, in taste, in life, in speech, you decide from feeling, and not from reason; that is, from the impression of a number of things on the mind, which impression is true and well-founded, though you may not be able to analyze or account for it in several particulars.[10]

De Quincey's affective bias was not so absolute as

to include without hesitation the straight run of Hazlitt's opening list. Nor did he, while admitting difficulty, oust analysis, but used it to seek explanations for the peculiar actions and components of his experience. Reviewing one of the most crucial points in his life, for the second time in his 1856 version of the Confessions, De Quincey not only reveals his consistent attempt to solve such mysteries of his past, but also affirms the centrality of the relationship between the autobiographer and his reader to this cause. Assumed in that relationship is a distinction between two levels of value which motivate the attempt at explanation. Considering the difficult decision he made as an adolescent in rebelling against his mother and running away from home De Quincey writes:

> *Inexplicable* I have allowed myself to call this fatal error in my life, because such it *must* appear to others; since even to myself, so often as I fail to realise the case by reproducing a reflex impression in kind, and in degree, of the suffering before which my better angel gave way - yes, even to myself this collapse of my resisting energies seems inexplicable.[11]

Difficulty of communication for De Quincey pertains to both a private and a public relevance. Likewise, the value of analysing, defining and setting literary limitations upon experience must conform to both considerations. Of course, the two will by no means always coincide. Translating the degree, the intensities and the presiding nature of the combinations involved in his life presents the greatest challenge to his powers of communication. Often it is the extent of the emotional impact required that exceeds the words available. This is especially true in the case of an assessment rather than a recreation of dreams. As De Quincey explains in the Confessions:

> This and all other changes in my dreams were accompanied by deep-seated anxiety and funereal melancholy, such as are wholly incommunicable by words. I seemed every night to descend - not metaphorically, but literally to descend - into chasms. ... why should I dwell upon this. For indeed the state of gloom which attended these gorgeous spectacles, amounting at last to utter darkness, as of some suicidal

despondency, cannot be approached by words.[12]

Such a claim against the powers of language, of course, can be manipulated as a device to convince the reader of the depth of the very material deemed beyond articulation. It also conforms to De Quincey's firm sense of the distinction to be drawn between literature and experience; between experiences which can and those which cannot be adequately handled by language. The province of his autobiography, nevertheless, remains for the most part defiantly in those borderline areas which are likely to provide as much failure as success.

Difficulty may arise because De Quincey deals with these marginal areas either trying to communicate from the isolated peculiarity of his own experience or simply attempting the communication of a shared often common experience which is not normally articulated. These are the two main circumstances producing his frequent admissions of failure or the inadequacy of words to fulfil his task. Between these two there is a radical difference in the way in which the autobiographer is involved with his reader. In the former he affirms the singularity of his experience, seeks sympathy and social acceptance; in the latter he establishes his contact with a public stance seeking confirmation and recognition. In this latter process the autobiographer is most likely to assert his superiority as an artist over his public by overtly proclaiming the potency and general value of his specialist technique.

De Quincey was not alone in his attempt to push back the boundaries of experiences, both normal and abnormal, that could be handled by literature. Nor was the potential conflict of the artist with his public, as a result of incorporating the two polarities mentioned above, exclusively his. Of more significance, undoubtedly, in this respect was Wordsworth's example in <u>The Prelude</u>. In that poem the admissions of difficulty in communicating intense experiential phenomena straddle the two extremes we have already mentioned, and have serious implications for the very nature of the poetic imagination itself. On a number of significant occasions Wordsworth checks himself in mid-statement to question his own poetic role and to guard himself against those two extremes. In Book III he states:

> This is, in truth, heroic argument,
> This genuine prowess, which I wished to touch
> With hand however weak, but in the main

It lies far hidden from the reach of words.
Points have we all of us within our souls
Where all stand single; this I feel, and make
Breathings for incommunicable powers;
But is not each a memory to himself?[13]

while in Book V he questions himself at the opposite end of the scale:

Why call upon a few weak words to say
What is already written in the hearts
Of all that breathe? - what in the path of all
Drops daily from the tongue of every child,
Wherever man is found?[14]

Similarly he asks, 'Why should I speak of what a thousand hearts/Have felt, and every man alive can guess?'[15] and 'whereof speak of things/Common to all?'.[16] Wordsworth realises that the very nature of his imagination militates against his democratic purpose. To speak either of those experiences in which he stands single, or to proclaim the universal nature of others, involves an assertion or an achievment which inevitably places the poet above his audience. The irony in this situation is evident in the following passage, where the power of magic is used metaphorically to describe how he will rid certain common areas of experience of their mystery:

And as, by simple waving of a wand,
The wizard instantaneously dissolves
Palace or grove, even so could I unsoul
As readily by syllogistic words
Those mysteries of being which have made,
And shall continue evermore to make,
Of the whole human race one brotherhood.[17]

And so 'Imagination', which is 'the Power so called/ Through sad incompetence of human speech',[18] if it takes on this kind of exploratory task and achieves any success, is seen to rise above that shared 'incompetence of human speech'. In De Quincey's autobiography also, successful communication, where difficulty is so evident, tends to devolve to the egocentric character of the autobiographer if not mediated by his democratic concern and a humility towards his own craft.

Naturally, the type of exploration De Quincey undertakes determines the extent of linguistic opportunities open to him. Where his interest lies amongst unprecedented or undocumented descriptions, as in his drug addiction, he might well be expected to realise his insight in his essays on 'Language' that: 'New ideas, new aspects of old ideas, new relations of objects to each other, or to man - the subject who contemplates those objects, - absolutely insist on new words'.[19] But since, as we have seen, many of De Quincey's explorations are psychologically referential, they impress us as much as triumphs of expression as acts of invention. Thus, although De Quincey spoke of 'the frailty of languages'[20] and sensed that 'a real danger seems to lie in the insensible corruption going on forever within all languages, by means of which they are eternally dying away from their own vital power',[21] even his accounts of dream visions, which he described as unprecedented, and which have traditionally been viewed as ornate, even obscure creative fantasies, are primarily conceived of as acts of communication. They deliberately confront the reader in areas where success is often thought to be in spite of the literary medium employed. In order to do this they make good use of their own context, as we shall see in Chapter Five. Their exploration of mysteries often demand to be substantiated from the reader's own experience. Difficulty of communication can often be bypassed by using this relationship.

For this relationship to function the mysteries of De Quincey's own experience must necessarily be objectified, abstracted to some extent. That aspects of experience are treated as generalisations is not simply the result of De Quincey seeking to secure relevance for his reader: his aim is as much to ratify the importance of the generalisations. In the following passage from an essay which purports to comment on recent scientific advances De Quincey makes use of an opportunity to pursue this aspect of his experiential concerns:

> Great is the mystery of Space, greater is the mystery of Time. Either mystery grows upon man, as man himself grows ... In reality, the depths and the heights which are in man, the depths by which he searches, the heights by which he aspires, are but projected and made objective externally in the three dimensions of space which are outside of him. He trembles at the abyss which his bodily eyes look down on, or look up; not knowing that abyss to be, not always consciously suspecting it to be, boding it to be, fearing it to be, and sometimes hoping it to be, the mirror to a mightier abyss

> that will one day be expanded in himself.[22]

The first sentence here isolates and capitalises the two major areas of difficulty in De Quincey's communication of experience: 'Space' being equatable with depth and intensity, 'Time' comprising the difficulty of accommodating types and the sense of duration of motion and process. The final sentence shows him trying to maintain the generalisation at the same time as applying it. It becomes protracted, attempting in its own rhythmical climax to suggest the emotional impact of experience, even though the verbs which dictate each successive unit seem to resist any greater particularity. As a result they appear to repeat one another. The difficulty is in moving between large generalisations and experiential veracity. De Quincey is aided here, of course, by the very analogy he talks of: it provides an external measure to his conviction. When a suitable analogy such as this is not available the situation is more difficult to overcome.

Stranded without an analogy in his autobiography De Quincey can also find that he is trapped in a situation where words not only fail to provide an escape, but are at the centre of his dilemma because they offer themselves as the very substance of his experience:

> *"Life is finished! Finished it is!"* was the hidden meaning that, half-unconsciously to myself, lurked within my sighs; and, as bells heard from a distance on a summer evening seem charged at times with an articulate form of words, some monitory message, that rolls round unceasingly, even so for me some noiseless and subterraneous voice seemed to chant continually a secret word, made audible only to my own heart - that "now is the blossoming of life withered for ever". Not that such words formed themselves vocally within my ear, or issued audibly from my lips: but such a whisper stole silently to my heart.[23]

Language and experience become subtly interfused when the nature of De Quincey's task is to articulate in expanded form just such a 'whisper' or a similar 'sigh'. In this passage from Suspiria de Profundis the very failure of language provides the platform for communication.

Similarly, where De Quincey forthrightly denies the possibility of articulation, rather than seeming to have reached an 'impasse' or to have deviated from his main theme, he is often at the very centre of his autobiographical concern, outlining the essential predicament of the autobiographer:

> The sentiment which attends the sudden revelation that *all is lost* silently is gathered up into the heart; it is too deep for gestures or for words; and no part of it passes to the outside. Were the ruin conditional, or were it in any point doubtful, it would be natural to utter ejaculations, and to seek sympathy. But, where the ruin is understood to be absolute, where sympathy cannot be consolation, and counsel cannot be hope, this is otherwise. The voice perishes; the gestures are frozen; and the spirit of man flies back upon its own centre.[24]

De Quincey directs his attention to these 'silent' experiences, using his autobiography to give voice to significant events in his past which would otherwise have no outlet. He can thus use his public medium to expose and illuminate both the fantastic and private occurrences of his social world. The results can surprise and shock the reader, especially since De Quincey, with Gothic sensationalism, claims amongst his subjects - '*Aporeta* ... things not utterable in human language or to human ears - things ineffable - things to be whispered - things to dream of not to tell'.[25] His interest in guilt and sin is another significant aspect of his autobiographical writings which connects domesticity to sublimity:

> Sin is that secret word, that dark *apporreton* of the human race, undiscoverable except by express revelation, which ... has ... blossomed into a vast growth of sublime ideas ... comprehending *all* functions of the Infinite operatively familiar to men. Yes I affirm that there is no form through which the Infinite reveals itself in a sense comprehensible by man and adequate to man; that there is no sublime agency which *compresses* the human mind from infancy so as to mingle with the moments of its growth, positively none but has been in its whole origin - in every part - and exclusively developed out of that tremendous mystery which lurks under the name of sin.[26]

Again, there is a movement between an assertive generalisation and its relevance to the complexity of experience. When De Quincey returns at the end of this passage to his word 'sin' we realise that it is a compromise attempting to solve the mystery; that it is an approximate 'tally' (to use Hazlitt's word) trying to distil the significance of the experience which, of course, is inevitably 'mingled with the moments of its growth': it does not correspond, but 'lurks under'.

De Quincey is faced with difficulty of communication because he is willing to accept, in relation to his past experience, the complexities involved in the organic notion of growth, but is still willing to define, analyse and categorise. In so doing he seeks to establish a public relevance from a private one, and thus confronts the following dilemma contemplated by Wordsworth in *The Prelude*:

> But who shall parcel out
> His intellect, by geometric rules,
> Split, like a province, into round and square?
> Who knows the individual hour in which
> His habits were first sown, even as a seed,
> Who that shall point, as with a wand, and say,
> "This portion of the river of my mind
> Came from yon fountain?"27

The various techniques and types of analogy that De Quincey adopted to accomplish his translation of experience need to be prefaced by a recognition of the difficulties involved, because, as we have seen, it is a subject which forms a significant part of the works themselves.

TECHNIQUES AND ANALOGIES

In his literary criticism De Quincey reveals his interest in the dual purpose of his autobiographical writing and outlines some of the possibilities attendant upon the degree to which literature deviates from experience. The combination of description and analysis of experience is resident, for example, in his distinction (which was examined in the last chapter) between the 'literature of knowledge' and the 'literature of power'. Using an encyclopaedia as an illustration of the former, De Quincey claims it 'speaks through the dead memory and unimpassioned understanding, which have not the repose of the higher faculties, but are continually enlarging their phylacteries'.[28] Although the constant movement of the world of knowledge here is not strictly equatable with that same quality in experience, it is nevertheless significant that De Quincey should single out 'repose' as belonging to faculties which presumably would include the literary imagination. It would seem that at least some form of reconciliation, of finality should pertain to a work of literature, that it should not simply be an act of process. This would be consistent with De Quincey's dictum: 'Style is the disentangling of thoughts or ideas reciprocally involved in each other'.[29] Such a debate between literature as an achieved, objective and therefore to some extent static representation of life, and literature as an expression of the movement of experience, is most evident in De Quincey's comments on the Greek drama. In his essay 'Theory of Greek Tragedy' he attempts to assert the essential difference between the two most acclaimed forms of drama:

> Shakspere - that is, English Tragedy - postulates the intense life of flesh and blood, of animal sensibility, of man and woman - breathing, waking, stirring, palpitating with the pulses of hope and fear. In Greek Tragedy, the very masks show the utter impossibility of these tempests or conflicts. Struggle there is none, internal or external: not like Hamlet's with his own constitutional inertia and his gloomy irresolution of conscience ... certain great *situations* - not passion in states of growth, of movement, of self-conflict - but fixed, unmoving *situations*, were selected; these held on through the entire course of one or more acts. ... the passion is essentially fixed throughout, not mantling and undulating with the breath of change, but frozen into marble life.[30]

Emotional content is still the centre of De Quincey's attention; the dramatic '*situation*' is particularly interesting to him because it is able to 'fix' the presiding 'passion'. Just what are the attendant consequences of 'fixing' experience, as suggested in the sculptural analogy at the end of that passage, De Quincey reveals in another essay on the same subject - 'The Antigone of Sophocles':

> What we read in sculpture is not absolutely death, but still less is it the fulness of

> life. We read there the abstraction of a life that reposes, the sublimity of a life that aspires, the solemnity of a life that is thrown to an infinite distance. This last is the feature of sculpture which seems most characteristic; the form which presides in the most commanding groups "is not dead but sleepeth": true, but it is the sleep of a life sequestrated, solemn, liberated from the bonds of space and time, and (as to both alike) thrown (I repeat the words) to a distance which is infinite. It affects us profoundly, but not by agitation. Now, on the other hand, the breathing life - life kindling, trembling, palpitating - that life which speaks to us in painting, this is also the life that speaks to us in English Tragedy.[31]

Clearly, De Quincey found in the Greek drama an example of a form of art which combined abstraction with solemnity, which could happily include his sense of the sublime and his need for objectivity. The profound effect achieved by such drama, according to De Quincey, does not result from the fluctuation of a long-term process, but is produced by a constant effect. Arguing that the ancient Greeks contemplated a life which was 'awful and still' De Quincey claims 'they felt it possible to present this mode of being in states of *suffering*, for suffering is enduring and indefinite, but never in states of *conflict*, for conflict is by its nature fugitive and evanescent'.[32] Continuity is the key factor here, inherent in both the passion and the situation. In his descriptions of Greek drama, which frequently use the analogy with sculpture, De Quincey intimates that the effect achieved is consistency, continuity at one level. It is thus an abstraction too, in the sense that it rules out the elements of change and variability. Both its abstract quality and its objectivity are interrelated. In particular, the emotional effects of awe and grandeur (effects in accordance with the notion of the sublime) are dependent upon this very kind of presentation. When De Quincey considers the part played by language in Greek drama he highlights the relationship between continuity and the production of an 'awesome' effect:

> over and above this original adaption of the Greek language to the Iambic metre, we have no doubt whatever that the recitation of verse on

> the Attic stage was of an artificial and semi-musical character. It was undoubtedly much more *sustained*, and intonated with a slow and measured stateliness, which, whilst harmonizing it with the other circumstances of solemnity in Greek Tragedy, would bring it nearer to music.[33]

De Quincey's comments on Greek drama provide a valuable illustration of how continuity, objectivity, 'grandeur', and music may be combined in a manner compatible with one side of his autobiographical demands. The musical formality of language can be manipulated to construct an elaborate tableau capable of reconciling or harmonising the raw material of experience. At the same time it can hold fast otherwise fugitive elements for analysis.

De Quincey recognises in Greek drama a specific type of vocabulary capable of fulfilling this purpose. It is a vocabulary he uses extensively in his own autobiographical work: 'in the first place, the dialogue is always ... severe, massy, simple, yet solemnized intentionally by the use of a select vocabulary, corresponding (in point of archaism and remoteness from ordinary use) to our own scriptural vocabulary'.[34] The very limited scope of such a 'select' vocabulary constitutes its strength where abstraction, continuity and uniformity are required. So, too, De Quincey's affective bias need not be compromised. Indeed, his central concern in this area is to isolate one specific kind of emotional effect. Musical continuity maintains that effect, allowing for variations on the theme, but precluding any other material which might threaten the uniformity of tone. To that extent such an effect is 'impassioned' - to use De Quincey's own terminology.

The use of a scriptural vocabulary is also connected with music in De Quincey's critical thinking, not only because it can produce a sustained solemnity, but because it is also a natural ally to the communication, or more particularly, to the revelation of truths. Music, rhythm, and this sort of language carry an emotional impact which is immediately recognisable as at once dignified and objective. In his essay 'Style' De Quincey refers to sociological evidence in order to make this point:

> Now, in the earliest states of society, all truth that has any interest or importance for man will connect itself with heaven. ... if it does not borrow its importance from its

> sanctity, then, by an inverse order, it will borrow a sanctity from its importance. Even agricultural truth, even the homeliest truths of rural industry, brought into connexion with religious inspiration, will be exalted (like the common culinary utensils in the great vision of the Jewish prophet) and transfigured into vessels of glorious consecration. All things in this early stage of social man are meant mysteriously, have allegoric values; and week-day man moves amongst glorified objects. So that, if any doctrine, principle, or system of truth, should call for communication at all, infallibly the communication will take the tone of a revelation; and the holiness of a revelation will express itself in the most impassioned form, perhaps with accompaniments of music, but certainly with metre.[35]

Where De Quincey suggests a technique for the communication of truths compatible with music (in his case often an aesthetic extreme) he approaches a description of his role as a moralist or an assertive public commentator. Again we witness De Quincey's awareness of how important communication is best achieved not directly, but through the artistic manipulation of specific techniques; emotion being carefully dictated, not released by a seemingly direct utterance. When he uses a sculptural analogy and, more importantly, musical analogies, he does so when discussing literature in its most abstracted and most elaborately constructed forms. While it is true to say that in his autobiographical writings De Quincey is interested in making accurate correspondences to experience, that is least likely to be the case where musical analogies are to be found. Although, speaking of diction in his essay 'Style', he says, 'there is not in the world so certain a guarantee for pure idiomatic diction, without tricks or affectation, as a case of genuine excitement. Real situations are always pledges of a real natural language',[36] the comments on Greek drama we have examined show that De Quincey was also conscious of an artistic alternative. A new, more sympathetic reading of The English Mail-Coach and parts of Suspiria de Profundis is possible if one applies these comments on drama to those of De Quincey's works which consistently use musical and scriptural language.

Alert to the fact that De Quincey's critical comments show him to be sensible of the artistic possibilities in the literary use of musical, sculptural and scriptural analogies, and not simply using them in an imitative capacity, one must question the extent to which De Quincey himself shies away from claims of artificiality. In a footnote to his translation of Richter's 'Dream-Vision of the Infinite as it reveals itself in the Chambers of Space',[37] De Quincey berates Richter's ability in the province of dream literature. This has been read in the past as a measure of De Quincey's commitment in providing accurate records of such experiences, of his concern as 'a purist in literary transcriptions of dream-work'.[38] The footnote reads:

> Neither should I much have sought to avoid alterations, if the original had been lying before me: for it takes the shape of a dream; and this most brilliant of all German writers wanted in that field the severe simplicity, that horror of the *too much*, belonging to Grecian architecture, which is essential to the perfection of a dream considered as a work of art. Too elaborate he was, and too artificial, to realise the grandeur of the shadowy.[39]

While De Quincey advocates 'severe simplicity' and talks of realising 'the grandeur of the shadowy', he does so in relation to 'a dream considered as a work of art'. He is contemplating here the proper use of suitable techniques for a deliberate construction which does not necessarily travesty the real nature of the dream experience, but which can most fully express the reality of that experience. Elaboration and artificiality, if not overplayed, can promote a more satisfactory correspondence. The indirect nature of both language and literature militates against direct communication; but the communication that is made in an artistic form can be both accurate and representative. De Quincey's interest in the analogies outlined so far seems to lie in the ability of abstract, objective forms to retain and communicate specific emotional intensities.

One of the problems in accounting for the particular analogies that can be used to describe De Quincey's prose is the mixed, sequential nature of his autobiographical works. Even the seemingly fantastic musical sections are, despite the frequent lack of narrative chronology and stylistic continuity, nearly always accommodated within a larger framework. They often form the culmination of a number of sections of prose.

This sequential aspect of De Quincey's autobiographical work was appreciated by Virginia Woolf who also outlined the peculiar difficulty besetting De Quincey's task. In her essay 'Impassioned Prose' she says, 'again and again, it is in returning to earth that De Quincey is undone. How is he to bridge the horrid transition? How is he to turn from an angel with wings of flame and eyes of fire to a gentleman in black who talks sense'.[40] She also takes us further towards an appreciation of how elaborate, seemingly artificial, but objective techniques such as De Quincey's use of the musical analogy, are central to the autobiographical purpose. In particular she suggests the disparate non-causal structure of his subject which is governed by movement and change:

> draw a little apart, see people in groups, as outlines, and they become at once memorable and full of beauty. Then it is not the actual sight or sound itself that matters, but the reverberations that it makes as it travels through our minds. These are often to be found far away, strangely transformed; but it is only by gathering up and putting together these echoes and fragments that we arrive at the true nature of our experience.[41]

In order to trace the 'reverberations' mentioned here by Virginia Woolf, De Quincey often finds himself offering his reader apparently whimsical connections. The difficulty of convincing the reader that they are not so is aggravated because the realism that is sought is psychological not objective, and any analogy that might be used in explanation might intrude and thereby destroy the subjective intimacy of the subject. De Quincey's subject is sometimes the vague connections made by a mind's movement, its line of associations 'half meditative, half capricious'.[42] At other times, but equally disturbing for his reader perhaps, his subjects are the dead-ends and disconnections of experience.

De Quincey's most successful analogies are fairly remote from the experience described. The qualities they need to have are fluid motion and a spatial dimension: they tend not to be visual or sensual images. Often they consist of reports of the working of natural phenomena, frequently abnormal in occurrence. The following quotation, which is just a fragment from De Quincey's uncollected writings, illustrates in a simple form how he can explain an experience through the use of such an analogy:

> The hatred of truth at first dawning - that instinct which makes you revolt from the pure beams which search the foul depths and abysses of error - is well illustrated by the action of the atmospheric currents, when blowing through an open window upon smoke. What do you see? Sometimes the impression is strong upon your *ocular* belief that the window is driving the smoke in. You can hardly be convinced of the contrary - scarcely when five or seven minutes has absolutely rarefied the smoke so much that a book-lettering previously invisible has become even legible. And at last, when the fact, the result, the experience, has corrected the contradictory theory of the eye, you begin to suspect, without any aid from science, that there were two currents, one of which comes round in a curve ↻[43]

Many of the difficulties of communicating experience are evident in this illustration. Characteristically, De Quincey's province here is contrary to visual phenomena, and yet he finds it necessary to resort to a diagram at the end. His aim is to convince the reader just as the 'experience' contradicts the previous 'theory'. His analogy must facilitate communication in difficult areas where preconceptions and disbelief are evident.

Having surveyed and anticipated both the difficulties involved and the possibilities available to De Quincey in his translation of experience, we can now approach two works of his which illustrate with varying degrees of success the problems and techniques looked at so far - Suspiria de Profundis and The English Mail-Coach.

THE ENGLISH MAIL-COACH

The English Mail-Coach was originally intended to form part of Suspiria de Profundis, but De Quincey subsequently recognised that it formed a unity of its own, and published it separately. His view was not accepted by critics of the day who found it difficult to perceive the connecting links between the different sections of the work, which are 'The Glory of Motion', 'The Vision of Sudden Death' and 'Dream-Fugue; Founded on the Preceding Theme of Sudden Death'. The first of these sections contains a mixture of casual personal reminiscence, social documentation and whimsical humour. The full significance of these different elements is not evident until the final sections have been read. 'The Vision of Sudden Death' consists of a factual account, narrated with the same detail as On Murder Considered as One of the Fine Arts, of a coach journey from Manchester to the Lake District. During this journey, his driver asleep and De Quincey seated on top of the coach at the back, he sees a gig on the road ahead and realises that a crash is imminent, but is powerless to act as the two vehicles collide. This event registers in a moment on De Quincey's consciousness; his coach continuing out of control into the distance. The final section - 'Dream-Fugue' - employs a musical prose to construct a dream experience in which most of the information related in the previous sections is to be found. A useful way of approaching The English Mail-Coach, in order to understand De Quincey's translation of experience, is to examine the causal links between these various sections.

Near the beginning of the work De Quincey would seem to offer an explanation of how the mail-coach came to play a part in his dreams. He offers this explanation unobtrusively, almost apologetically, calling it a 'circumstantial notice'.[44] Since it is introduced in this manner the following sentence can only surprise the reader. The reasons for the mail-coach's involvement in the 'anarchies' of his dreams are:

> first, through velocity, at that time unprecedented; they first revealed the glory of motion: suggesting, at the same time, an under-sense, not unpleasurable, of possible though indefinite danger; secondly, through grand effects to the eye between lamp-light and the darkness upon solitary roads; thirdly, through animal beauty and power so often displayed ... fourthly, through the conscious presence of a central intellect, that, in the midst of vast distances, of storms, of darkness, of night, overruled all obstacles into one steady co-operation in a national result.[45]

The most important in this list would appear to be the fourth which suggests a central unity in the subject matter that might be infused into the work itself. De Quincey elaborates on this unity, characteristically exhibiting his affective bias in connection with music:

> To my own feeling, this Post-office service recalled some mighty orchestra, where a thousand instruments all disregarding each other, and so far in danger of discord, yet all obedient as slaves to the supreme *baton* of some great leader, terminate in a perfection of harmony like that of heart, veins, and arteries, in a healthy animal organisation.[46]

This clearly anticipates the final 'Dream-Fugue' section of the work, and recalls De Quincey's comment in his preface to the Collected Writings of 1854, that the reader should be reminded of 'the perilous difficulty beseiging all attempts to clothe in words the visionary scenes derived from the world of dreams, where a single false note, a single word in a wrong key, ruins the whole music'.[47] This anticipation highlights a coincidence of subject and technique which develops as the work continues.

The way in which experience transforms and orders disparate material mirrors the literary process. We are told later, for example, that 'the victories of England in this stupendous context rose of themselves as natural *te deums*':[48] later he talks of 'the grandest chapter of our experience within the whole mail-coach service'.[49] Because there is this convergence De Quincey finds it difficult to isolate the causal links which make the transitions through to the final harmony.

After the list of explanations we have seen, he again attempts to make a claim for the singular importance of another 'particular element in this whole combination' - the 'political mission'[50] of the coaches. Such attempts seem in total opposition to the express nature of his subject which is one of metamorphosis and synthesis, and yet they appear to serve a valuable function in the work as a whole. Because the tendency is always towards synthesis the work would become less accessible. De Quincey explains: 'I find it necessary to relate the circumstances because they are such as could not have occurred unless under a singular combination of accidents'.[51] Clearly there is a serious threat to the whole credibility of the work offered in the very nature of its singularity. Unless its accidental nature is explained it may as well not have any causal structure at all. Similarly, De Quincey's use of insufficient explanations and conflicting claims of significance, though inevitable due to the nature of the subject, nevertheless serves to open it out and make it communicable where it might have passed as one obscure series, insoluble and continuous.

Aware of the difficulty facing his reader, De Quincey appended a notice to the front of the second instalment asking him to understand,

> this present paper, in its two sections of *the vision & C.*, and *The Dream-Fugue*, as connected with a previous paper on *The English Mail-Coach* ... The ultimate object was the Dream-Fugue, as an attempt to wrestle with the utmost efforts of music in dealing with a colossal form of impassioned terror. The Vision of Sudden Death contains the mail-coach, which really did occur, and did really suggest the variations of the Dream, here taken up by the Fugue, as well as other variations not now recorded. Confluent with these impressions ... were other and more general impressions, derived from long familiarity with the English mail ... From this function of the mail, arises naturally the introduction of Waterloo into the fourth variation of the Fugue; for the mail itself having been carried into the dreams by the incident of the Vision, naturally all the accessory circumstances of pomp and grandeur investing this national carriage followed in the train of the principal image.[52]

This would seem to suggest that The English Mail-Coach was conceived in reverse order to that of its publication, and that the underlying factor which dictated it should develop in this retrogressive manner was born out of a need for public communication. Starting from the 'Dream-Fugue' De Quincey retraced its various elements for the sake of explanation, following an experiential process back to its disparate foundations. Attempting to clarify, in logical terms, the transitions involved in this process, De Quincey may, ironically, have alienated and confused many of his readers. These logical explanations seem to have been taken by such readers as overriding the seemingly capricious and irrational development of the experience depicted. In his preface to the volume of his Collected Writings containing The English Mail-Coach De Quincey naturally expressed his surprise at a number of critics who failed to perceive the logical coherence of his work:

> one or two critics, not carelessly in conversation, but deliberately in print, professed their inability to apprehend the meaning of the whole, or to follow the links of the connexion between its several parts. I am myself as little able to understand where the difficulty lies, or to detect any lurking obscurity, as these critics found themselves to unravel my logic.[53]

De Quincey's final reaction to this problem is to become more intrenched in the experiential nature of his work, adamantly refusing to offer any means of approach, and humourously releasing himself from any share of the blame:

> if there be anything amiss - let the Dream be responsible. The Dream is a law to itself; and as well quarrel with a rainbow for showing or *not* showing, a secondary arch ... But the Dream knows best; and the Dream, I say again, is the responsible party.[54]

While he quite rightly points out that 'a circumstantial accuracy is essential to the effect of my narrative'[55] it becomes difficult for him to locate and assign one particular set of circumstances to a given effect, granted the inter-dependency of the agents involved. The limits of his subject are constantly expanding because his consciousness is still providing new variations. These developments become more and more difficult to ascribe to a specific number of causes. Because of this continuing metamorphic capacity of his own consciousness, effects which De Quincey thought he had successfully located suddenly produce unexpected lines of association and make him doubt his original pronouncement. This particular difficulty is evident in the following passage, where he again asserts the peculiarity of his experience, not in its constituent parts, but in the nature of their combination and their movement:

> This is the peculiarity that I wish the reader to notice as having first been made known to me for a possibility by this early vision of Fanny on the Bath road. The peculiarity consisted in the confluence of two different keys, though

> apparently repelling each other, into the music and governing principles of the same dream; horror, such as possesses the maniac, and yet, by momentary transitions, grief ... There was also a separate peculiarity in the quality of the horror. This was afterwards developed into far more revolting complexities of misery, and incomprehensible darkness; and perhaps I am wrong in ascribing any value as a *causative* agency to this particular case on the Bath road.[56]

Suddenly an assertion singled out for the reader's particular attention ends in uncertainty. De Quincey's difficulty is in deciding whether connections outlined in his experience (logical or not) represent true developments or lines of continuity, rather than simply being thrown up as aberrent inconsistencies or capricious suggestions.

Sometimes De Quincey is convinced of the connection only to find that the degree of strength of the effect is disproportionate to the circumstances. This presents more difficulty than may be thought because, as we have already seen, for him the emotional intensity of an experience distinguishes or creates the reality of that experience. It was probably for this reason that he omitted the following passage from his revised text of The English Mail-Coach:

> the dream-horror which I speak of is far more frightful. The dreamer finds housed within himself - occupying, as it were, some separate chamber in his brain - holding, perhaps from that station with a secret and detestable commerce with his own heart - some horrid alien nature - What if it were his own nature repeated - still, if the duality were distinctly perceptible, even *that* - even this mere numerical double of his own consciousness - might be a curse too mighty to be sustained. But how,if the alien nature contradicts his own, fights with it, perplexes, and confounds it? How, again, if not one alien nature, but two, but three, but four, but five, are introduced within what once he thought the inviolable sanctuary of himself? These, however, are horrors from the kingdoms of anarchy and darkness, which, *by their very intensity, challenge the sanctity of concealment, and gloomily retire from exposition.* Yet it was necessary to mention

> them, because the first introduction to such appearances (whether causal, or merely casual) lay in the heraldic monsters, which monsters were themselves introduced (though playfully) by the transfigured coachman of the Bath mail.[57] (my italics)

The problem of finding adequate explanations for complexly combined experiences would seem to operate on two levels: offering the reader a means of approaching though not solving the difficult experiential subject; and attempting to appreciate the true line of development undergone by a particular experience. Neither of these seeks to subordinate the intrinsic nature of the experience to their incomplete generalisations. This is not only generally true of De Quincey's autobiographical works, but possesses a special relevance in the case of The English Mail-Coach where it is reinforced thematically. For this work asserts the importance of organic, subjective experiential knowledge over the facts of mechanical, external knowledge. The unity achieved by the mail-coach system in spreading the latest news of the Napoleonic wars across the country, is one in which an individual recognises the important part which can be played in such a method of communication. More particularly, an individual can not only comprehend his part in that extensive unity, but can feel the very means by which it is achieved. De Quincey makes this very clear, drawing a sharp distinction between the past and the present, aware that he is documenting a by-gone social institution in the middle of an autobiographical work which examines a private world of dreams and guilt-stricken conscience:

> The modern modes of travelling cannot compare with the mail-coach system in grandeur and power. They boast of more velocity, but not however as a consciousness, but as a fact of our lifeless knowledge, resting upon *alien* evidence; as, for instance, because somebody *says* that we have gone fifty miles in the hour ... The vital experience of the glad animal sensibilities made doubts impossible on the question of our speed; we heard our speed, we saw it, we felt it as thrilling; and this speed was not the product of blind insensate agencies; that had no sympathy to give, but was incarnated in the fiery eyeballs of an animal, in his dilated nostril, spasmodic muscles, and echoing hoofs.[58]

The English Mail-Coach laments the fact that 'vital experience' is no longer the measure of an individuals's link with society, and, at the same time, shows how the expansive nature of an individual mind accommodates various layers of the social and private worlds, moulding them and reconciling them to its own individual predicament. The work considers both the triumphs and dangers of the mind's self-responsibility and metamorphic capacity. In the first section it celebrates the joys of events where the primacy of experience is allowed to flourish alongside national unity. But even here it anticipates the dangers latent in such a precarious union, demonstrating how things whimsical and humorous can be transformed in the subconscious into agents of horror and guilt.

As we have seen, De Quincey is faced with the difficulty of articulating the stages of these transformations because they are not simply linear, but always accumulating and incorporating new elements. This is not only true of the transformations which take place but also of the unity which is depicted. The unity depicted in the first section of *The English Mail-Coach* (naturally considering the title) is one which is brought about by movement: it is a unity made possible by an expansive process, relying not only on the actual coincidence of an individual and a social mechanism, but on the associative and empathic powers of the mind. De Quincey finds two different analogies to describe this unity both of which require movement and a spatial dimension denying any definite formulaic characteristic which would destroy their affinity with experiential process:

> The half-slumbering consciousness that, all night long and all the next day - perhaps for even a longer period - many of these mails, like fire racing along a train of gunpowder, will be kindling at every instant new successions of burning joy, has an obscure effect of multiplying the victory itself, by multiplying to the imagination into infinity the stages of its progressive diffusion. A fiery arrow seems to be let loose, which from that moment is destined to travel, almost without intermission, westwards for three hundred miles - northwards for six hundred; and the sympathy of our Lombard Street friends at parting is exalted a hundredfold by a sort of visionary sympathy with the approaching sympathies, yet unborn,

> which we were going to evoke.[59]

The unity contemplated here is created by an anticipatory act of imaginative sympathy. Later on in this work the same kind of projection becomes a threat to De Quincey, representing a hideous form of inevitability which is capable of paralysing his will:

> The palsy of doubt and distraction hangs like some guilty weight of dark unfathomed remembrances upon my energies, when the signal is flying for *action*. But, on the other hand, this accursed gift, I have, as regards *thought*, that in the first step towards the possibility of a misfortune, I see its total evolution: in the radix I see too clearly and too instantly its entire expansion; in the first syllable of the dreadful sentence, I read already the last.[60]

A potentially creative act of mind is here found to have seriously damaging results. De Quincey describes such a possibility both in terms of his own mental experience, and in terms of his own literary experience. Such an effect is both horrific to him in certain circumstances which ask for action, and hazardous for his very translation of such an incident into words.

This threat of inevitability seems to lie behind the whole structure of The English Mail-Coach. From the final section 'Dream-Fugue' (which presents in a condensed, restricted form a type of dream experience) back to the whimsical introductory paragraphs its evolution seems to have been one of de-restriction. It breaks down the elements of inevitable continuity for the purpose of communication and analysis. The chronologial movement of the work, as it appears to the reader, on the other hand, runs parallel to the cumulative nature of experience and the similar workings of the literary imagination. The difficulties facing De Quincey's technical accomplishment are, in part, consequent upon undertaking this complex act of reassembly.

Because The English Mail-Coach gradually moves towards the final synthesis of the 'Dream-Fugue', musical prose providing its climax, and because it tries to provide tangential deviations from the main theme to break the continuity, repetition and prefiguration of certain 'types' are amenable to its purpose. As well as drawing attention to the change undergone by different aspects of experience, and using such explanatory statements to effect transitions in the work, others are not drawn openly into the comments on its own genesis, but are allowed to stand effectively by themselves. In these cases the experiences do indeed 'speak for themselves', to use De Quincey's terminology. In so doing, however, they often serve to undercut the most elaborate forms of De Quincey's artistry.

The 'impassioned' rhythmical prose of the later sections is used humourously in the opening parts of the work. For example, De Quincey ridicules his own sort of exclamation of difficulty to the reader, saying 'What words, then, could express the horror, and the sense of treason, in that case, which *had* happened'.[61] In the same way, but more importantly, De Quincey presents us with a report of an incident which prefigures the accident dealt with in the section on 'Sudden Death', in which his coach crashes into the gig containing the young girl. In this prefiguration the reader is presented with what appears to be a whimsical 'tour de force', a pleasant digression. By the end of the work it turns out to have been both a reminder of the irony of De Quincey's own cruel fortune, and another example of how the mind in retrospect can invest the elements of an innocuous past experience with the traumatic emotions of a present one. It both substantiates De Quincey's later feelings of guilt and responsibility and strengthens the impression of inevitability. The humour of the following passage will rebound for the reader, just as De Quincey claims it did for himself:

> Sometimes after breakfast his majesty's mail would become frisky; and in its difficult wheelings amongst the intricacies of early markets, it would upset an applecart, a cart loaded with eggs, & Co. Huge was the affliction and dismay, awful was the smash, though, after all, I believe the damage might be levied upon the hundred. I, as far as was possible, endeavoured in such a case to represent the conscience and moral sensibilities of the mail; and, when wildernesses of eggs were lying poached under our horses' hoofs, then would I stretch my hands in sorrow saying ... "Ah! wherefore have we not time to weep over you?" which was quite impossible, for in fact we had not even time to laugh over them ... could the royal mail pretend to undertake the offices of sympathy and condolence? Could it be expected

> to provide tears for the accidents of the road? If even it seemed to trample on humanity, it did so, I contended, in discharge of its own more peremptory duties.
>
> Upholding the morality of the mail, *a fortiori* I upheld its rights, I stretched to the uttermost its privilege of imperial precedency, and astonished weak minds by the feudal powers which I hinted to be lurking constructively in the charters of this proud establishment.[62]

At the other extreme The English Mail-Coach does not enact or display the nature of its transitions, but simply refers to the kind of transition involved. Any straightforward narrative technique is not available. After describing a number of related incidents De Quincey draws them together and is able to move on to the next aspect of his subject by explaining that:

> These were among the gaieties of my earliest and boyish acquaintances with mails. But alike the gayest and the most terrific of my experiences rose again after years of slumber, armed with preternatural power to shake my dreaming sensibilities; sometimes, as in the slight case of Miss Fanny on the Bath road ... through some casual or capricious association with images originally gay, yet opening at some stage of evolution into sudden capacities of horror; sometimes through the more natural and fixed alliances with the sense of power so various lodged in the mail system.[63]

Whereas before the reader was dramatically led through the transformation of the experience, and felt the shock of De Quincey's own horror, here the transition is simply stated because, as he says, it is either 'casual' or 'capricious' and 'various'. Although The English Mail-Coach uses such a mixture of techniques, and does not hide from the fact that some of those techniques are inadequate, and that its author finds difficulty in employing others, it nevertheless succeeds in that variety. As the reader follows the circumlocutions, apparent digressions, admissions of failure and mixture of styles, it can be argued that they provide not only an accommodating framework, but a subtle examination of one incident hidden in the complexities of experiential process. The digressions and circumlocutions are resolved to a unity due to the prepossessing importance of that single incident.

SUSPIRIA DE PROFUNDIS

Suspiria de Profundis exists only in a fragmented form, but as the title suggests, its unity is thematic, not structural. It consists of a series of sections which explore and reveal the significance of traumatic experience involved in dreams. Each of these sections varies considerably, much as the sections in *The English Mail-Coach* exhibit a number of techniques. Unlike that work it does not concentrate intensively on one incident which is capable of maintaining an important centrality. It does not use its various techniques to consider the ramifications of a single experience. Rather than proclaiming the unity of its own literary achievement it sets out to reveal the unity of conscious and subconscious experience. Its very fragmentary character, De Quincey argues, is dictated by the precedency it gives to moments or processes which illustrate such psychological unity or continuity. Using a method of selection the work claims to expose privileged vantage points which reveal otherwise unapparent links between seemingly disparate and inchaote experiences:

> The fleeting accidents of a man's life, and its external shows, may indeed be irrelate and incongruous; but the organising principles which fuse into harmony, and gather about fixed predetermined centres, whatever heterogeneous elements life may have accumulated from without, will not permit the grandeur of human unity greatly to be violated, or its ultimate repose to be troubled in the retrospect from dying moments, or from other great convulsions.[64]

This statement reveals that De Quincey's perception of unity in experience is based on abstraction, on the fundamental laws of process - the 'organising principles'. The valuable generalisations which arise out of his autobiographical exploration manifest themselves in the concrete and particularised examples of his own past life.

In *Suspiria de Profundis* De Quincey finds that the private significance of these 'great convulsions' often conflicts with the universal principles they are supposed to illustrate. The individual importance for the autobiographer often seems to become inseparable from the publicly valuable assertion which confronts his reader. De Quincey sensed the danger which this coincidence offered to his purpose of providing his audience with valuable new truths. He deliberately denies idiosyncrasy in himself the autobiographer: 'what I point to are not peculiarities of temperament or of organisation, so much, as peculiar circumstances and incidents through which my own separate experience had revolved'.[65] By arguing for public relevance here De Quincey finds himself ironically describing his own exception to the rule, his isolation.

Likewise, De Quincey apologises for digressional material at the same time as drawing a distinction between the personal and public relevance of his autobiography:

> But the reader of more kindness ... will perceive that it is not for the mere facts that the case is reported, but because these facts move through a wilderness of natural thoughts or feelings; some in the child who suffers; some in the man who reports; but all so far interesting as they relate to solemn objects.[66]

De Quincey is not simply altering the emphasis of the different types of significance to be expected in his work, but its very subject. For this reason, he refers to 'solemn objects' at the end of the sentence rather than impressing the reader finally with 'thoughts and feelings'. He attempts to aid the reader in making this difficult step and so provides us with 'objects' to conform to the idea of a subject. In so doing he deflects attention from the fact that his subject does not consist of fixeties but is bound by the movement of process. De Quincey is reversing the usual conventions of autobiography in which 'I' is the subject, and even if at one remove, is to be recognised as the autobiographer. He wishes to dissolve such an absolute correspondence between his past self and his role as an autobiographer. It is his past experience not his past identity which is drawn before the reader. Likewise the autobiographer appears to us not so much as the man who experienced as the artist who now translates.

In the section of Suspiria de Profundis entitled 'Our Ladies of Sorrow' De Quincey takes this inversion to its most extreme form. Instead of abstracting the significance from the autobiographical material, he takes that significance and presents it overtly to the reader in an abstract form. He has invented suitable female figures:

> These sisters - by what name shall we call them? If I say simply "The Sorrows", there will be a chance of mistaking the term; it might be understood of individual sorrow, - separate cases of sorrow - whereas I want a term expressing the mighty abstractions that incarnate themselves in all individual sufferings of man's heart, and I wish to have these abstractions presented as impersonations, - that is, as clothed with human attributes of life, and with functions pointing to flesh. Let us call them, therefore, *our ladies of sorrow*.[67]

Having set up these fictions he is at liberty to delineate clearly his role of interpreter, and then centre our attention on his difficulty of communicating experience. The autobiographer's dilemma is one of literary technique, not one of identity: the 'Ladies of Sorrow'

> utter their pleasure, not by sounds that perish, or by words that go astray, but by signs in heaven - by changes on earth - by pulses in secret rivers - heraldries painted on darkness - and hieroglyphics written on the tablets of the brain. *They* wheeled in mazes; *I* spelled the steps. *They* telegraphed from afar; *I* read the signals. *They* conspired together; and on the mirrors of darkness *my* eye traced the plots. *Theirs* were the symbols - *mine* are the words.[68]

Even though such elaborate techniques are employed the autobiographical concern remains central: the difficulty contemplated with the use of these personifications is nevertheless accurate correspondence to past experience.

The way in which Suspiria de Profundis directs attention away from the autobiographer as a personality and centres attention on him as an artist dealing with the communication of complex experience is consistent with De Quincey's restrospective notice to his earlier Confessions. Defending himself against critics he denies that the subject of that work is opium and, more significantly perhaps, does not even entertain as a possibility the proposition that his own personality might be the subject:

> I tell my critic that the whole course of this narrative resembles and was meant to resemble, a *caduceus* wreathed about with meandering ornaments, or the shafts of a tree's stem hung round and surmounted with some vagrant parasitical plant. The mere medical subject of the opium answers to the dry withered pole, which shoots all rings of the flowering plants, and seems to do so by some dexterity of its own; whereas in fact, the plant and its tendrils have curled round the sullen cylinder by mere luxuriance of *theirs* ... Not the flowers are for the pole, but the pole is for the flowers ... The true object of my "Opium Confessions" is not the naked physiological theme ... but those wandering musical variations upon the theme - those parasitical thoughts, feelings, digressions, which climb up with bells and blossoms round about the arid stock.[69]

This recalls us to the revelatory nature of De Quincey's act of composition, when as a result of the resistance offered in his subject new possibilities are made available. To be successful his writing must seek to accommodate and record the movement of his mind in this extempore situation. In this attempt to arrest the rapid phenomena of his immediate consciousness he duplicates his previous aim of exploring, disentangling and expanding brief moments and delicate processes of his past life. This double operation, the 'facility of impression' over both the long-term and short-term, allows him to undertake his role of interpreter. Like the Greek chorus he is then able to 'recall you to your own lurking thoughts - hidden for the moment or imperfectly developed ... in immediate connexion with groups vanishing too quickly for any effort of meditation on your own part'.[70] He shows this ability even while he is in the act of accomplishing it technically; it arises as he attempts to define assimilated events in his past. For this reason also the autobiographer is seen as a literary artist not as a personality: we accompany him in the voyage of his discoveries.

Even though we grant this subordination of the autobiographer to the importance of his experience, the difficulty of depicting the intensity of experience is still paramount. For the types of experience De Quincey translates inevitably lead him back to the particularities and unique circumstances of his own life. In order to release his subject from that particularity, and to register its intensity, De Quincey outlines the following proposal which describes the method of The English Mail-Coach:

> It is impossible, with respect to any memorable grief, that it can be adequately exhibited so as to indicate the enormity of the convulsion which really it caused without viewing it under a variety of aspects - a thing which is almost necessary for the effect of proportion to what follows: 1st, for instance, in its immediate pressure, so stunning and confounding; 2ndly, in its oscillations, as in its earlier agitations, frantic with tumults, that borrow the wing of the winds; or in its diseased impulses of sick languishing desire, through which sorrow transforms itself.[71]

In Suspiria de Profundis these three aspects are quite clearly exploited; the first in 'The Affliction of Childhood', the third, arguably in such sections as 'The Daughter of Lebanon' and 'Savannah-la-Mar'. But it is the second, the 'oscillations', which dominate and dictate the form of the various 'suspiria' as De Quincey tries to explain not simply portray the psychological transformations attendant upon suffering. Because he undertakes an act of explanation De Quincey needs to create a sophisticated and specific relationship with his reader, as we shall see. The first significant evidence of this relationship in Suspiria de Profundis is the following notice, forewarning us that the structure and movement of the 'suspiria' are dependent upon the oscillatory nature of experience:

> Here pause, reader! Imagine yourself seated in some cloud-scaling swing, oscillating under the impulse of lunatic hands; for the strength of lunacy may belong to human dreams, the fearful caprice of lunacy ... Seated in such a swing, fast as you reach the lowest point of depression, you may rely on racing up to a starry altitude of corresponding ascent. Ups and downs you will see, heights and depths, in our fiery course together, such as will sometimes tempt you to look shyly and suspiciously at me, your guide, and the ruler of these oscillations.[72]

Although the reader is prepared in this way De Quincey still needs to provide considerable aid in the form of analogies such as the swing. Because, as he says, he is dealing with capricious impulses, he may find that the very authority of his role as guide is likely to deteriorate as his work continues, despite the pact with the reader set up in the quotation above. De Quincey seems particularly worried about the credibility of these 'oscillations' in his experience; for this reason he needs to bring familiar authorities and analogies to support himself, even though they might be alien to his own autobiographical content. Ironically, by doing so, he inevitably alerts the reader to the danger of digression. The following passage, for instance, opens with the introduction of knowledge very likely to make the reader suspicious. It consolidates the authority of De Quincey's oscillations by a dense grouping of analogies, only returning to its main concern at the very end. In its defence of accommodating the capricious turns of experience it comes perilously close to digression itself. In that mimetic quality lies its success:

> As sometimes, upon the English lakes, waterfowl that have careered in the air until the eye is wearied with the eternal wheelings of their inimitable flight - Grecian simplicities of motion, amidst a labyrinthine infinity of curves that would baffle the geometry of Appolonius - seek the water at last, as if with some settled purpose (you imagine) of reposing. Ah, how little have you understood the omnipotence of that life which they inherit! *They* want no rest; they laugh at resting; all is 'make believe', as when an infant hides its laughing behind its mother's shawl. For a moment it is still. Is it meaning to rest? Will its impatient heart endure to lurk there for long? Ask rather if a cataract will stop the fatigue. Will a sunbeam sleep on its travels? Or the Atlantic rest from its labours? As little can the infant, as little can the waterfowl of the lakes, suspend their play, except as a variety of play, or rest unless when nature compells them. Suddenly starts off the infant, suddenly ascend the birds, to new evolutions as incalculable as the caprices of a kaleidoscope; and the glory of their motions, from the mixed immortalities of beauty and inexhaustible variety, becomes at least pathetic to survey. So also, and with such life of variation, do the *primary* convulsions of nature - such, perhaps,

> as only *primary* formations of the human system can experience - come round again and again by reverberating shocks.[73]

In this passage De Quincey provides suitable analogies and then simulates his reader's present, and his own former bewilderment. He builds up a series of questions around his familiar analogies, then answers them rhetorically in his role of guide. This kind of movement is clearly intended to convince the reader. But because it reveals so obviously the rhetorical skill of the autobiographer (and his knowledge of experience as well as his expertise) it heightens his authority over the reader where he only appeared to be seeking to avoid difficulty in his communication of common experience. This situation arises because De Quincey asserts the complexity of common experience, and is not satisfied to rest within the bounds of commonplace observation. He challenges his reading public by offering it a picture of its own experience in a more complex form than is usually accepted. He then declares the abiding significance of that complexity. At times, therefore, he naturally risks offering platitudes in an elaborate manner. Much of his success is achieved because he is able to move so close to commonplace observations and invest them with a new intensity and significance:

> The collisions with alien interests or hostile views, of a child, boy, or very young man, so insulated as each of these is sure to be, - those aspects of opposition which such a person *can* occupy, are limited by the exceedingly few and trivial lines of connexion along which he is able to radiate any essential influence ... Far otherwise is the state of relations connecting an adult or responsible man with the circles around him as life advances. The network of those relations is a thousand times more intricate, the jarring of these intricate relations a thousand times more frequent, and vibrations a thousand times harsher which these jarrings diffuse.[74]

So much depends on De Quincey's ability to suggest the complexity, and register the intricacy of experience. A delicate balance needs to be maintained if the importance of that intricacy is to be ratified. He needs to find ways and illustrations which can adequately express the intangible realities of movement, expansion and repetition.

In *Suspiria de Profundis* the 'wheeling' of the wild duck is echoed many times, since it combines in one formula all those three qualities. De Quincey claims again that, 'In some potent convulsion of the system, all wheels back into its earliest elementary stage',[75] and suggests, in relation to sorrow suffered by his reader, that 'Many years are gone since that darkness settled on your head; many summers, many winters; yet still its shadows wheel round upon you at intervals, like these April showers upon this glory of bridal June'.[76] In this last sentence the insubstantiality and transience of experiential process is reinforced by both 'shadows' and 'April showers'. De Quincey frequently uses his knowledge of abnormal atmospheric phenomena, probably gleaned from his reading of eighteenth century travel literature,[77] to effect the same result. The most dramatic example of this sort forms a whole section within *Suspiria de Profundis* - 'The Apparition of the Brocken'. This has important bearings on De Quincey's relationship with his reader, to be dealt with later on in Chapter Five. Ironically, because De Quincey's prime concern is the intricacy and intensity of experience it leads him to find analogies which might equal the obscurity and finely balanced characteristics of his experience. Located in the very technique of *Suspiria de Profundis*, in these analogies, is the central dilemma of De Quincey the autobiographer - his isolation which promotes a search for sympathy and mediation. In this area there is but a fine dividing line between success and failure. The intricacy of his analogies can betray the very gulf they seek to fill between author and reader.

De Quincey's attempts in *Suspiria de Profundis* to communicate the principles and processes underlying the hidden unity of experience show that his position of translator involves two abilities which are often at variance with each other. His act of translation requires him to dictate to his reader at the same time as being at his mercy. He needs to demonstrate as well as record accurately. Each of these two extremes may be dominant depending on the type of unity under consideration; for in *Suspiria de Profundis* De Quincey handles both progressional continuities in experience - the developing links of process - and absolute, though often brief, unities which may be the consummations of a particular process. The latter, corresponding to the final 'Dream-Fugue' section of *The English Mail-Coach* contain no linear progression: 'in a moment, in the twinkling of an eye, every act - every design of her past life lived again, arraying themselves not as a succession, but as parts of a coexistence'.[78] De Quincey's difficulty here lies in providing suitable access to the experience, in dismantling its continuity. At the other extreme he is faced not with too rigid a union, but with no true centre at all:

> Even in our daily life is exhibited, in proportions far more gigantic, that tendency to swell and amplify itself into mountains of darkness, which exists oftentimes in germs that are imperceptible. An error in human choice, an infirmity in the human will, though it were at first less than a mote, though it should swerve from the right line by an interval less than a thread
>
> 'That ever spider twisted from her web', sometimes begins to swell, to grow, to widen its distances rapidly, travels off into boundless spaces remote from the true centre, spaces incalculable and irretraceable, until hope seems extinguished and return impossible. Such was the course of my own opium career. Such is the history of human errors every day.[79]

Again, De Quincey's own unusual experience is subordinated to common human experience, providing an example for a universal psychological phenomenon; not asserting its own particularity or deviation from the norm. The movement is towards social affirmation, not egotistical independence. Lack of success in his act of translation leaves De Quincey isolated, reinforcing his statement that 'The solitude in life is deep for those who suffer by secret and incommunicable woe and have none to pity them'.[80] Suspiria de Profundis explores not only the isolation of suffering, but also the literary attempts to make such suffering communicable.

An examination of De Quincey's translations of experience reveals the precedency of his need to communicate. Even where his work exhibits ornate and seemingly artificial forms of expression it appears to be governed by a requirement which asks for the most appropriate means of articulating experiential veracity to a specific public. De Quincey gives 'substance and life to what he feels'[81] in order to promote this communicative purpose: there is little evidence of him, 'enshrining/... the spirit of the Past/for future restoration'.[82] As he adopts the role of the public commentator he necessarily enters the realm of Hazlitt's 'common sense'; though differing considerably from Hazlitt's view of abstraction:

> There is nothing more distinct than common sense and vulgar opinion. Common sense is only a judge of things that fall under common observation, or immediately come home to the business and bosoms of men. This is of the very essence of its principle, the basis of its pretensions. It rests upon the simple process of feeling, it anchors in experience. It is not, nor it cannot be, the test of abstract, speculative opinions.[83]

He engages his reader in an area which needs to 'supervene upon dutiful attentiveness',[84] where 'common sense' is enforced with more than its usual intensity. For De Quincey to operate upon this shared ground he needs to de-particularise and depersonalise his own experience. The reason why he refers to 'common sense' is to verify the importance of a principle abstracted from that experience. He operates for much of the time within the boundaries of a popular consciousness; his periodical context at a slight, though significant remove from the workings of the daily press. In such close proximity De Quincey is able to voice an attack against that popular consciousness as well as expanding its boundaries by supervening upon its 'common sense'. On the subject of newspapers De Quincey wrote:

> Were there no other section in it than simply that allotted to the police reports, oftentimes I stand aghast at the revelations there made of human life and the human heart - at its colossal guilt, and its colossal misery; at the suffering which oftentimes throws its shadows over palaces, and the grandeur of mute endurance which sometimes glorifies a cottage. Here transpires the dreadful truth of what is going on for ever under the thick curtains of domestic life, close behind us, and before us, and all around us. Newspapers are evanescent, and are too rapidly recurrent, and people see nothing great in what is familiar, nor can ever be trained to read the silent and the shadowy in what, for the moment, is covered with the babbling garrulity of daylight.[85]

In order to deliver common truths drawn from his own experience, De Quincey needs to be suspicious of familiarity, deflecting his reader's attention away from the usual, and therefore staled ways of viewing experience. His techniques of communication are by no means direct or easily accessible. This leads to the dilemma of the public commentator recognised and experienced by Carlyle who was also capable of satirising it in Sartor Resartus:

> Singular Teufelsdrockh, would thou hadst told thy singular story in plain words! But it is fruitless to look there, in those Paper-bags, for such. Nothing but innuendoes, figurative crotchets: a typical Shadow, fitfully wavering, prophetico-satiric; no clear logical Picture. "How paint to the sensual eye", asks he once, "what passes in the Holy of Holies of Man's Soul; in what words, known to these profane times, speak even afar-off of the unspeakable?" We ask in return: Why perplex these times, profane as they are, with needless obscurity, by omission and by commission? Not mystical only is our Professor, but whimsical; and involves himself, now more than ever, in eye-bewildering *chiaroscuro*.[86]

Where Carlyle's deliberate tactic is often to cultivate obscurity in order to expand the popular consciousness, De Quincey's indirectness attains greater objectivity and artistic control over obscure or whimsical experience. Where Carlyle argues that, 'In a symbol there is concealment and yet revelation: here therefore, by Silence and by Speech acting together, comes a double significance ... the commonest Truth stands out to us proclaimed with quite new emphasis'[87] De Quincey consistently seeks access to the complexities of common experience. De Quincey's translation of experience recognises the vitality of the human consciousness - its variety, its movement, and its subtlety; and from that recognition undertakes a difficult task of correspondence. Hazlitt speculated on just such a richness, outlining a meditative motion of the mind akin to De Quincey's act of contemplation in the midst of composition:

> How many ideas and trains of sentiment, long and deep and intense, often pass through the mind in only one day's thinking, or reading, for instance! How many such days are there in

> a year, how many years in a long life, still occupied with something interesting, still recalling some old impression, still recurring to some difficult question and making progress in it, every step accompanied with a sense of power, and every moment conscious of "the high endeavour or the glad success" *for the mind fixes chiefly on that which keeps it employed, and is wound up to a certain pitch of pleasurable excitement or lively solicitude by necessity of its own nature.*[88] (my italics)

De Quincey's problem in The English Mail-Coach and Suspiria de Profundis results from his attempt to follow the 'trains of sentiment' in his own past life, tracing continuities and acts of assimilation which have transposed themselves in his consciousness. Many of his difficulties arise because he attempts to handle long-term experiential processes. In the next chapter we shall analyse specific 'moments' in his autobiographical writings, where transitions can be more successfully exploited; and where the dense texture of experience can be handled within more limited confines.

NOTES

1. Thomas De Quincey, The Collected Writings of Thomas De Quincey, David Masson (ed.) (14 vols., Edinburgh, 1889-90), vol. I, p. 39.
2. Ibid., p. 10.
3. Thomas De Quincey, The Posthumous Works of Thomas De Quincey, A.H. Japp (ed.) (London, 1893), vol. II, p. 27.
4. Masson, vol. III, p. 332.
5. William Hazlitt, The Complete Works of William Hazlitt, P.P. Howe (ed.) (London, 1932), vol. XII, pp. 277-278.
6. Masson, vol. X, p. 274.
7. Hazlitt, The Complete Works, vol. XIII, p. 335.
8. Ibid., vol. VIII, p. 40.
9. Masson, vol. III, p. 315.
10. Hazlitt, The Complete Works, vol. VIII, p. 31.
11. Masson, vol. III, pp. 271-272.
12. Ibid., p. 435.
13. William Wordsworth, The Prelude, Ernest De Selincourt (ed.) (London, 1959), Second Edition, 1850 version, Book III, lines 184-191.

14. Ibid., Book V, lines 184-188.
15. Ibid., Book IV, lines 44-45.
16. Ibid., Book VIII, lines 518-519.
17. Ibid., Book XII, lines 81-87.
18. Ibid., Book VI, lines 592-593.
19. Masson, vol. X, p. 246.
20. Ibid., vol. VII, p. 126.
21. Ibid.
22. Ibid., vol. VIII, p. 15.
23. Ibid., vol. I, p. 28. (originally part of Suspiria de Profundis).
24. Ibid., vol. XIII, p. 338.
25. Thomas De Quincey, The Uncollected Writings of Thomas De Quincey, James Hogg (ed.) (London, 1890), vol. I, p. 303.
26. A.H. Japp (ed.), Posthumous Works, vol. I, pp. 226-227.
27. Wordsworth, The Prelude, 1805 version, Book II, lines 208-215.
28. Masson, vol. XI, p. 59.
29. A.H. Japp (ed.), Posthumous Works, vol. I, p. 225.
30. Masson, vol. X, pp. 348-349.
31. Ibid., p. 375.
32. Ibid., pp. 340-341.
33. Ibid., p. 358.
34. Ibid., p. 357.
35. Ibid., p. 173.
36. Ibid., p. 145.
37. Ibid., vol. VIII, p. 33.
38. Alethea Hayter, Opium and the Romantic Imagination (London, 1971), p. 74.
39. Masson, vol. VIII, p. 33.
40. Virginia Woolf, 'Impassioned Prose', in Granite and Rainbow (London, 1958), p. 36.
41. Ibid., p. 40.
42. Masson, vol. X, p. 92.
43. A.H. Japp (ed.), Posthumous Works, vol. I, p. 201.
44. References to The English Mail-Coach and Suspiria de Profundis are made, in this chapter, to their initial form of publication in Blackwood's Edinburgh Magazine. Thomas De Quincey, Blackwood's Edinburgh Magazine (October 1849), p. 485.
45. Ibid.
46. Ibid., p. 486.
47. Masson, vol. I, p. 14.
48. Blackwood's (October 1849), p. 486.
49. Ibid., p. 496.
50. Ibid., p. 486.
51. Masson, vol. XIII, p. 305 (not in the

Blackwood's version).

52. Blackwood's (December 1849), p. 741.
53. Masson, vol. XIII, pp. 328-330.
54. Ibid.
55. Blackwood's (December 1849), p. 743.
56. Ibid. (October 1849), p. 495.
57. Ibid., p. 496.
58. Ibid., p. 497.
59. Ibid.
60. Ibid. (December 1849), p. 747.
61. Ibid. (October 1849), p. 486.
62. Ibid., p. 490.
63. Ibid., p. 491.
64. Ibid. (June 1845), p. 742.
65. Ibid. (March 1845), p. 272.
66. Ibid., pp. 272-273.
67. Ibid. (June 1845), p. 745.
68. Ibid.
69. Ibid. (March 1845), p. 273.
70. Ibid. (June 1845), p. 750.
71. Ibid. (April 1845), p. 496.
72. Ibid., pp. 501-502.
73. Ibid., pp. 496-497.
74. Ibid. (July 1845), p. 44.
75. Ibid. (June 1845), p. 743.
76. Ibid., p. 749.
77. See H.A. Eaton (ed.), A Diary of Thomas De Quincey (New York, 1927), pp. 155 and 182.
78. Blackwood's (June 1845), p. 742.
79. A.H. Japp (ed.), Posthumous Works, vol. I, pp. 22-23.
80. Ibid., p. 28.
81. Wordsworth, The Prelude, 1850 version, Book XII, line 284.
82. Ibid., line 286.
83. Hazlitt, The Complete Works, vol. VIII, p. 37.
84. John Holloway, The Victorian Sage (New York, 1965, first published London, 1953), pp. 4-5.
85. Masson, vol. I, p. 102.
86. Thomas Carlyle, Sartor Resartus, Collected Works, vol. I, Library Edition (London, 1869), p. 179.
87. Ibid., pp. 212-213.
88. Hazlitt, The Complete Works, vol. VIII, p. 28.

Chapter 4

SUSPENDED MOMENTS

De Quincey's autobiographical writings contain depictions of critical moments of experience which have to a large extent determined his status as a Romantic writer. His reputation has long been thought to rest on his ability to describe elaborately the traumatic moments of his life. In the past an appreciation of this aspect of his work has frequently been blurred by the accompaniment of that traditional dismissive label 'prose stylist'. A disproportionate estimate of De Quincey the autobiographer is likely to arise if such moments are viewed without due regard to their own immediate textual context and the related larger context of the periodical press. The full significance of such moments is denied if they are considered in isolation. For the full effect of their 'suspension' does not simply consist in their being more circumscribed than the sequential experiences we dealt with in the last chapter. They form interruptions to the narrative, chronological, or progressive movement of the text - the very movement which is capable of substantiating the link between the periodical writer and his audience. In addition to the severance of that direct link, the experiential content of the moment frequently emphasises the departure from the everyday norm. The multiple nature of the 'suspension' can be even further supported if the writer creates a personality which is at odds with or remote from his audience.

If one takes into account the relevance of 'suspension' to these related points of view one can estimate more fully the tactics exploited by De Quincey the periodical writer, and define more precisely the nature of the various 'moments concerned. It becomes easier to see both the possibilities and difficulties confronting De Quincey. The difficulties are then not simply the result of the critic creating islands within the text. Such cautionary remarks are needed to define the important issues entangled in the following statements of a reviewer who confidently reminds the public of the agreed qualities of De Quincey's talent:

> Suspended moments! In greater or less degree they determine every characteristic of the essential De Quincey: style, supernatural arrest, addiction to dreams, humour ... The inability to pass from one experience to the next begets an extraordinary musical development of the original experience ... this huge impact of the single revelation that fixes experience and will reverberate through a lifetime.[1]

The 'essential De Quincey' offered here is severely limited: even though it alludes to the problematical nature of such an area, it fails to provide a discriminating critical vantage point. The same sort of confident, popular estimate of De Quincey is to be found in Leslie Stephen's Hours in a Library: 'He appeals to our terror of the infinite, to the shrinking of the human mind before astronomical distances and geological periods of time. He paints vast perspectives, opening in long succession, till we grow dizzy in the contemplation.'[2] Again we seem to have lost sight of the periodical writer. One needs to examine the extent to which the periodical writer disappears, if he disappears at all in handling these high points of experience. Leslie Stephen's remarks are pertinent, but lack the incisiveness which might penetrate beyond that initial 'dizziness'.

De Quincey's excitement at these 'suspended moments' of his autobiography is sponsored by their imaginative impact, as apparent facts of his experience, and not by his interest in the mechanism of their production. In this denial of the scientific he is, of course, typically Romantic. Intense moments of experience are valued by the periodical writer and opium-eater combined: they even become the starting points from which he preaches to his public:

> It is certain, howsoever it may be explained psychologically that the fierce compression of mental activities which takes place in ... struggle ... has the effect of suddenly

> unlocking cells in the brain ... Pain, and conflicts with suffering are ministrations of development to the human intellect.[3]

Although the delivery is almost arrogantly assertive, the basis is Romantic in its insistence on the primacy of intense experience. De Quincey's presentation of these 'climactic moments' is evidence of his excitement as a Romantic autobiographer at the prospect of experience. He frequently acknowledges its complexity by considering one moment rather than by following a process. Alternatively one moment may conclude, or contain, a number of linked processes in experience. The complexity of a moment is drawn to our attention because of its intensity. Coleridge was obviously excited by this fact of his experience: 'What a swarm of thoughts and feelings, endlessly minute fragments ... lie compact in any one moment!'[4] As Georges Poulet says, 'the present moment ... is so intensely experienced that it seems as if transience gives way to everlastingness, as if time stands still and becomes eternity'.[5] He claims this is current in all Romantic poetry and draws attention to Keats' statement that 'nothing startled [him] beyond the Moment'.[6] Such moments are thus 'suspensions' in that they are interruptions or alternatives to the usual awareness of experience. Poulet writes of 'the essential belief ... of nearly all Romanticists ... in the continued existence of the past'[7] which is supported by these moments which provide 'rare glimpses, disconnected reminiscences, of this immense treasure stored in a remote place in our soul'.[8] He highlights the difficulty of handling these moments. As in the last chapter, part of the difficulty is in suggesting or recreating the fullness and complexity of experience. Poulet sees the imagination 'confronted at once with such an infinity of detail, it could not but perceive them as details, that is, one after another, without possibility of taking in the whole'.[9] Sufficient respect must be paid to the organic nature of experience: abstraction and dislocation must be apologised for.

A terminology which takes into account some of these difficulties, and rules out others, is that subsumed under the notion of the 'sublime'. It is a notion which combines a religious sense with a psychological awareness. It is concerned with the intensity of experience and recognises a difficulty involved with that intensity. Indeed, the difficulty of contemplating the intensity of certain key points in experience again refers us to the idea of a suspension from the usual methods of apprehension, quantification and rationalisation. So, too, De Quincey's idea of the 'literature of power', which was examined in Chapter Two, may be viewed profitably in relation to the sublime, showing how 'resistance' and 'power' operate together.

De Quincey's relationship to other Romantic writers, particularly Wordsworth, is very persuasive when one attempts to handle this aspect of his autobiography. In the past it appears to have been too persuasive. Perhaps this is why De Quincey's reputation has rested in this area and why his identity as a periodical writer has been specifically denied at the same time. Certainly there are fruitful comparisons to be made between the 'moments' and their method of 'suspension' in Wordsworth's The Prelude and the 'suspended moments' of De Quincey's autobiographical writing. How fruitful such comparisons are would seem to depend on how great is the recognition of difference between the two cases.

The restorative agency - the 'efficacious spirit' that is associated with Wordsworth's 'spots of time' passage in The Prelude[10] is linked, as Geoffrey Hartman intimates, to Wordsworth's specialist concern with the Imagination. He says it 'renews the poet vis-a-vis nature. He again meets the world with a sensitive, creative soul, as in his youth.'[11] Jonathan Wordsworth has pointed to the significance of an earlier version of this passage where Wordsworth pointed more obviously to his specialist interest in creativity by writing 'fructifying virtue'[12] instead of 'vivifying Virtue' in the 1805 version and 'renovating virtue' in the 1850 version. Furthermore, this earlier version said not simply, and perhaps inclusively, that 'our minds/Are nourished and invisibly repair'd' but inserted the important clause, 'Especially the imaginative power'.[13] Wordsworth's insistence on value in this respect (through his adjectives 'efficacious' and 'fructive') differentiates him from De Quincey who is obviously not specialised in the same way - in talking about the imagination.

De Quincey's analogous experiential concern as an autobiographer with 'suspended moments' may be viewed most profitably by considering the tension available to him in the periodical context. We should look for an interaction, a potentially useful friction, between the claims made on him as a magazine personality or presence, and as a translator of experience. Again, these by no means mutually exclusive functions become polarised because of an assumption that a text cannot act in an explanatory, discursive manner and at the same time progress in terms of its actual presentation. This is especially true when non-fictional prose is concerned. In De Quincey's case it is a question of deciding when that friction spoken of earlier is really useful or whether it is finally destructive.

When Virginia Woolf attacks De Quincey as an autobiographer it would seem that she fails to allow for any fruitful possibilities in his special relationship with his readers: 'He was profusely and indiscriminately loquacious. Discursiveness - the disease that attacked so many of the nineteenth century English writers - had him in her coils.'[14] Having pinpointed what she considers to be De Quincey's greatest defect as an autobiographer it is consistent that the quality she praises in that area of his work is localised, and precludes any continuous reading of the text. Virginia Woolf finds a special sympathy for De Quincey because, as she says, 'he was capable of being transfixed by the mysterious solemnity of certain emotions: of realising how one moment may transcend in value fifty years'.[15] In another essay on De Quincey, similarly, she highlights some of the traits of a periodical writer which are clearly at odds, despite her sympathy for the subject, with her own selective concern:

> He required, too, endless leisure and ample elbow-room. He wanted time to soliloquise and loiter; here to pick up some trifle and bestow upon it all his powers of analysis and decoration; here to brush aside such patient discrimination and widen and enlarge and amplify until nothing remains but the level sands and the immense sea.[16]

Admittedly, it might be argued that these are the traits of a periodical writer taken to an extreme - that such loiterings and amplification went beyond the immediate need for communication and the degree of leisure afforded to the essay. Nevertheless, Virginia Woolf isolates the 'solemnity of certain emotions' and 'transcendent moments' from the whole range and movement of De Quincey's autobiographical works and in so doing draws attention to the problem he faced in one area of his translation of experience. Although she appears to see other solutions to these problems than were afforded to De Quincey in his more public and non-fictional context, her diagnosis of his problem is refreshing:

> A prose writer may dream dreams and see visions, but they cannot be allowed to lie scattered, single, solitary upon the page. So spaced out they die. For prose has neither the intensity nor the self-sufficiency of poetry. It rises slowly off the ground; it must be connected on this side and on that. There must be some medium in which its ardours and ecstasies can float without incongruity, from which they receive support and impetus. Here was a difficulty which De Quincey often faced and often failed to solve ... he must descend from these happy heights to the levels of ordinary existence. And, again and again, it is in returning to earth that De Quincey is undone. How is he to bridge the horrid transition? How is he to turn from an angel with wings of flame and eyes of fire to a gentleman in black who talks sense?[17]

Such a marked contrast as Virginia Woolf contemplates in that last sentence is considerably reduced if one keeps in mind the overt contact with the reader which is a significant feature of De Quincey's writing, and which will be assessed in the next chapter. The reader can also be summoned more directly (if crudely at times) than is implied by a gradual transition. The impetus supplied in this manner is certainly more abrupt than that operating in a traditionally fictional text, and as a result can be as demanding in its own way. With less space available there is not always time for a gradual transition: the reader must be forced along quickly, even if it means breaking up the text, both within a narrative sequence and more obviously by separating it under different headings. The fact that such operations take place under a degree of necessity provides the requisite tension for De Quincey's autobiography.

Most of the attention so far has centred on how to accommodate 'spots of time' or 'suspended moments'. Cautioned by Virginia Woolf's awareness of the difficulty in this area, we might still consider that such moments can provide a method of scrutinising experience (given a belief in its organic nature) which is available within the context of the periodical magazine. With this initial appreciation of 'suspension' rather than deviation, we should now be able to analyse a variety of key moments in De Quincey's autobiography, giving more attention to their experiential content and judging the different 'suspensions' that take place.

ANARCHIC MOMENTS

The key moments in De Quincey's autobiography can be viewed most profitably in relation to 'value'. De Quincey differs significantly from Wordsworth in this respect due to the latter's insistence on value, which is in accordance with his specialised concern with the imagination. While De Quincey, too, is clearly operating in a specialised field, as an autobiographer with an affective bias, the nature of his specialisation often militates against direct evaluation, particularly in the case of suspended moments. Virginia Woolf's statement that De Quincey was 'capable of being transfixed by the mysterious solemnity of certain emotions' is again pertinent. The emphasis is to be on presentation, communication where intensity is sometimes all-important. We are presented with an account, rendered in artistic terms, of the initial wonder and excitement of experience. Even though De Quincey's handling of these moments, as already suggested, may include much that is explanatory, abstractive, and interpretive, direct evaluations are scarce. Most assertive claims involve the movement from personal truth to generalisation.

Where the major Romantic poets, including Wordsworth, frequently focus on the power of the imagination, De Quincey the autobiographer, seemingly at one slight remove from this interest in artistic creativity, concentrates his attention on the powers of the individual consciousness. These powers, as we have already seen (particularly in Chapter One), can be anarchic and capricious. Clearly, there is an ambivalence rooted in the word 'power': whether applied to consciousness generally or imagination particularly, there is a recognition of potential danger. De Quincey's 'suspended moments' refer us to experiences which may be best described and distinguished by thinking of them in two categories: not directly creative, but anarchic or restorative.

In his <u>Confessions</u> De Quincey claims he had both 'the advantage of a prodigious memory, and the far greater advantage of a logical instinct for feeling in a moment the secret analogies and parallelisms that connected things else apparently remote'.[18] The last 'advantage' is evidence of the mind's ability to perceive unity. In De Quincey's case it can be threatening. This 'logical instinct' provides sudden realisations of impending disaster. In his short stories and his historical essays, as well as in his autobiographical writings, De Quincey is particularly fascinated by the suddenness with which apparent domestic security can be shattered. His fascination and his fear were so strongly attached to such an event because his vision of the insulated household group is at the centre of his vision of society, and fundamental to his understanding of the individual. This is especially true of his essay 'The Theban Sphinx'. Our attention is focused on the specifically individual nature of the evil exemplified in Oedipus, described as 'loaded with an insupportable burthen of pariah participation in pollution and misery, to which his will had never consented'.[19] At the same time, there is a fascination with the related destruction of the household:

> Mysterious also is the pomp of ruin which this revelation of the past descends upon that ancient house of Thebes. Like a shell from modern artillery, it leaves no time for prayer or evasion, but shatters by the same explosion all that stand within its circle of fury. Every member of that devoted household, as if they had been sitting not around a sacred domestic hearth, but around the crater of some surging volcano, - all alike, father and mother, sons and daughters, are wrapt at once in fiery whirlwinds of ruin.[20]

The key phrase here is 'revelation of the past'. The moment of destruction is simultaneously one of recognition: the past must be totally re-considered and re-deciphered according to the new insight, as in the case of the Sphinx's riddle. The nexus between past and present, the organic unity of experience, becomes nightmarishly vigorous in its logic. The anarchy and destructive power evident in such a moment is emphasised by the remote nature of the connection that is made. This is implied in its remoteness. De Quincey is often led to exclaim retrospectively upon this appearance of disparity: 'Upon what slender accidents hang oftentimes solemn life-long results'.[21] However, in these sudden destructive moments, although they may confirm in all their terribleness the links between experiences or circumstances, there is a strong sense of alienation. Before the latest revelation has been assimilated, its agency and its connection with the past appear to be externalised, divorced from the individual who perceives them.

This kind of alarming externalisation and the accompanying insecurity is considered in De Quincey's short story 'The Household Wreck'. Here melodramatic narration is prefaced by emotive generalisations which serve to focus and justify a place for the sentimental heart of the tale. Among these urgent preparatory remarks is the following lament for the anarchy and insecurity of human experience, although (as the subsequent tale makes clear) it is sponsored, ironically, by an all too vigorous, and therefore destructive logic:

> What is life? Darkness and formless vacancy for a beginning, or something beyond all beginning; then next a dim lotos of human consciousness, finding itself afloat upon the bosom of waters without a shore; then a few sunny smiles and many tears; a little love and infinite strife; *whisperings from paradise and fierce mockeries from the anarchy of chaos*; dust and ashes, and once more darkness circling round, as if from the beginning, and in this way rounding or making an island of our fantastic existence.[22]
> (my italics)

The sense of disproportion here appears almost as injustice and has been externalised in the italicised phrase. This kind of naming process, though it may seem overcharged in its rhetoric, is a rudimentary form of subjective mythologising. The translation of experience involves the use of abstract figurative devices. This is particularly so when De Quincey is dealing with the sudden destructive transformations of a single moment, as in this further passage from 'The Household Wreck':

> Yet in the lowest deep there still yawns a lower deep; and in the vast halls of man's frailty there are separate and more gloomy chambers of a frailty more exquisite and consummate ... Cases there are, and those not rare, in which a single week, a day, an hour, sweeps away all vestiges and landmarks of a memorable felicity; in which the ruin travels faster than the flying showers upon the mountain side, faster "than a musician scatters

> sounds"; in which "it was" and "it is not" are words of the self-same tongue in the self-same minute.[23]

The overt insistence of metaphor, the elaborate construction 'halls of man's frailty' so as to give a spatial dimension, and the two illustrations which signify transience (the latter significantly in quotation marks) all increase the complexity of the moment. 'Exquisite' is a key word in this aspect of De Quincey's work; it frequently highlights difficulty of communication. Nevertheless, the style is still, of course, assertive and declamatory because the destructive moment is also a moment of recognition - a revelation of sorts. De Quincey frequently projects an image of himself by using the authority such an insight affords. A slight suggestion of this 'ability' is present in the following statement from 'The Household Wreck':

> the hollowness visible amid the very raptures of enjoyment to every eye which looks for a moment underneath the draperies of the shadowy *present*, the hollowness, the blank treachery of hollowness, upon which all the pomps and vanities of life ultimately repose.[24]

In a number of short stories (some translated from German) and in his novel Klosterheim De Quincey incorporates this awareness of 'blank treachery' with his delight in exploring the secret and subtle machinations of Gothic melodrama. Other stories illustrate his related fascination with the fatality of choice, as in the case of 'The Dice' and 'The Fatal Marksman'. Although these fictional works display various approaches to anarchic moments, their concern is almost entirely with the final effects or mechanisms of destruction. There is little interest in motives of any sort, which is in keeping with De Quincey's lack of psychological interest in 'character'. This is so even when the subject is murder.

One of the most gruesome of these short stories is 'The Avenger', in which the security of a whole community is destroyed by a series of murders that are both masterfully executed and inexplicable. The tale exploits the macabre nature of the murders and the mystery which surrounds them. Explanation finally takes the form of a revelation of identity which, in its turn, stems from the remote history of the community. The main focus of attention, however, is on the unresolved mystery and terror: the final explanation provides no resolution, but convinces the reader only of the aberrant nature of the actions that have been perpetrated. De Quincey's interest is typified by the following comment:

> - the sense of mystery, when ten cases of total extermination, applied to separate households, had occurred, in every one of which these precautionary aids had failed to yield the slightest assistance. The horror, the perfect frenzy of fear, which seized upon the town after that experience, baffles all attempt at description.[25]

A fascination with the disruption of domestic peace from within is again present in this tale: 'the city in its more stationary and native classes would very soon have manifested *their* awful sense of things, of the hideous insecurity for life, and of the unfathomable dangers which had undermined their hearths before their very feet.'[26]

In these fictional works, as one might expect, De Quincey's interest in anarchic processes and their sudden manifestations is evidenced by intricacy of plot and the very actions of the tales. Moments of revelation are simply presented or reported, rarely elaborated on or suspended within the text as they are in the autobiographical works. In the 'Postscript' section of <u>On Murder Considered as One of the Fine Arts</u> we move away from the orthodox fictional techniques and stylisations of short story or novel as practised by De Quincey, but still remain in the area of mystery, suspense and murder. This text, which exploits its relation to real events, provides a link between the anarchic actions of the short stories and the anarchic suspended moments of the autobiographical works.

In this 'Postscript' De Quincey recreated with the help of contemporary newspaper accounts two scenes of murder which took place in London many years before. His reconstruction of the probable course of events is sponsored throughout by an insistence of facts and plausibility that is, at times, reminiscent of Defoe. The text exploits this factual foundation; it uses a mixture of dramatic reconstruction and inquisitive explanation to be both provocative and disturbing. After a good deal of information introducing the situation of the first set of murders (involving a shopkeeper named Marr and his household) De Quincey suddenly shifts the reader's attention to Marr's female servant with the following transition. Significantly, the accommodation of a moment within the text, in all its abruptness, heightens the relationship between the periodical writer and his reader:

> Meantime, at this point, let us leave the murderer alone with his victims. For fifty minutes let him work his pleasure. The front-door, as we know, is now fastened against all help. Help there is none. Let us, therefore, in vision, attach ourselves to Mary; and, when all is over, let us come back with *her*, again raise the curtain, and read the dreadful record of all that has passed in her absence.[27]

The imaginative projection is then, as promised, used to concentrate on the particularly dramatic moment when Mary arrives at the front door and rings the bell. By focusing on this one viewpoint and thereby creating a sense of drama this moment represents a departure from the previous methods of narration. The primarily logical detective work, which progresses chronologically, is suspended to provide a moment seen from an individual point of view and thus affording some psychological insight. Furthermore, because the moment concerned is fairly complex, containing both subtle and simultaneous components, its place in the text appears to be extended, despite its 'real' brevity. De Quincey's depiction of this moment involves a lengthy as well as continuous suspension: keeping a sense of the moment alive, while alternating between comment on Mary's situation and an attempted recreation of it:

> But all such reflections this way or that were swallowed up at this point in overmastering panic. That her double summons *could* have been unnoticed - this *solitary fact in one moment made a revelation of horror*. One person might have fallen asleep, but two - but three - *that* was a mere impossibility. And, even supposing all three together with the baby locked in sleep, still how unaccountable was this ... utter silence! Most naturally at this moment something like hysterical horror overshadowed the poor girl, and now at last she rang the bell with the violence that belongs to sickening terror. This done, she paused: self-command enough she still retained, though fast and fast it was slipping away from her, to bethink

> herself ... still, even in that case Mrs. Marr and her infant would be left, and some murmuring reply, under any extremity, would be elicited from the poor mother. To pause, therefore, to impose stern silence upon herself, so as to leave room for the possible answer to this final appeal, became a duty of spasmodic effort. Listen, therefore, poor trembling heart; listen, and for twenty seconds be still as death! Still as death she was; and during that dreadful stillness, when she hushed her breath that she might listen, occurred an incident of killing fear, *that to her dying day would never cease to renew its echoes in her ear*. She ... heard at last ... a sound within the house. Yes, now beyond a doubt there is coming an answer to her summons. What was it? On the stairs ... was heard a creaking sound. Next was heard most distinctly a footfall: one, two, three, four, five stairs ... Then the dreadful footsteps were heard advancing along the little narrow passage ... The very breathing can be heard of that dreadful being who has silenced all breathing ... in the house. There is but a door between him and Mary ... The unknown murderer and she have both their lips upon the door, listening, breathing hard; but luckily they are on different sides of the door; and upon the least indication of unlocking or unlatching she would have recoiled into the asylum of general darkness.[28] (my italics)

The starting point for this moment - a sudden recognition - is combined with the investigatory nature of the whole piece so that it is 'a solitary fact' which makes 'a sudden revelation of horror'. In De Quincey's autobiographical works this kind of sudden recognition is frequently retrospective rather than being dramatically realised in the present, as it is here. Nevertheless, a suggestion of the usual autobiographical standpoint is present because of De Quincey's inclusion of the telling phrase, 'that to her dying day would never cease to renew its echoes in her ear'. The continued presence and re-assessment of the past, coupled with the possibility of menace, underlines the significance of the moment.

Apart from these two biographical inclusions, the effectiveness of this suspended moment also depends on its heightened depiction of danger in the very midst of society, revealing the frailty of those barriers which might provide protection. This threat of sudden disaster from within shared by some of the short stories, differentiates the passage quoted above from the moment De Quincey considers in his critical essay 'On the Knocking at the Gate in *Macbeth*'. Although critics[29] have tended to concentrate on the similarity between the two cases, in the 'Postscript' section of *On Murder Considered as One of the Fine Arts* and in 'The Household Wreck' our attention is drawn to the proximity of destruction to the usual or domestic 'goings-on of the world'. In contrast, De Quincey's description of the scene in *Macbeth* highlights the juxtaposition of two sharply separated areas of activity. The shock of recognition which gives significance to the knocking is provided by bridging the gap between the two areas:

> The murderers and the murder must be insulated - cut off by an immeasurable gulf from the ordinary tide and succession of human affairs - locked up and sequestered in some deep recess; we must be made sensible that the world of ordinary life is suddenly arrested, laid asleep, tranced, racked into a dread armistice; time must be annihilated, relation to things without abolished; and all must pass self-withdrawn into a deep syncope and suspension of earthly passion. Hence it is that, when the deed is done, when the work of darkness is perfect, then the world of darkness passes away like a pageantry in the clouds: the knocking at the gate is heard, and it makes known audibly that the reaction has commenced; the human has made its reflux upon the fiendish; the pulses of life are beginning to beat again; and the re-establishment of the goings-on of the world in which we live first makes us profoundly sensible of the awful parenthesis that had suspended them.[30]

In this case the emphasis is clearly on 'insulation', described in terms which are tantalisingly close to the psychological language of a Romantic autobiographer. 'Tranced', 'self-withdrawn', 'syncope' and 'pulses' all indicate that isolation might be substituted for 'insulation'. His observation on Shakespeare's drama reminds us of those moments in De Quincey's autobiography which in terms of consciousness, rather than artistic technique, might best be referred to as 'reveries'. They frequently conclude, as we shall see later in this chapter, with a noise which brings the 'dreamer' back to the immediate action of the present. De Quincey's consideration of this moment in a critical essay, while being intimately connected with the anarchic moments discussed so far, differs from them because of its insistence on separation. The threat resident in those anarchic moments derives from the fluid interchange between usually self-contained and carefully defined areas. Just as rigidity or inflexibility can be frightening for De Quincey the autobiographer, causing isolation and offering no hope of alternative possibilities, so movement and growth may appear to be without rationale or purpose, offering no promise of an intermittent stasis. A review of past experience may uncover threads of experience leading out from a seemingly insignificant event. This kind of aberrant organic principle is present in the 'Postscript' to Murder Considered when De Quincey exclaims: 'Upon what slender accidents hang oftentimes solemn life-long results! ... And yet upon these trivial circumstances depended Mary's life'.[31] Because the principle of growth in experience may be frighteningly fluid, and capable of establishing a link which excludes other possibilities, De Quincey also focuses his autobiographical vision on crucial moments of choice.

The moment of choice, as depicted by De Quincey, is often characterised by helplessness or passivity at a time of crisis. Experience seems to impose itself on the individual rather than vice versa. The subordinate role of the individual described in the following passage from the Confessions parallels the inevitability of the destructive workings of fate in the short stories:

> "It comes then to this", thought I, "that in myself only there lurks any arrear of help": as always for every man the ultimate reliance should be on himself. But this *self* of mine seemed absolutely bankrupt; bankrupt of counsel or device - of effort in the way of action, or of suggestion in the way of plan.[32]

Apart from this inability to draw upon the fundamental resources of individual identity, the reasons for this helplessness also include (most importantly for the autobiographer) a lack of knowledge about the past, and more specifically, an inability to designate the areas or moments of most importance. The autobiographer and the individual alike can find that they have been basing their estimate of experience on a false premise. Stability is lost with the sudden revelation, in a crisis, of a hitherto unknown starting-point. Such a crisis can only be explained by following the route of an anarchic process leading back to a previous moment of error. In his 'Revolt of the Tartars' De Quincey focuses on just this sort of negative impulse: a destructive premise lies hidden from the people who are to suffer its consequences.

> Hence it happened that this astonishing Exodus of a whole nation, before so much as a whisper of the design had begun to circulate amongst those whom it most interested, before it was even suspected that any man's wishes pointed him in that direction, had been definitely appointed for January of the year 1771. And almost up to the Christmas of 1770 the poor simple Kalmuck herdsmen and their families were going nightly to their peaceful beds, without even dreaming that the *fiat* had already gone forth from their rulers which consigned quiet hordes, together with the peace and comfort which reigned with them, to a withering desolation, now close at hand.[33]

From this initial 'fiat' the work follows the destructive impulse through elaborate and exotic descriptions until it culminates in the spectacle of a massacre. Just before this final set-piece De Quincey, as in the episode from Murder Considered, suddenly changes the perspective by viewing the scene of carnage at a distance through the eyes of the Chinese Emperor. Our attention is drawn to the fatal attraction of the destructive course of events. Again we are presented with a passive response to a climactic situation:

> From this pass, elevated about two thousand feet above the level of the water, they continued to descend, by a very windy and difficult road, for an hour and a half; and during the whole of this descent they were compelled to be inactive spectators of the fiendish spectacle below.[34]

In his autobiographical works De Quincey, as we shall see in the next chapter, invites the reader to share in this passivity, so that both autobiographer and reader become 'inactive spectators' of the past experience. This example from the 'Revolt of the Tartars' delivers in a historical and prospective narrative an instance of the kind which in autobiography is usually viewed retrospectively with a descriptive and explanatory evocation in the past tense of such mysterious and anarchic impulses.

Because there is this sense of mystery, the descriptive and explanatory aspect of the autobiography is able to accommodate a certain amount of heterogeneity in its use of metaphor. Again, as in the passage from 'The Household Wreck', a series of seemingly remote comparisons may serve to define a moment of past experience, and yet, ultimately, point to its inexplicability, as in the following elaborate suggestion from the later version of the Confessions:

> But now, at last came over me, from the mere excess of bodily suffering and mental disappointments, a frantic and rapturous re-agency. In the United States the case is well known, and many times has been described by travellers, of that furious instinct which, under a secret call for saline variations of diet, drives all the tribes of buffaloes for thousands of miles to the common centre of the "Salt licks". Under such a compulsion does the locust, under such a compulsion does the leeming, traverse its mysterious path. They are deaf to danger, deaf to the cry of battle, deaf to the trumpets of death. Let the sea cross their path, let armies with artillery bar the road, even these terrific powers can arrest only by destroying; and the most frightful abysses, up to the very last menace of engulfment, up to the very instant of absorption, have no power to alter or retard the line of their inexorable advance.[35]

Having ranged widely in these comparisons De Quincey switches economically to make the link with his own experience:

> Such an instinct it was, such a rapturous command - even so potent, and alas! even so blind - that, under the whirl of tumultuous indignation and of new-born hope, suddenly transfigured my whole being. In the twinkling of an eye, I came to an adamantine resolution - not as if issuing from any act or any choice of my own, but *as if passively received from some*

> *dark oracular legislation external to myself.*[36]
> (my italics)

Wide-ranging destructive impulses are thus implied in the recognition of a single moment, just as alienation or 'externalisation' is suggested due to a choice which cannot be rationalised, and therefore appears to be no choice at all. Part of the complexity of a moment of experience derives from its power to dictate a whole course of later events. The fact that it has been designated a 'moment' by the autobiographer points not to its isolation but to its continued significance in the intricate web of experience.

Since that significance may be harmful in its nature, and it may also be revealed suddenly, its destructive impact on the *status quo* of the autobiographer is doubled. The harmful nature of a past moment is renewed as it spreads to accommodate new experiences. The organic growth of consciousness assures its continued presence. In this way a moment of past error becomes inescapable, and the frightening possibility arises that its most traumatic significance may not yet have arrived. The continued existence of the past, normally a source of both comfort and creativity to the Romantic autobiographer, thus also proves to be negative. When De Quincey handles this possibility, in the later version of the Confessions, he rhetorically invokes the very method of his autobiographical task:

> Oh, spirit of merciful interpretation, angel of forgiveness to youth and its aberrations, that hearkenest for ever as if to some sweet choir of far-off female intercessions! will ye, choir that intercede - wilt thou, angel that forgivest - join together, and charm away that mighty phantom, born amidst the gathering mists of remorse, which strides after me in pursuit from forgotten days - towering for ever into proportions more and more colossal, overhanging and overshadowing my head as if close behind, yet dating its nativity from hours that are fled by more than half-a-century? Oh heavens! that it should be possible for a child not seventeen years old, by a momentary blindness, by listening to a false, false whisper from his own bewildered heart, by one erring step, by a motion this way or that, to change the currents of his destiny, to poison the fountains of his peace, and in the twinkling of an eye to lay

> the foundations of a life-long repentence![37]

This attempt at a ritualistic exorcism of the past may appear to be stilted, but the threat provided by a link between the present and a past moment can also be expressed humourously by means of a comic inversion:

> For, if a man indulges himself in murder, very soon he comes to think little of robbing, and from robbing he comes next to drinking and Sabbath-breaking, and from that to incivility and procrastination. Once begin upon this downward path, you never know where you are to stop. Many a man dated his ruin from some murder or other that perhaps he thought little of at the time.[38]

Here, again, the compulsion to 'date' moments of experience is particularly characteristic of the autobiographer. It reveals a tendency to require more than the usual stability afforded by past experience, and a fear of its intrinsic laws of growth. The autobiographer's task of translating experience within the limitations and powers of language is inextricably linked to the threat provided by the ever-changing meaning of a past moment. When De Quincey considers the problem of a choice in relation to that last idea, it is language which takes pride of place:

> This thought turned upon the fatality that must often attend an evil choice. As an oracle of fear I remembered that great Roman warning, *Nescit vox missa reverti* (that a word once uttered is irrevocable), a freezing arrest upon the motions of hope too sanguine that haunted me in many shapes. Long before that fifteenth year of mine, I had noticed, as a worm lying at the heart of life and fretting its security, the fact that innumerable acts of choice change countenance and are variously appraised at varying stages of life - shift with the shifting hours. Already, at fifteen, I had become deeply ashamed of judgments which I had once pronounced, of idle hopes that I had once encouraged, false admirations or contempts with which once I had sympathised. And, as to acts which I surveyed with any doubts at all, I never felt sure that after some succession of years I might not feel withering doubts about

> them, both as to principle and as to inevitable results.[39]

This passage from the later version of the Confessions introduces a type of experience illustrated by the effect of the Whispering Gallery in St. Paul's Cathedral. Just as in the episode from the 'Postscript' to Murder Considered - 'that to her dying day would never cease to renew its echoes in her ear'[40] - a moment of error from the past suddenly manifests itself in an amplified form. Typically, the autobiography suggests an articulate or near articulate form - 'whispers' or 'words' - for the significance of experience.

Once again, there is an ambivalence at the heart of De Quincey's creativity as an autobiographer. The menace provided by these anarchic moments from the past necessarily reflects his objectives as a translator of his own experience. He refers us to instants and instances which specifically refuse to comply with the fixing or recording aspect of his task. Although, as a Romantic autobiographer, he insists on the process of experience, its dynamics, its inter-relationship and the organic nature of its unity, his interest in moments generally, whether anarchic or restorative, is a denial of that kind of constant flux. He desires at least a period of sure foundation upon which to make both statements and evaluations. If its claims are absolute rather than relative the retrospective vision of the autobiographer has its authority questioned by the continuing developments of experience. De Quincey is frequently caught up in an autobiographical dilemma: a moment from the past is irretrievable, but its significance is constantly changing. This dilemma is highlighted when De Quincey turns his attention to those threatening moments of choice - threatening because, as he suggests, a choice itself is 'arbitrary':

> every intricate and untried path in life, where it was from the first a matter of arbitrary choice to enter upon it or avoid it, is effectually a path through a vast Hercynian forest, unexplored and unmapped, where each several turn in your advance leaves you open to new anticipations of what is next to be expected, and consequently open to altered valuations of all that has been already traversed. Even the character of your own absolute experience, past and gone, which (if anything in this world) you might surely answer for as sealed and settled

> for ever - even this you must submit to hold in suspense, as a thing conditional and contingent upon what is yet to come - liable to have its provisional character affirmed or reversed, according to the new combinations into which it may enter with elements only yet perhaps in the earliest stages of development.[41]

Clearly, such a statement is contradictory to the basic autobiographical impulse. It implies that the authority of autobiography must be provisional and its method accepted as a necessary and workable compromise.

Because the consequences of a past moment of choice or decision are subject to continued assessment and development from differing perspectives the autobiographer is likely to place great value on his very ability to isolate, describe or even perceive those moments of origin, as in De Quincey's case. The Confessions constantly urges the reader to connect the present state of the opium-eater, however disproportionate it might seem, with the particularised moments from his past. One of the most problematical characteristics of this work, its attempt at excuse or justification, hinges on the value which De Quincey attaches to various turning-points in the past. The emphatic quality of the following statement is typical: 'The morning came which was to launch me into the world; that morning from which, and from its consequences, my whole succeeding life has, in many important points, taken its colouring'.[42]

One of the most thoroughly and elaborately described moments of choice or decision in De Quincey's work occurs only in the later version of the Confessions. It concerns the move from Wales to London in the wanderings of the young De Quincey. The sustained focus on this one moment is due to the complexity of its consequences. In the depiction or attempt at recreation of this incident, at least, there is something of a guaranteed significance. Although its importance may alter as it combines with succeeding events, its value as a source remains constant. We are again confronted with passivity, so that a change in the course of events, though in the context of a choice, appears to be imposed rather than the result of a decision. In this case, the way in which London, or the idea of London, is described accords with Burke's notion of the sublime which we dealt with in Chapter Two:

> Rightly, and by a true instinct, had I made my farewell adieus to summer. All through the day, Wales and her grand mountain ranges ... had divided my thoughts with London. But now rose London - sole, dark, infinite - brooding over the whole capacities of my heart. Other object, other thought, I could not admit.[43]

Burke describes, as we have seen, the sublime state in which 'the mind is so entirely filled with its object, that it cannot entertain any other, nor by consequence, reason on that object which employs it'.[44] Significantly, too, Burke writes: 'the power of the sublime ... anticipates our reasonings, and hurries us on by an irresistable force'[45] which aptly suggests the passivity of De Quincey's case. Apart from these concurrences with the notion of the sublime, however, there is in De Quincey's description an equally significant deviation or inversion of the usual object which produces a sublime effect. The 'grand mountain ranges' have been replaced by the metropolis of London. A remnant of the usual Romantic sublime setting - 'precipice' - provides the starting-point, in a metaphorical capacity, for De Quincey's full description of this moment:

> More than ever I stood upon the brink of a precipice; and the local circumstances around me deepened and intensified these reflections, impressed upon them solemnity and terror, sometimes even horror ... The unusual dimensions of the rooms, especially their towering height, brought up continually and obstinately, through natural links of associated feelings or images, the mighty vision of London waiting for me afar off. An altitude of nineteen or twenty feet showed itself unavoidably upon an exaggerated scale in some of the smaller side-rooms - meant probably for cards or for refreshments. This single feature of the rooms - their unusual altitude, and the echoing hollowness which had become the exponent of that altitude - this one terrific feature (for terrific it was in the effect), together with crowding and evanescent images of the flying feet that so often had spread gladness through these halls on the wings of youth and hope at seasons when every room rang with music: all this, rising in tumultuous vision, whilst the dead hours of night were stealing along, - all around me, household and town, sleeping, - and whilst

> against the windows more and more the storm outside was raving, and to all appearance endlessly growing, - threw me into the deadliest condition of nervous emotion under contradictory forces, high over which predominated horror recoiling from that unfathomed abyss in London into which I was now so wilfully precipitating myself. Often I looked out and examined the night. Wild it was beyond all description, and dark as "the inside of a wolf's throat". But at intervals, when the wind, shifting continually, swept in such a direction as to clear away the vast curtain of vapour, the stars shone out, though with a light unusually dim and distant. Still, as I turned inwards to the echoing chambers, or outwards to the wild, wild night, I saw London expanding her visionary gates to receive me, like some dreadful mouth of Acheron (*Acherontis avari*). Thou also, Whispering Gallery! once again in those moments of conscious and wilful desolation didst to my ear utter monitorial sighs. For once again I was preparing to utter an irrevocable word, to enter upon one of those fatally tortuous paths of which the windings can never be unlinked.[46]

Not only are the consequences of this experience 'tortuous', but so too is De Quincey's description of it. Although the basis of his description is, typically, to show the connection between the external 'local circumstances' and his own internal 'reflections', there is no overriding principle to simplify that connection or assure us of any one significance throughout. So the sentence that starts with 'This single feature' continues, punctuated only by a series of dashes, for a hundred and fifty words, its whole purpose being to combine various elements together, and all the time refusing to separate or isolate. Nothing in the actual depiction of the moment is reconciled or resolved. The variety of components and their different processes simply continue. Although De Quincey switches attention a number of times in his usual fashion from the individual to 'household and town', to the night sky, and finally back again to the mental vision of London, there is no rationale to those movements. A composite picture of the past moment is the overriding prerogative.

Evaluation of this moment finally arrives with the archaic address to the 'Whispering Gallery'.

Its significance is overtly described, but not made implicit or built into the passage. The autobiographical act of interpretation is delivered boldly to the reader. This is partly due to the fact that De Quincey is handling an experience which relies upon the peculiar coincidence of its various components. They obviously occur together, but the combination they form may best be described as exquisite or accidental. It is certainly no vision of unity. We are again presented with a frightening vision of growth. The threat of London is reinforced by the appearance of the immediate setting in which the storm is 'endlessly growing', and the wind is 'shifting continually'. De Quincey's repetition of 'wilful' also serves, ironically, to highlight the element of caprice in the whole experience, depicting, as he says, the effect of 'contradictory forces'.

In its insistence on unreconciled process - its suspension of process - and its related awareness of the horrific potentialities of growth, this passage has clear affinities with the anarchic moments already considered. Such a moment is not prized by De Quincey the autobiographer because of these qualities, but almost despite them. He does not ask the reader to appreciate only the intrinsic nature of the experience, but refers him to a significance which can only be assessed by the autobiographer. We are asked to make connections between such moments and other remote or intricately connected experiences of the autobiography.

These moments draw attention to the relationship between the nature of the experience (whether it is anarchic or restorative) and the possibilities or shortcomings of the autobiographical technique. By handling a moment rather than following an experiential process, the different techniques of the autobiographer are drawn into a more abrupt alignment with each other. By offering his reader a composite picture of a moment of experience De Quincey often exposes his autobiographical method so that the difference between presentation and explanation is emphasised. It is likely that in autobiography rather than in fiction, an anarchic moment will induce interpretative assertions in the text. Credibility in this case rests not on presentation but on the degree to which the autobiographer is supposed to be manipulating his reader's sympathy.

The anarchic moments discussed above point us once again to the problems of translating and communicating experience. As we have seen, they may contain evidence of anarchic or disruptive forces, or they may, as in this last instance, be symptomatic of incommunicable, expanding links between other related areas of experience. In this latter form they simplify the fundamental principles of autobiography - its capacity to select, and its ability to rest securely in the significance of that selection. They outline the parallelism that exists between experiential knowledge and stylistic technique in De Quincey's field of Romantic creativity. A consideration of moments in his autobiographical works draws special attention to the ambivalent nature of that creativity, where its powers might terrify as in the last case, or offer comfort or invigoration, as in the next.

RESTORATIVE MOMENTS

As we have seen, one of the central issues facing De Quincey the autobiographer in his handling of experiential process is the choice between fixity and movement. Whereas the anarchic moments of his autobiography point us to the frightening possibilities of growth, the restorative moments we are to examine are characterised not by stasis, but by a suspension of process. Here we are not presented with continuous growth, but given an indication of activity within a stabilising framework of balance or equipoise. To deny movement altogether as in a stasis is to tip the scales once more into the danger area. As has been suggested already, the 'moments' of De Quincey's autobiography highlight the polarisation of what he deems to be the creative powers of his own consciousness. On one side is the horrific possibility of 'blankness', on the other the menace of renegade growth.

This duality of response to what appears to be creative 'power' is paralleled in De Quincey's connections with the notion of the sublime. As we saw in Chapter Two, one kind of sublime effect is abrupt and leads to horror: another, while still all-consuming, is unified and leads to awe. This latter kind of sublime effect is related to the restorative moments of De Quincey's autobiography and is carefully described in his essay 'System of The Heavens':

> It was the Memnon's head, then recently brought from Egypt. I looked at it, as the reader must suppose in order to understand the depth which I have ascribed to the impression, not as human,

> but as a symbolic head; and what it symbolised to me were:- 1. The peace which passeth all understanding. 2. The eternity which baffles and confounds all faculty of computation; the eternity which *had* been, the eternity which *was* to be. 3. The diffusive love, not such as rises and falls upon waves of life and mortality, not such as sinks and swells by undulations of time, but a procession - an emanation from some mystery of endless dawn. You durst not call it a smile that radiated from the lips; the radiation was too awful to clothe itself in adumbrations or memorials of flesh.
>
> In that mode of sublimity, perhaps, I still adhere to my first opinion, that nothing so great was ever beheld. The atmosphere for *this*, for the Memnon, was the breathlessness which belongs to a saintly trance; the holy thing seemed to live by silence.[47]

This mode of sublimity as defined by De Quincey centres on the power produced by contemplating an object which is fixed and characterised by peace and silence: these qualities determine that power. In another Romantic version of the sublime, Shelley wrote, 'Power dwells apart in its tranquillity/ Remote, serene and inaccessible'.[48]

The symbolic impact of the Memnon's head is worthy of De Quincey's celebration because it evidences an awe-inspiring power issuing from a serene and tranquil centre. The threat of a power eddying further and further away from the central principle is no longer present. That alternating and divisive movement of an anarchic moment of choice has been replaced by the stability of a central unity. In the Confessions De Quincey focuses on Wordsworth's phrase and applies it to his own case: '"*The senselessness of joy*": this it was, joy - headlong - frantic - irreflective - and (as Wordsworth truly calls it), for that very reason, *sublime* - which swallowed up all capacities of rankling care or heart-corroding doubt'.[49]

Despite this statement of the 'swallow[ing] up' of corrosive agencies, De Quincey's restorative moments usually recognise the negative side of things. It is more correct to talk of replacement or suspension than a straightforward omission. Indeed, as we shall see, the restorative moments are defined and balanced against the antithetical idea of anarchy.

The sense of tranquillity and the depiction of harmony in De Quincey's restorative moments rely upon the recognition of discordant forces. The vision of tranquillity is given greater power by showing how it offers resistance to such forces. In the same way, a climactic moment may hold in check a potentially dangerous or wayward vision of multiplicity. An otherwise alarming variety can be united under one head. As we shall see, a moment of trance-like vision may be born out of an impending crisis. The restorative moment is suspended between an awareness of impending disaster and its actual occurrence. The following description might well presage a moment of calm reflection and eerie stillness:

> Then suddenly would come a dream of far different character - a tumultuous dream - commencing with a music such as now I often heard in sleep - music of preparation and of awakening suspense. The undulations of fast-gathering tumults were like the opening of the Coronation Anthem; and, like *that*, gave the feeling of a multitudinous movement, of infinite armies. The morning was come of a mighty day - a day of crisis and of ultimate hope for human nature, then suffering mysterious eclipse, and labouring in some dread extremity.[50]

In this way a crisis may pull a variety of actions together, and then, through contrast, allow a brief space for a moment of stillness. One side feeds off the other in a form of counterpoint. De Quincey was aware not only of a simple contrast, but of an interpenetration of two opposing areas. His sense of beauty was inextricably linked to his sense of decay. In the following quotation it can be seen that this is so not only in a general sort of way, but specifically as he is an autobiographer with a particular psychological bias. The two poles of his creative consciousness appear in all their starkness as they gradually emerge from the initial defensive discourse on beauty.

> There is a feeling, - morbid it may be, but for which no anodyne is found in all the schools from Plato to Kant, - to which the human mind is liable at times: it is best described in a little piece of Henry More, the Platonist. He there represents himself as a martyr to his own too passionate sense of beauty, and his

> consequent too passionate sense of its decay. Everywhere, - above, below, around him, in the earth, in the clouds, in the fields, and in their garniture of flowers, - he beholds a beauty carried to excess; and this beauty becomes a source of endless affliction to him, because everywhere he sees it liable to the touch of decay and mortal change. During one paroxysm of this sad passion, an angel appears to comfort him; and, by the sudden revelation of her immortal beauty, does, in fact, suspend his grief. But it is only a suspension; for the sudden recollection that her privileged condition, and her exemption from the general fate of beauty ... restores his grief ... Profitless rebellion against the laws which season all things for the inexorable grave! Yet not the less we rebel again and again; and, though wisdom counsels resignation and submission, yet our human passions, still cleaving to their object, force us into endless rebellion.[51]

At this stage in the paragraph De Quincey suddenly changes direction, thereby making what has gone before appear to be no more than an illustration to his real subject:

> Feelings, the same in kind as these, attach themselves to our mental powers, and our vital energies. Phantoms of lost power, sudden intuitions, and shadowy restorations of forgotten feelings, sometimes dim and perplexing, sometimes by bright but furtive glimpses, sometimes by a full and steady revelation, overcharged with light, - throw us back in a moment upon scenes and remembrances that we have left full thirty years behind us. In solitude, and chiefly in the solitudes of nature; and, above all, amongst the great and *enduring* features of nature ... under these circumstances it is, that such evanescent hauntings of our past and forgotten selves are most apt to startle and to waylay us. These are *positive* torments from which the agitated mind shrinks in fear; but there are others *negative* in their nature, that is, blank mementos of power extinct, and of faculties burnt out within us.[52]

Here the formulation '*positive* torments' might seem perplexing, but it suggests a retrospective vision which can make good artistic use of those incidents which previously had led only to fear and agitation. As we have seen, agitation and fear are prominent components of the anarchic moments, just as frightening as the possibility of 'power extinct'. The restorative moments frequently point us to the fact that, at a later stage, the agitation may cease and, with its significance relatively assured, the experience may then be seen to contain a balance between the two opposing forces. De Quincey's autobiography does not present a simple contrast between these two sides: they are subtly related to each other in the record of fluid psychological process which constitutes the autobiography.

Although there is a reference to landscape in this last passage, it is quickly passed over. Natural settings constitute no more than a convenient back-drop for the required solitude. De Quincey's interest is of an abstract kind being satisfied with only a scant 'features of nature', and not requiring any concrete particularities. The real stage is still reserved for the 'mental powers' and 'vital energies': the tension resides largely in that subjective or psychological area, and not fundamentally in the relationship between an observer and the landscape. This can be seen in the following episode from the 1856 version of the Confessions where the general features of the setting, not the particularised ones, point us once again to an effect of equipoise just before a moment of crisis. Surrounded by the processes of anarchy we have already examined lies a vision of tranquillity:

> The day on which I left Oswestry ... was a day of golden sunshine amongst the closing days of November. As truly as Jessica's moonlight ... this golden sunshine might be said to *sleep* upon the woods and the fields; so awful was the universal silence, so profound the death-like stillness. It was a day belonging to a brief and pathetic season of farewell summer resurrection ... It is that last brief resurrection of summer in its most brilliant memorials ... like the lambent and fitful gleams from an expiring lamp, mimicking what is called the "lightning before death" in sick patients, when close upon their end. There is the feeling of a conflict that has been going on between the lingering powers of summer and the strengthening powers of winter, not unlike that which moves by antagonist forces in some deadly

> inflammation hurrying forwards through fierce struggles into the final repose of mortification. For a time the equilibrium has been maintained between the hostile forces; but at last the antagonism is overthrown; the victory is accomplished for the powers that fight on the side of death; simultaneously with the conflict, the pain of conflict has departed: and thenceforward the gentle process of collapsing life, no longer fretted by countermovements, slips away with holy peace into the noiseless deeps of the Infinite. So sweet, so ghostly, in its soft, golden smiles, silent as a dream, and quiet as the dying trance of a saint, faded through all its stages this departing day, along the whole length of which I bade farewell for many a year to Wales, and farewell to summer. In the very aspect and the sepulchral stillness of the motionless day, as solemnly it wore away through morning, noontide, afternoon, to meet the darkness that was hurrying to swallow up its beauty, I had a fantastic feeling as though I read the very language of resignation when bending before some irresistable agency. And at intervals I heard - in how different a key! - the raving, the everlasting uproar, of that dreadful metropolis which at every step was coming nearer, and beckoning (as it seemed) to myself for purposes as dim, for issues as incalculable, as the path of canon-shots fired at random and in darkness.[53]

The emphasis here is certainly negative rather than positive; De Quincey articulates a process of decay which offers some consolation - even if it is melancholic in its peacefulness. This is effectively juxtaposed with the menacing and arbitrary discord of the 'metropolis'. In this episode the vision of tranquillity is still involved in a process: we witness a gradual slowing down rather than a genuine suspended moment. Nevertheless, the way in which the stillness of the day is used to register the psychological significance of the departure, and the way in which that stillness contrasts with anarchic movements operating alongside it, brings us one step closer to those suspended moments of a tranquil kind.

In June 1841 Blackwood's published an article by De Quincey entitled 'Russia as it was in the Summer and Winter of 1812'. This was largely a translation of Arndt's Erinnerungen (1840), except that it contained a few memorable passages of De Quincey's own invention. One of these interrupts the fairly routine documentary of events leading up to Napoleon's ill-fated military campaign. Suddenly we leave behind Arndt's description of his meetings with the notable personages on the Russian side, and we are presented with a moment which makes good use of its contrast with the impending military conflict. Once again stillness and silence are the main characteristics of De Quincey's contribution. The scene he sets is clearly defined in terms of distance, but it is not essentially a visual description. De Quincey is not so much interested in the realisation of a particular landscape as in setting a brief scene in order to particularise and credibilise the workings of the mind in a certain state of reverie:

> One day - I turn for the sake of variety, and of a larger experience, from high regions of society to the lowest - one day, finding myself perfectly wearied and exhausted by the never-ending successions of troops streaming onwards to the west, I moved round the skirts of the town, until I reached a situation so distant from the great tumult, that no sound could be caught even of trumpets and kettledrums; the roar of baggage-waggons died away upon the wind, the groaning of heavy artillery oppressed the ear no longer. It was noon day - sultry as usual; and that peculiar silence, so breathless, solemn, and Pan-like, which sometimes belongs to deep noon, disposed even the thoughtless man to reverie. I had flung myself upon a soft, lawny couch of heathy ground: no one moving object was in sight; indeed, no living creature whatever, except some peaceful cattle tranquilly reposing under the shade of umbrageous trees half a mile distant. Solemn forests could be seen skirting the backgrounds in one direction; and the eye could dimly penetrate the gloomy recesses, which their openings revealed. The imagination peopled those awe-inspiring solitudes with corresponding inhabitants; but to the mere bodily eye, all was silent, motionless, breathless as the grave.[54]

At this point, just after the 'bodily eye' has almost been decried and the imagination praised, De Quincey, while not dismissing the setting, relegates it to a subordinate position in order to promote the psychological act of association:

> Such being the external scene, it was inevitable that one's thoughts should revert to the tremendous scenes of havoc, struggle, and carnal fury, just now in the very crisis of opening. Then came the antagonist thought presenting the utter stillness, the inaudible tread, of that final grave which was so surely stealing onwards to swallow up, in one common abyss of darkness, the horse and his rider, the master and the slave[55]

That such associations are not really dramatic but retrospective is suggested by the intrusion of a question revealing De Quincey's privileged historical vantage-point as he writes in 1840:

> Five and twenty years hence, thought I, say in the year 1840, what will have become of these innumerable captains, marshals, plumed cavaliers, so stately and exulting? The earth shakes beneath their sounding tread on this day of August 1812. But if the curtain of time could draw up on the sad wrecks of those brilliant armies ... if - but just at that moment rose a solemn breathing of wind from the forests, so sad, so full of woe in its sound, half between a sigh and a groan, that I was really startled, as if mute nature had understood and answered my ejaculation. It was a sound, beyond all I ever heard, that expressed a requiem and a lamentation over the pomps and glories of man - so noble in his aspirations, so full of beauty and power for the moment - yet so inevitably lying down, after one generation, in dust and ashes, that I sank deeper into abstractions gloomy and full of tears.[56]

Here De Quincey's involvement in a historical narrative parallels his own retrospective vision as an autobiographer. At a completely safe distance from the dangerous events now in motion, he can insert a moment of calm reflection through which even the forces of destruction can be accommodated, and then defined in a more balanced framework. At its best this leads to a fairly complex appreciation of the dynamics of the situation, deeply rooted in a sense of power which is psychological in origin.

Once again 'beauty' and 'power' are linked to

their negative opposites of decay and death, almost before there is time for their celebration. De Quincey clearly sees them as bound up in the process of experience. As a result, such a moment ultimately points to the transient nature of those vital energies: an appreciation of the intensity of a momentary experience is expressed as a 'requiem'. In this instance the historical context affords De Quincey his usual autobiographical position in which he must face the irrevocable nature of the past. At the same time it represents the familiar situation of radical discontinuity between past and present - the possible contrast between past vitality and present inertia. This gap, which is integral to the act of autobiography, is partly responsible for De Quincey's dual response to creativity. It informs the 'antagonist thoughts' of the restorative moments where process is temporarily suspended in order to allow for a balanced appreciation of both sides.

This kind of antithesis or 'antagonism' is further illustrated in the later version of the Confessions where De Quincey feels obliged to explain why a number of his key experiences contain the same components - summer skies and death:'the light and the appearances of the declining and the setting sun', he argues,

> are much more fitted to be types and characters of the infinite; and, thirdly (which is the main reason), the exuberant and riotous prodigality of life naturally forces the mind more powerfully upon the antagonist thought of death, and the wintry sterility of the grave.[57]

Typically, De Quincey offers us no acceptable middle ground, only the stark contrast of two extremes. It is not simply life which is opposed to 'wintry sterility', but a dubious, certainly excessive 'exuberant and riotous prodigality'.

In this way - by the juxtaposition of opposite extremes - the restorative moments of De Quincey's autobiography constitute a relief from the one-sidedness of the anarchic moments which only stress the threat of prodigality. They function in the text by virtue of a tension produced by the alternation of those two extremes, and not as a result of any kind of reconciliation. Furthermore, the basic pattern of a moment of stillness punctuating a series of climactic events is reinforced in miniature both by De Quincey's overt commentary referring us to 'antagonist thoughts' and by subtle and economic description of the setting.

In the last episode, for example, there is a characteristic interplay between the setting and De Quincey's reflections upon it. Just as his musings and questionings are about to reach a crescendo, there is a melodramatic interruption: 'if - but just at that moment rose a solemn breathing of wind'. This apparent intrusion then turns out to be a reinforcement and a continuation of De Quincey's train of thought. The wind is described as 'so sad, so full of woe in its sound, half between a sigh and a groan', and it appears 'as if mute nature had understood and answered [his] ejaculation'. From this point of daring, perhaps strained, metaphorical substitution, the moment concludes with a generalised statement which is accredited to the sound of the wind which 'expressed a requiem and lamentation over the pomps and glories of man'.

The main effect is again achieved by a kind of counter-definition. 'Silence and desolation', De Quincey wrote, 'are never felt so profoundly as when they are interrupted by solemn sounds, recurring by uncertain intervals, and from distant places'.[58] In other words, such intermittent interruptions maintain the impression of a suspension. De Quincey's insight into this effect is most clearly illustrated, as one might expect, in his essay 'On the Knocking at the Gate in Macbeth', where he supports his appreciation of the incident in the drama with the following information, delivered in his characteristic form of address to the reader:

> If the reader has ever witnessed a wife, daughter, or sister in a fainting fit, he may chance to have observed that the most affecting moment in such a spectacle is *that* in which a sigh and a stirring announce the recommencement of suspended life. Or, if the reader has ever been present in a vast metropolis on the day when some great national idol was carried in funeral pomp to his grave, and ... has felt powerfully, in the silence and desertion of the streets, and in the stagnation of ordinary business, the deep interest which at that moment was possessing the heart of man, - if all at once he should hear the death-like stillness broken up by the sound of wheels rattling away from the scene, and making known that the transitory vision was dissolved, he will be aware that at no moment was his sense of the complete suspension and pause in ordinary human concerns

> so fully and affecting as at that moment when the suspension ceases, and the goings-on of human life are suddenly resumed. All action in any direction is best expounded, measured, and made apprehensible by reaction.[59]

This effect holds true not only for the moments as they are dramatically depicted in their settings, but also for their settings within the text as they change the pace and the intensity of the autobiographical focus.

The use of definition provided by 'reaction' and the related change in pace of the autobiography are well illustrated in 'The Affliction of Childhood' where De Quincey concentrates on a trance-like vision he experienced after his sister's death.[60] He tells how he crept guiltily to see her corpse in an upstairs room on a summer's day; and then interrupts his narrative to explain the special significance he attaches to deaths and summer skies, since, as we have seen, the latter 'express types of infinity'. This digression successfully stalls the reader's expectations, drawing out the attention given to the moment. Then, having returned to the young De Quincey standing in the room, the next impetus to the episode is provided by the familiar sound of the wind which utters a 'hollow, solemn, Memnonian, but saintly swell', worthy of being called a 'vast Æolian intonation'. This is immediately followed by a brief description of the trance in which 'some mighty relation between God and death dimly struggled to evolve itself from the dreadful antagonism between them'. Finally, he awakes, still standing by his sister's bed, and the 'wandering suspension of [his] perfect mind' concludes with the sound of a foot on the stairs.

Sound clearly plays an important part in De Quincey's tranquil moments, not only in emphasising the eerie effect of silence and stillness, but also, as we noted in the Russian episode, playing a part in allowing De Quincey to attach special significance to the moment. The sound of the wind is spoken of as 'expressing' or 'articulating' a 'requiem'. One of the most frequent symbols of Romantic creativity is used in a metaphorical capacity in De Quincey's case to affirm the importance of the autobiographical moment.

Sound plays a key role in one of De Quincey's most elaborate descriptions of momentary experience to be found in his essays on the Lakes and the Lake poets. Here it not only dictates the symbolic meaning of the experience in the way we have already seen, but provides the very link by which the autobiography draws our attention to the assimiliation of past experience. De Quincey focuses on the repetition of a single sound, and fashions out of its changed significance another elaborate 'requiem'. At least in terms of autobiographical technique, this sound acts as a platform on which to assemble the movement between past statement, present statement and moralistic conclusion. Since this movement is located in the sound it has the effect of masking the outright declarations of the autobiographer. For in this instance we witness the very formulation of the 'requiem', seeing how a potentially anarchic discontinuity with the past has eventually attained its final place in the history of the autobiographer.

Although De Quincey is handling the repeated effect of the one sound the whole passage is drawn together in his usual manner by the employment of long and involved sentences. The openings to these sentences also comply by denying any real separation: most of them begin with the conjunction 'but':

> But often and often, in years after all was gone, I have passed old Brathay, or have gone over purposely after dark, about the time when, for many a year, I used to go over to spend the evening; and, seating myself on a stone, by the side of the mountain river Brathay, have staid for hours listening to the same sound to which so often Charles Lloyd and I used to hearken together with profound emotion and awe - the sound of pealing anthems, as if streaming from the open portals of some illimitable cathedral; for such a sound does actually arise, in many states of the weather, from the peculiar action of the river Brathay upon its rocky bed; and many times I have heard it, of a quiet night, when no stranger could have been persuaded to believe it other than the sound of choral chanting - distant, solemn, saintly. Its meaning and expression were, in those earlier years, uncertain and general; not more pointed or determined in the direction which it impressed upon one's feelings than the light of setting suns: and sweeping, in fact, the whole harp of pensive sensibilities, rather than striking the chord of any one specific sentiment. But since the ruin or dispersion of that household, after the smoke had ceased to ascend from their hearth, or the garden walks to re-echo their

> voices, often times, when lying by the river side, I have listened to the same aerial saintly sound, whilst looking back to that night, long-hidden in the frost of receding years, when Charles and Sophia Lloyd, now lying in foreign graves, first dawned upon me, coming suddenly out of rain and darkness; then - young, rich, happy, full of hope, belted with young children ... and standing apparently on the verge of a labyrinth of golden hours. Musing on that night in November, 1807, and then upon the wreck that had been wrought by a space of fifteen years, I would say to myself sometimes, and seem to hear it in the songs of this watery cathedral - Put not your trust in any fabric of happiness ... Sometimes even I was tempted to discover in the same music a sound such as this - Love nothing, love nobody, for thereby comes a killing curse in the rear. But sometimes also, very early on a summer morning, when the dawn was barely beginning to break, all things locked in sleep, and only some uneasy murmur or cockcrow, at a faint distance, giving a hint of resurrection for earth and her generations, I have heard in that same chanting of the little mountain river a more solemn if a less agitated admonition - a requiem over deparated happiness[61]

Most significant for our purposes of defining the relationship between the anarchic and the restorative moments of De Quincey's autobiographical writings is the last change to 'a less agitated admonition' which can, as a result, be termed a 'requiem'. The disturbance caused by the destruction of a household has at last been accommodated by De Quincey's retrospective vision. He can reflect on a harrowing experience from the past and also contemplate a discontinuity in his past, now that he stands at a safe distance from the event. In short, this last episode not only shows the benefits of a solitary contemplative position like the other restorative moments we have considered, but also manages to combine with that position the analogous stance of the autobiographer. Indeed, we saw in the Russian episode how De Quincey could fabricate one from the other. Both constitute a relief from the burden of immediate events and their consequences, in which imagination can formulate a statement 'recollected in tranquillity', to use Wordsworth's phrase. 'How much solitude', De Quincey wrote, 'so much power';[62] a statement which should remind us that a requisite pause in the course of events is being considered and not any release.

The extent to which a suspended moment can evidence 'power' and embrace rather than exclude the otherwise discordant, agitating elements of experience, can best be seen in the Liverpool reverie in the Confessions. Once again, solitude and silent contemplation are the means to that power. In this case there is relief not only from the course of everyday, external events, but also from a psychological burden of emotions. There is a temporary lack of self-consciousness. Although De Quincey speaks of a respite from the problem of his own identity, the moment nevertheless centres around the movement from an external scene to an internal state of mind. This does not involve the imposition of personality on the external world, however, for our attention is focused, as it frequently is in De Quincey's autobiographical writing, specifically on the mechanism of the mind. De Quincey feared certain of his opium dreams in case 'some dropsical state or tendency of the brain might thus be making itself (to use a metaphysical word) *objective*; and that the sentient organ might be projecting itself as its own object'.[63] Clearly such a possibility is as likely to be anarchic as it is restorative. As far as it illustrates a major element in the following reverie, however, it must be deemed positive, for this is the most celebratory of De Quincey's restorative moments, and the one which articulates most clearly a balanced appreciation of a potentially dangerous 'power':

> I will admit that markets and theatres are not the appropriate haunts of the opium-eater, when in the divinest state incident to his enjoyment. In that state crowds become an oppression to him; music, even, too sensual and gross. He naturally seeks solitude and silence, as indispensable conditions of those trances, or profoundest reveries, which are the crown and consummation of what opium can do for human nature ... At that time I often fell into such reveries after taking opium; and many a time it has happened to me on a summer night - when I have been seated at an open window, from which I could overlook the sea at a mile below me, and could at the same time command a view of some great town ... that from sunset to sunrise ... I have continued motionless, as if frozen, without consciousness of myself as of an object

> anywise distinct from the multiform scene which I contemplated from above. Such a scene in all its elements was not unfrequently realised for me on the gentle eminence of Everton. Obliquely to the left lay the many-languaged town of Liverpool; obliquely to the right, the multitudinous sea. The scene itself was somewhat typical of what took place in such a reverie. The town of Liverpool represented the earth, with its sorrows and its graves left behind, yet not out of sight, nor wholly forgotten. The ocean, in everlasting but gentle agitation, yet brooded over by dove-like calm, might not unfitly typify the mind, and the mood which then swayed it. For it seemed to me as if then first I stood at a distance aloof from the uproar of life; as if the tumult, the fever, and the strife, were suspended; a respite were granted from the secret burdens of the heart, - some sabbath of repose, some resting from human labours. Here were the hopes which blossom in the paths of life, reconciled with the peace which is in the grave; motions of the intellect as unwearied as the heavens, yet for all anxieties a halcyon calm; tranquillity that seemed no product of inertia, but as if resulting from mighty and equal antagonisms; infinite activities, infinite repose.[64]

Most of the components of De Quincey's suspended moments are present in this instance; including one of the most important characteristics of his work as an autobiographer: abstractions such as 'antagonism' and 'repose' issue from his psychological interest, not arguing for the specificity of his own experience, but reaching out from it to claim wider significance. There is excitement and a celebration at work here partly because of the way in which this kind of experience breaks free from its local bounds and appears to be both unlimited - 'infinite' - and representative. The words which must bear the weight in this last respect are 'represented', 'typify' and 'it seemed to me'; all of them forced to carry, not enact, the significance claimed by the autobiographer. They are the raw metaphors supporting the whole moment, which, in another context, either purely poetical or fictional, could afford to be manifestations and not simply statements.

To the extent that these moments of De Quincey's autobiography incorporate meditative, or reflective experiences often located in a natural setting, and from this basis or immediate context reach out to claim special and representative significance for the nature of the experience, it could be argued that they are De Quincey's counterparts to many Romantic lyric poems. The fact that they incorporate material which can best be classified under the notion of the sublime, and that they include the related, more specific, components of Æolian winds, lights of setting suns, and, in the last example, a prospect from a window, certainly seems to substantiate such an argument, in which Coleridge's 'Conversation Poems' and Wordsworth's 'Lines Composed Above Tintern Abbey' would seem to offer the most compelling similarities. But such a reading, even disregarding other considerations, would only be able to appreciate these moments as fragments.

It is precisely because those episodes in De Quincey's autobiography are not self-contained that certain words in the last example have to bear a certain amount of strain. This is lessened, however, if one thinks of the moment as not complete in itself, but suspended in the supportive framework of the text, in which specialised arguments are taking place. This last episode does not stand alone, but furthers an argument the purpose of which is to illustrate the power of opium. In the same way, the moment dealing with the sound of the river Brathay and the death of Charles Lloyd builds into a crescendo which rather than closing the passage off from the rest of the text, breaks out in a direct appeal to the reader. De Quincey's awareness of the dramatic potential of 'suspension', on various levels, of how it can be defined by a recall to the world of everyday events, finds support in his autobiographical writings where the recall is to his readership, or, more particularly, to his 'reader'.

After such moments in the autobiography De Quincey needs to make overt contact with his reader again, especially since he may have alienated him by depicting an extraordinary experience, enraged him if the suspension appeared to be no more than a digression, and may even have used him in a moment of suspense. De Quincey's relationship with the reader can be threatened due to the very nature of the autobiographical task. In so far as they represent the most intense and extreme of De Quincey's experiences, the 'suspended moments' test that relationship, resolute as they are in 'showing what things occur in the realities of experience which a novelist could not venture to imagine'.[65]

NOTES

1. G.W. Stonier, _Statesman and Nation_, vol. XXXV, no. 893 (1948), p. 316, reviewing a new edition of De Quincey's _Recollections of the Lakes and the Lake Poets_, E. Sackville-West (ed.).
2. Leslie Stephen, _Hours in a Library_ (London, 1874), p. 245.
3. John E. Jordan, _Thomas De Quincey, Literary Critic_ (Berkeley and Los Angeles), p. 40.
4. S.T. Coleridge, _Anima Poetae_, E.H. Coleridge (ed.) (London, 1895), p. 425.
5. Georges Poulet, 'Timelessness and Romanticism', _Journal of the History of Ideas_, vol. XV, No. 1 (1954), p. 6.
6. Ibid., p. 5.
7. Ibid., p. 11.
8. Ibid.
9. Ibid.
10. William Wordsworth, _The Prelude_, Ernest De Selincourt (ed.) (London, 1959), Second Edition, 1805, Book XI, lines 258-273.
11. Geoffrey Hartman, _Wordsworth's Poetry 1787-1814_ (New Haven and Yale, 1964), p. 213.
12. Jonathan Wordsworth, 'Fructifying Spots of Time', _TLS_ (November 1977), p. 1330.
13. Ibid.
14. Virginia Woolf, 'De Quincey's Autobiography', in _The Common Reader_ (London, 1965), p. 136.
15. Ibid., p. 138.
16. Virginia Woolf, 'Impassioned Prose', in _Granite and Rainbow_ (London, 1958), pp. 36-37.
17. Ibid., pp. 35-36.
18. Thomas De Quincey, _The Collected Writings of Thomas De Quincey_, David Masson (ed.) (14 vols., Edinburgh, 1889-90), vol. III, p. 332.
19. Ibid., vol. VI, p. 142.
20. Ibid., p. 149.
21. Ibid., vol. XIII, p. 83.
22. Ibid., vol. XII, p. 158.
23. Ibid.
24. Ibid., p. 157.
25. Ibid., p. 235.
26. Ibid.
27. Ibid., vol. XIII, p. 85.
28. Ibid., p. 87 ff.
29. See John E. Jordan, 'De Quincey's Dramaturgic Criticism', _ELH_ (1951); Vincent A. De Luca, 'De Quincey's "Knocking at the Gate in _Macbeth_": Dream and Prose Art', _ELN_, 13 (1976).

30. Masson, vol. X, p. 393.
31. Ibid., vol. XIII, p. 83.
32. Ibid., vol. III, p. 276.
33. Ibid., vol. VII, p. 378.
34. Ibid., p. 414.
35. Ibid., vol. III, p. 278.
36. Ibid.
37. Ibid., p. 232.
38. Ibid., vol. XIII, p. 56.
39. Ibid., vol. III, p. 296.
40. Ibid., vol. XIII, p. 88.
41. Ibid., vol. III, pp. 314-315.
42. Ibid., p. 294.
43. Ibid., p. 346.
44. See Chapter 2.
45. Ibid.
46. Masson, vol. III, pp. 346-347.
47. Ibid., vol. VIII, p. 17.
48. P.B. Shelley, 'Mont Blanc', <u>Poetical Works</u>, Thomas Hutchinson (ed.) (Oxford, 1970), p. 532, lines 96-97.
49. Masson, vol. III, p. 279.
50. Ibid., p. 446.
51. Thomas De Quincey, <u>Recollections of the Lakes and the Lake Poets</u>, David Wright (ed.) (Harmondsworth, 1970), pp. 91-92; <u>Tait's Edinburgh Magazine</u> (September, October and November 1834, and January 1835).
52. David Wright (ed.), <u>Recollections of the Lakes and the Lake Poets</u>, p. 92.
53. Masson, vol. III, pp. 343-344.
54. Thomas De Quincey, <u>Blackwood's Edinburgh Magazine</u> (June 1841), p. 743.
55. Ibid.
56. Ibid., pp. 743-744.
57. Masson, vol. III, p. 444.
58. Ibid., vol. II, pp. 403-404.
59. Ibid., vol. X, pp. 392-393.
60. Ibid., vol. I, pp. 38-44.
61. David Wright (ed.), <u>Recollections of the Lakes and the Lake Poets</u>, pp. 332-333.
62. Masson, vol. XIII, p. 335.
63. Ibid., vol. III, p. 440.
64. Ibid., pp. 394-395.
65. David Wright (ed.), <u>Recollections of the Lakes and the Lake Poets</u>, p. 282.

Chapter 5

DE QUINCEY AND THE READER

THE READER'S ROLE AS MEDIATOR

If Confessions of an English Opium-Eater is considered with emphasis on the word 'confessions' we might find the opening sentence to be perplexing. Instead of immediately appealing to the reader to listen to a justification of experience open to censure, De Quincey would have us believe that his history is, by and large, sealed up, a carefully constructed artefact intended for both amusement and instruction:

> I here present you, courteous reader, with the record of a remarkable period of my life; according to my application of it, I trust that it will prove not merely an interesting record, but, in a considerable degree, useful and instructive.[1]

The promise of an insulated autobiographical work is reinforced by the intimation of a specialist intention conveyed confidently by 'my application'. If De Quincey claims a specific purpose, the reader might well expect to be directed towards, or obliged to be engaged in the delivery of this ulterior purpose. And since De Quincey links his 'application' to the instructive quality of the work it would appear that he intends us to consider its purpose to be distinct from personal justification.

The very complication of this opening address suggests that the Confessions is not a mere presentation of experience, but a more enterprising and flexible structure involving a creative interaction with the reader. The use De Quincey makes of his reader is connected with the confessional aspect of the work which implies that the reader might act as mediator. After the initial appeal quoted above it soon becomes apparent that he or she is to be actively engaged; sometimes reprimanded, sometimes flattered, and often used. Even before displaying his actual record before the public De Quincey continues and develops his appeal in the opening notice headed 'From the Author to the Reader'. We soon see the way in which he wishes to expand the meaning of that first 'courteous reader'.

When De Quincey uses his favourite question technique for the first time in referring to 'the whole class of opium-eaters' he highlights the suggested social implication behind the word 'courteous'. Social context is given to himself and his subject by a concerned appeal through the delivery of which he reinforces his previous reference to courtesy:

> But who are they? Reader, I am sorry to say, a very numerous class indeed. Of this I became convinced some years ago, by computing, at that time, the number of those in one small class of English society (the class of men distinguished for talent, or of eminent station) who were known to me, directly or indirectly, as opium-eaters; such, for instance, as the eloquent and benevolent William Wilberforce; the late Dean of Carlisle; Lord Erskine; Mr. ---, the philosopher; a late undersecretary of state (viz., Mr. Addington, brother to the first Lord Sidmouth ...); Mr. Samuel Taylor Coleridge; and many others, hardly less known, whom it would be tedious to mention.[2]

This second direct address is followed by information which places the anonymous opium-eating scholar in an eminent public social milieu. It also creates a fascinating tension between the open and public, and the darker recesses of private life. Because of this tension De Quincey can use such information in a mediatory capacity, giving his work contemporary relevance, social acceptability, and a genial compliance with a certain type of reading class. At the same time he can also rest secure in the individuality of his account; he recognises but breaks with the decorum he has gestured towards. In its turn this convinces the reader that the autobiographer is in earnest, serves to justify the work before him, and raises his curiosity. Essentially, this introductory notice establishes a common or, at least, a recognisable ground between author and reader. It appeals to some of the achnowledged, acceptable literary and social decorums of the time while relying on the unacknowledged ones for support. De Quincey consolidates his reader's interest in things private, exotic, and perhaps immoral, at the same time as flattering a regard for good taste.

By using such appellations as 'courteous' De Quincey also constructs his own reader. His impulse to stabilise, to render acceptable and understandable, serves not so much to tone down the remarkable, morally dubious nature of the subject as to engage the writer with the reader so that the two stand together sharing, or assuming they share, a common store of values. This engagement is sponsored by a basic need of the autobiographer: De Quincey openly urges his reader to carry out a mediatory process for him. Periodically he calls us to 'sympathise', to 'imagine',[3] to 'picture to ourselves'.[4] The effect of this engagement between autobiographer and reader, declaring as it does the self-conscious literary process of the work, is to create a decisive split between the autobiographer and his experiences. Not only does De Quincey gain his reader's sympathy: he also manages to dissociate himself from his past history. In turn this promotes a closer liaison between autobiographer and reader: the two join together in a discriminating retrospective judgement.

After this initial call for mediatory aid De Quincey can then refer to 'the public (into whose private ear I am confidentially whispering my confessions)'.[5] This statement, made in the confidence of his reader's sympathy, is significantly followed by instructions to the reader to rely on pictorial imagination to produce an image of the author. The reader is asked to work, to fill in the gaps of the autobiographical commentary. In this instance De Quincey takes further liberties by advising, even humourously flattering the reader's own imaginative powers while retaining his anonymity:

> If the public ... should chance to have framed some agreeable picture for itself of the opium-eater's exterior, should have ascribed to him, romantically, an elegant person or a handsome face, why should I barbarously tear from it so pleasing a delusion - pleasing both to the public and to me? No; paint me, if at all, according to your own fancy; and, as a painter's fancy should teem with beautiful creations, I cannot fail, in that way, to be a

> gainer. And now, reader, we have run through all the ten categories of my condition as it stood about 1816-17.[6]

That the Confessions are constructed around this use of the reader might suggest that the personality of the autobiographer remains largely unrevealed. However, the very terms of address begin to formulate the identity of the autobiographer, so that the words 'courteous',[7] 'logical',[8] 'humane',[9] and 'generous'[10] remain as much with De Quincey as with ourselves. At least from this aspect of the work, the tendency is to see the autobiographer at one with the values of his society. The genial, mannered discourse between writer and reader flatters and confirms the values of both parties.

De Quincey maintains his anonymity at the same time as aligning himself with the reader on the grounds of social gentility. This is promised at the very opening of the work where the reason for his retreat is placed at the hands of his relationship with the reader. In the opening notice De Quincey apologises for 'breaking through that delicate and honourable reserve which, for the most part, restrains us from the public exposure of our own errors and infirmities'.[11] Already, he collaborates with the reader by his use of 'us' and 'our', but the necessity to join with him is made stronger by an appeal to patriotic feeling,

> Nothing, indeed, is more revolting to English feelings than the spectacle of a human being obtruding on our notice his moral ulcers or scars and tearing away that "decent drapery" which time or indulgence to human frailty may have drawn over them: accordingly, the greater part of *our* confessions (that is, spontaneous and extra-judicial confessions) proceed from demireps, adventurers or swindlers.[12]

The extent to which De Quincey forced his contemporary reader to accept a respectable set of values with regard to autobiographical writing is rather difficult to define. Certainly Crabb Robinson - by no means a standard or reliable authority - maintained that he was most impressed by the 'morality' he found in the Confessions.[13] His reaction shows how De Quincey's claim of moral instruction for the Confessions was readily maintained, despite the obvious retraction in the work itself and in the later revised edition. The likelihood of a class of his readers resting assured in the morally upright stance of the autobiographer would seem to be strengthened by the conformity of his address to the reader.

That the values suggested in the definition of the reader might represent a challenge which may either be accepted or declined at the reader's own peril, also seems a pertinent question, especially since the initial confrontation with the autobiographer continues and develops subsequent to the initial appeal for sympathy. Having taken the reader into his own hands De Quincey throws out a challenge by anticipating questions and forestalling objections. The way he does so is directly related to his having a real, unknown and various audience on the one hand, and a constructed particularised reader on the other. He can carefully dictate and deflect anticipated reactions - 'Here let me stop for a moment to check my reader from any erroneous conclusions'[14] - 'if I talk in this way the reader will think I am laughing; and I can assure him that nobody will laugh who deals with opium'.[15] The way in which his own fictive reader allows him to assume control is revealed in the repeated 'wills' of the following anticipations: 'In so mighty a world as London it will surprise my reader';[16] 'Meantime the reader who takes any interest in such a question will find';[17] 'Any attentive reader, after a few moments' reflection will perceive'.[18]

These anticipations and forestallings show De Quincey aiming at one aspect of his reader's mind. He splits his reader up into various readers, each characterised by one approach which makes it easy for him to put down any objections. The logical reader will be catered for at one point, the courteous at the next, the practical at another. Such a rhetorical dialogue allows De Quincey to justify and explain his narrative piece by piece. Precisely because the reader is split up into various categories, no actual reader is likely to take offence. On the contrary, this device is likely to engage the actual reader more closely with the autobiographer so that by an economical manoeuvre De Quincey and the actual reader stand together realising the one-sidedness of the fabricated reader's objection. Sometimes the fictive reader is reprimanded in order to make the actual reader realise the relationship between the text and the past experience. By using this tactic De Quincey can make obvious the irrevocable nature of past action and the earnestness of his continued self-examination: 'O reader, urge not the crying arguments that spoke so tumultuously against me. Too sorrowfully I feel them'.[19] De Quincey is eager to point out that any judgements the reader might make are made from the privileged retrospective position: the autobiographer can now meet those objections, granted the same distance.

The creation of this flexible fictive reader through such rhetorical engagements, maintaining a further level of discourse within the framework of the text, represents a characteristic tendency of autobiography to refer to a mid-way authority between author and reader. In De Quincey's case this does not stand in isolation, but promotes other mediatory processes taking place within the work. This relationship heightens the distinction between the text and the experience, between the writing now and the experience then, thus giving the autobiographer a historical perspective which may placate a desire for greater objectivity. By engaging the reader De Quincey is able to define the measure of authorial awareness and control; he is able to communicate the very process of his autobiographical writing - that there are essential distinctions to be made between primary experience, that experience seen in retrospect and then transfigured for delivery to another person in a public context. For example, when he describes his flight from Manchester Grammar School which constituted a rebellion against his guardians, De Quincey reveals the nature of the continued autobiographical process:

> Oh, wherefore, then, was it - through what inexplicable growth of evil in myself or in others - that now in the summer of 1802 ... some dark sympathising movement within my own heart, as if echoing and repeating in mimicry the political menaces of the earth, swept with storm-clouds across that otherwise serene and radiant dawn which should have heralded my approaching entrance into life? *Inexplicable* I have allowed myself to call this fatal error in my life, because such it *must* appear to others; since, even to myself, so often as I fail to realise the case by reproducing a reflex impression in kind, and in degree, of the suffering before which my better angel gave way - yes, even to myself this collapse of my resisting energies seems inexplicable.[20]

By seeming to allow the reader into the private workings of this process De Quincey necessarily draws attention to the difficulties which beset his work.

The more explanatory remarks that are offered the more the reader is likely to be distanced from the central autobiographical experiences, and to sympathise with the dilemma of the autobiographer. The split between author and reader is emphasised at the same time as a sharper distinction is drawn between the autobiographer's past self and his present writing self. His apparent compliance with the reader does not detract or intrude upon the curiously private role of autobiographer; he still manages to maintain his position as sole authority. By dismissing the objections and forestalling the questions of his reader, as we have seen, De Quincey appears to be carrying out a dialogue with himself. There can, of course, be no real interchange at work. When he has met the objections and answered the questions he naturally assumes the authoritarian standpoint which such an activity suggests. While he allows his reader to follow him past these very objections and questions, there can be no real equality upon this point. The role of the reader is as intermediary only; it allows him to reach the unknown public by fabricating and satisfying definite demands. He supposedly places his reader in a temporarily privileged position in order to reach for a more personal and particularised interaction. Granting these privileges might be thought to lead to a reduction in the authority of the autobiographer, but this is offset by anonymity. No concession being made on that account the reader must retreat from any thought of real compliance.

Nevertheless, the degree of compliance with the reader which does take place tends to lessen the egocentric concern of the autobiographer. By referring to his reader as a mediatory agent De Quincey dilutes the usual tendency of autobiographical writing towards pride and vanity. The reader readily joins with the autobiographer to look at his secretive and anti-social activity of opium-eating. Due to this bond the reader accepts the sub-title of the work - that these confessions are but 'An Extract from the Life of a Scholar',[21] and are not meant to represent the whole man or the sum total of his experience. Though problematical, the inference is strong that apart from this extract the scholar conforms readily with the type of reader he has depicted. De Quincey uses his reader as a means of establishing a norm of social acceptability. With this common ground, he is at greater liberty to express his more personal and obscure autobiographical experience. Greater credence is thus given to what might have been dismissed as mere eccentricity. Simply by showing an awareness of the demands of his audience, that audience is more likely to respond sympathetically.

De Quincey's demand for sympathy reveals the dilemma he was confronted with due to lack of a friend who could act in a mediatory capacity by vouching for the veracity of the autobiographical account. When he wrote articles on his friendship with the Wordsworths for Tait's Magazine in the 1830s he could cite his friend Professor Wilson as a helpful authority: 'In whatever I say or shall say of Miss Wordsworth, the reader may understand me to have the entire sanction and concurrence of Professor Wilson. We both knew Miss Wordsworth well'.[22] Approaching a dangerous section in his assessment of Wordsworth's character De Quincey again brings in Wilson to aid him, as he interrupts his narrative in an aside to the reader,

> But one thing it is highly necessary that I should explain, and the more so because a grand confession which I shall make at this point, as in some measure necessary to protect myself from the appearance of a needless mystery and reserve, would, if unaccompanied by such an explanation, expose me to the suspicion of having, at times, yielded to a private prejudice, so far as to colour my account of Wordsworth with a spirit of pique or illiberality. I shall acknowledge then, on my own part - and I feel that I might even make the same acknowledgement on the part of Professor Wilson, (though I have no authority for doing so)[23]

Without someone to testify to the fact that evidence does exist, that a course of action was justified by a number of circumstantial details spanning a number of years, De Quincey is faced with a dilemma - which he recognises - of either running his narrative to an inordinate length in order to justify himself, or of failing to impress his reader that he possessed just cause to pursue a certain course of action. The confessional aspect of the Confessions is founded on such a point.

That the motive for his taking of the drug was one of alleviating pain and not one of luxurious indulgence is the turning point of De Quincey's personal moral standing in the eyes of the public. Here he comes to the centre of a problem facing every autobiography which is an act of persuasion based on experiential knowledge. With logical questions or questions of fact, De Quincey the scholar can refer to written authorities, but on a question of experience his is obviously the sole testimony. Sensing this problem in the middle of the Confessions he pauses to explain:

> This is the point of my narrative on which, as respects my own self-justification, the whole of what follows may be said to hinge. And here I find myself in a perplexing dilemma: Either, on the one hand, I must exhaust the reader's patience by such a detail of my malady and of my struggles with it as might suffice to establish the fact of my inability to wrestle any longer with irritation and constant suffering; or, on the other hand, by passing lightly over this critical part of my story, I must forgo the benefit of a stronger impression left on the mind of the reader and must lay myself open to the misconstruction of having slipped, by the easy and gradual steps of self-indulging persons, from the first to the final stage of opium-eating.[24]

Although openly avowed the problem is laid to the blame of the reader; it is with respect to the reader's 'patience' and 'comfort' that the detail is not given. Having placed the onus on the reader in this way the dilemma is not resolved, but remains disconcertingly at the mercy of his sympathy. Having stated again that any drawing up of the details is out of the question De Quincey concludes on this point with:

> It remains, then, that I *postulate* so much as is necessary for my purpose. And let me take as full credit for what I postulate as if I had demonstrated it, good reader, at the expense of your patience and my own. Be not so ungenerous as to let me suffer in your good opinion through my own forbearance and regard for your comfort. No, believe all that I ask of you, namely, that I could resist no longer - believe it liberally, and as an act of grace.[25]

The necessity for the reader to believe in the veracity of his account is a crucial element of the Confessions, especially since veracity is thought to lie in the wealth of detail of De Quincey's past experience. While the work claims to be an extract, it asks the reader to supply the remedial sympathy to counter the inevitable distortion arising from the process of selection. De Quincey's fear that selection is likely to jeopardise the authenticity and sincerity of his account seems to be based on an assumption that many of his experiences are out of the range of logical explanation. If his autobiography were a history of intellectual development dealing with ideas and attempting to justify those ideas, his task would be an easier one, but logic is not the overriding principle of his work - the one which determines the reader's sympathy. Indeed, of the readers whom De Quincey invokes, the logical reader appears to be the one most easily dismissed as insufficient, and also the one most likely to lead to a realisation of the ultimate inexplicability of certain autobiographical experiences.

That section of the Confessions which deals with dreams as evidence of suffering experienced by the author naturally leads towards explanatory remarks: 'All this, and much more than I can say, the reader must enter into before he can comprehend the unimaginable horror which these dreams of oriental imagery and mythological tortures impressed upon me'.[26] Less expected is the following case, from the section of the Confessions entitled 'Pleasures of Opium', where De Quincey attempts to describe the pleasure he received from witnessing the Saturday night entertainment of London's workers:

> On this subject I am afraid I shall be rather obscure, but, I can assure the reader, not at all more so than Marinus in his life of Proclus or many other biographers and autobiographers of fair reputation. This pleasure, I have said, was to be had only on a Saturday night. What, then, was Saturday night to me more than any other night? I had no labors that I rested from, no wages to receive; what needed I to care for Saturday night more than as it was a summons to hear Grassini? True, most logical reader; what you say is unanswerable. And yet so it was.[27]

The pleasure he obtained through mixing with the London crowds was dependent, as he later explains, upon sympathising with their situation. It is the action of sympathy which he describes indirectly as 'obscure' and 'unanswerable'. Although his account rests upon such sympathy De Quincey seems to remain uncertain and unhappy about justifying his own past actions upon such emotions alone. Previous to this statement he claims that his descriptions of these London evenings are supporting evidence in order that 'the reader may judge of the degree in which opium is likely to stupefy the faculties of an Englishman'.[28] He adds that he shall treat the question 'illustratively, rather than argumentatively'.[29] Justification is dependent upon wealth of presentation not logic. De Quincey is forced to operate upon principles of sympathy of which he is both unsure and suspicious - a fact which he draws to the reader's attention:

> I give this account at the risk of being pronounced a crazy enthusiast or visionary, but I regard that little. I must desire my reader to bear in mind that I was a hard student, and at severe studies for all the rest of my time.[30]

De Quincey asks for sympathy from his reader whose objections he hopes to have met by both sharing his awareness of them, and then forthrightly maintaining his own position. He uses the reader as a means of both stabilising his narrative in the eyes of the public and as a means of declaring his own individuality; he defines himself by referring to a definite social norm, and then egotistically declaring his deviance from it. Generally, it is his dialogue delivered directly at the reader which allows him to approach that norm.

The section of the _Confessions_ which deals with De Quincey's poverty in London and which describes his friendship with the girl prostitute Anne deserves special attention because it provides the most striking example of De Quincey and his reader enjoying the benefits of a shared experience. So, too, it foreshadows a different relationship between author and reader which De Quincey was to exploit later in _On Murder Considered as One of the Fine Arts_. Sharing the same London landscape made specific by place names, De Quincey and his reader, at this point in the _Confessions_, at last have a further testimony to the veracity of the autobiographical account. This shared landscape also has the effect of bringing the past into sharp juxtaposition with the present. It is this near approximation of autobiographical narrative to the actual world of the reader which De Quincey turns to such memorable account.

Although Oxford Street and Piccadilly make

public the autobiographical landscape, the gap in time, especially when De Quincey deliberately makes it so, becomes an immeasurable gulf. The reader is led so far and then denied. If it is not time which denies complete involvement then it is De Quincey's reluctance (partly justified for reasons of libel) to give complete identification to both scene and character. The way in which anonymity is both a natural product of the subject and a result of the reserve of the autobiographer is typified by De Quincey's treatment of the lawyer who lets him a room:

> But who, and what, meantime, was the master of the house himself? Reader, he was one of those anomalous practitioners in lower departments of the law who - what shall I say? - who, on prudential reasons or from necessity, deny themselves all the indulgence in the luxury of too delicate a conscience (a periphrasis which might be abridged considerably, but *that* I leave to the reader's taste); ... The inner economy of such a man's daily life would present a most strange picture if I could allow myself to amuse the reader at his expense.[31]

Ironically, the success of such a passage depends upon the edge given to it by treating the subject obliquely: it has all the weight of a world impending, but held back. While it opens ostensibly with De Quincey about to begin to conciliate his demanding reader, the final outcome is a denial. This effect of fabricating the autobiographical commentary around the expectations of the reader, expressed in the form of questions, invariably results in disappointment. It is a challenge set in motion precisely because De Quincey makes the claim for real detail at the same time as engaging his reader. The two are linked together so that expectations are raised. This effect is well illustrated by the following extract:

> This house I have already described as a large one. It stands in a conspicuous situation and in a well-known part of London. Many of my readers will have passed it, I doubt not, within a few hours of reading this. For myself, I never fail to visit it when business draws me to London. About ten o'clock this very night, August 15, 1821, being my birthday, I turned

> aside from my evening walk, down Oxford Street, purposely to take a glance at it. It is now occupied by a respectable family, and by the lights in the front drawing room, I observed a domestic party assembled, perhaps, at tea and apparently cheerful and gay - marvelous contrast, in my eyes, to the darkness, cold, silence, and desolation of that same house eighteen years ago, when its nightly occupants were one famishing scholar and a neglected child.[32]

The passage opens with a direct attack upon the reader's curiosity, only to be followed by a description of the difference between past and present. The reader is soon aware of being excluded from the autobiographical account. However, as we have seen, De Quincey's use of the reader as mediator leads to a fine awareness of the distinction between past and present, and, in particular, between the present time of writing and the past time of experiencing. Here the autobiography gains extra vitality from that involvement of the literary present. It both sponsors and is a product of the engagement with the reader.

The manner in which this literary present openly proclaims itself in its connection with the reader also assists De Quincey with his problem of selection mentioned earlier. Apart from troubling him over the question of justification, selection also provides some structural difficulties. Although the autobiography repeatedly expresses its purpose of dealing with one aspect of his life, and accepts the consequent imposition upon its time structure, De Quincey nevertheless uses his reader to make the inevitable leaps in the time sequence more acceptable. When, in the _Confessions_, he moves from his Oxford days to his time at Grasmere, he does so by making his familiar address:

> Courteous and, I hope, indulgent reader (for all my readers must be indulgent ones, or else, I fear, I shall shock them too much to count on their courtesy), having accompanied me thus far, now let me request you to move onwards, for about eight years, that is to say, from 1804[33]

In the same way that he seemed to appeal to the reader and then deny the expectations aroused by that appeal in his description of the London scenes,

De Quincey now goes one step further. In the midst of unpretending civilities the reader's sympathy and apparent involvement are mockingly returned when De Quincey justifies his addiction by direct confrontation:

> And what am I doing amongst the mountains? Taking opium. Yes, but what else? Why, reader, in 1812, the year we are now arrived at, as well as for some years previous, I have been chiefly studying German metaphysics in the writings of Kant, Fichte, Schelling, etc. And how and in what manner do I live? In short, what class or description of men do I belong to? I am at this period, namely, in 1812, living in a cottage, and with a single female servant ... And how do I find my health after all this opium-eating? In short, how do I do? Why, pretty well, I thank you, reader; ... and I hope sincerely that the quantity of claret, port, or in particular Madeira which, in all probability, you, good reader, have taken and design to take for every term of eight years during your natural life, may as little disorder your health as mine was disordered by opium.34

Though the reader may act as a mediatory agent, it is one against which De Quincey maintains superiority and one against which he adopts attacking rather than defensive tactics. It is the reader who must make concessions if the autobiography is to work. The first of those concessions is granting De Quincey the freedom to fictionalise his own reader.

Anticipating an unfavourable moralistic response concerning the justification of his opium-eating in the <u>Confessions</u>, De Quincey pauses to deliver another challenge which clearly exploits the comic potential issuing from his superiority over the reader:

> Here I take the liberty of an Eclectic philosopher, and I look out for some courteous and considerate sect that will condescend more to the infirm condition of an opium-eater, - that are pleasant men and courteous, such as Chaucer describes, to hear confession or to give absolution, and will show some conscience in the penances they inflict, or the efforts of abstinence they exact from poor sinners like myself. An inhuman moralist I can no more endure, in my

> nervous state, than opium that has not been boiled. At any rate, he who summons me to send out a large freight of self-denial and mortification upon any cruising voyage of moral improvement must make it clear to my understanding that the concern is a hopeful one. At my time of life (six-and-thirty years of age), it cannot be supposed that I have much energy to spare; in fact, I find it all little enough for the intellectual labours I have on my hands; and, therefore, let no man expect to frighten me, by a few hard words, into embarking any part of it upon desperate adventures of morality.[35]

The mediatory agency provided by the reader allows De Quincey to proceed with his narrative, at the same time as he, in turn, cuts away any further involvement. The effect is to insulate the autobiography rather than 'publicise' it. De Quincey's recognition of the reader and of the society to which he belongs is a recognition of the difference imposed upon the autobiography by that society.

In the essay entitled 'The Affliction of Childhood' which was originally intended for incorporation in Suspiria de Profundis De Quincey is struck by this distinction between his experiences as his own property, and his experiences as seen by the public. Describing his affection in early childhood for his sister, he is drawn beyond his own analytical curiosity:

> Could a child, little above six years of age, place any special value upon her intellectual forwardness? Serene and capacious as her mind appeared to me upon after review, was *that* a charm for stealing away the heart of an infant? Oh no! I think of it *now* with interest, because it lends, in a stranger's ear, some justification to the excess of my fondness.[36]

The central dilemma of De Quincey's involvement with the reader in the Confessions is neatly encapsulated in that phrase 'in a stranger's ear', which reiterates his statement in the Confessions themselves when he talks of 'confidentially whispering' into the 'private ear' of 'the public'.[37] De Quincey's public visions are at the same time curiously private. His depiction of London concentrates on loneliness and separation, the narrative in his short story 'The Household Wreck' revolves around the very insularity of man's groupings in society, and the hidden side of ordinary life forms the basis of his concern in the Confessions. De Quincey attempts to bring dreaming and opium-eating out into the open without laying himself bare before the public. His real concern is to implicate the public in his autobiographical wanderings so that he does not stand alone. He acknowledges his kinship with the secret and furtive goings-on of life, and urges the reader to follow him in making that acknowledgement. In the next section of this chapter both acknowledgements are examined, showing how De Quincey's prior involvement entails a further use for the reader, so that what had been compliance in the Confessions becomes complicity in On Murder Considered as One of the Fine Arts.

'PASSIVE OBSERVER': THE READER'S PARTICIPATION

Involving the reader as mediator in the autobiographical writings naturally presupposes that the writer is assumed to be making a defence of some kind or an act of persuasion linked to a particular argument, rather than simply formulating a statement. When De Quincey is less preoccupied with justification and more concerned with observation and analysis, when he seems to be more firmly in command of his subject and less at the peril of his public, the reader is required to recognise and justify the statements of the autobiographer. The reader's role changes as the autobiography becomes more intent on describing past experiences, rather than arguing a case to defend a past course of action.

Such an occasion takes place in the Confessions with De Quincey's journey to Wordsworth's home at Grasmere in 1806, and his failure to make the acquaintance of the poet at that time. Although this appeal to the reader has a motive in the sense that it clears De Quincey of irrationality, immaturity or cowardice, it does not involve the depth of moral censure potentially attendant upon opium-eating. It is a measure of De Quincey's confidence in his handling of the experience that he can make the following suggestion to his reader:

> If you, reader, were a devout Mahometan, throwing gazes of mystical awe daily towards Mecca, or were a Christian devotee looking with the same rapt adoration to St. Peter's at Rome, or to El Kodah, the Holy City of Jerusalem (so

> called even amongst the Arabs, who hate both Christian and Jew), - how painfully would it jar upon your sensibilities if some friend, sweeping past you upon a high road, with a train (according to the circumstances) of dromedaries or of wheel carriages, should suddenly pull up, and say, "Come, old fellow, jump up alongside of me; I'm off for the Red Sea, and here's a spare dromedary, ... Seasonable and convenient it might happen that the invitation were; but still it would shock you that a journey which, with or without your consent, could not *but* assume the character eventually of a saintly pilgrimage, should arise and take its initial movement upon a casual summons, or upon a vulgar opening of momentary convenience.[38]

The relaxed, digressional nature of this suggestion to the reader with its humour does not carry the earnestness of appeal of a writer unconvinced as to the motive of his action. It does not detract from the seriousness of his statement, but aids him in asking his reader to take notice of an important observation which he is proud to put before his audience. There is a significant difference between this use of the reader and that in the Confessions where De Quincey uses the London landscape. When referring to the house owned by the lawyer mentioned previously, De Quincey writes: 'It stands in a conspicuous situation, and in a well-known part of London. Many of my readers will have passed it, I doubt not, within a few hours of reading this'.[39] The reader is led to involvement here by a secondary branch of the autobiographical statement; sympathy is brought in under cover of a tacit acceptance of realism: it is assumed in the autobiographer's act of justification.

In the second instalment of the Suspiria de Profundis, which appeared in Blackwood's for April 1845, De Quincey, having described the death of his sister in childhood and its effect upon himself, suddenly brings his account to a close to make the following announcement:

> Here pause, reader! Imagine yourself seated in some cloud-scaling swing, oscillating under the impulse of lunatic hands; for the strength of lunacy may belong to human dreams, the fearful caprice of lunacy, and the malice of lunacy, whilst the *victim* of those dreams may be all the more certainly removed from lunacy;

> even as a bridge gathers cohesion and strength from the increasing resistance into which it is forced by increasing pressure. Seated in such a swing, fast as you reach the lowest point of depression, may you rely on racing up to a starry altitude of corresponding ascent. Ups and downs you will see, heights and depths, in our fiery course together, such as will sometimes tempt you to look shyly and suspiciously at me, your guide, and the ruler of the oscillations.[40]

While this notice prepares for De Quincey's next switch in time sequence, it also defines a special involvement with the reader. De Quincey shares his autobiography with the reader, they go through the narrative together, but as guide the autobiographer is in command. By asking the reader to imagine himself seated in the swing, De Quincey is really asking two things: the first is for the reader to picture his situation at the hands of the irrational process of dreams; the second is to submit to the capricious turns of the autobiographer. Through the use of this analogy De Quincey communicates the fact that participation necessarily involves a submission. When he is most interested in gaining real participation from his reader De Quincey inevitably assumes an authoritarian voice. That he desires this kind of participation shows him to be confident about his presentation of experience. Instead of proving or justifying De Quincey is now revealing or interpreting; his main concern is the communication of autobiographical material, the value of which is evident.

The important distinction between experience and text developed as a result of involving the reader comes to the fore when assessing De Quincey the interpreter's relationship with the participating reader. When De Quincey describes his sorrow as a child he records it in his main text simply by saying 'I felt'.[41] The evidence for the distinction appears in the footnote to this 'I felt' where De Quincey reveals to his reader what is obvious to himself:

> The reader must not forget, in reading this and other passages, that, though a child's feelings are spoken of, it is not the child who speaks. *I* decipher what the child only felt in cipher. And so far is this distinction or this explanation from pointing to any thing metaphysical or doubtful, that a man must be

> grossly unobservant who is not aware of what I am here noticing, not as a peculiarity of this child or that, but as a necessity of all children. Whatsoever in a man's mind blossoms and expands to his own consciousness in mature life, must have pre-existed in germ during his infancy. I, for instance, did not, as a child, *consciously* read in my own deep feelings these ideas. No, not at all; nor was it possible for a child to do so. I the child had the feelings, I the man decipher them. In the child lay the handwriting mysterious to *him*; in me the interpretation and the comment.[42]

This footnote reveals the dual nature of the autobiographer's responsibility as interpreter. There are at least two levels of 'interpretation' operating simultaneously; for himself and the reader. De Quincey realises that self-interpretation does not always coincide with intelligibility.

The section of Suspiria de Profundis entitled 'The Apparition of the Brocken' provides dramatic evidence of De Quincey possessing this awareness and then asking his reader to participate. Before discussing its striking use of reader participation it is necessary to explain (as he explains in a footnote) the natural phenomenon which suggested itself as a suitable vehicle. The 'Spectre of the Brocken' (so named from having been first observed in 1780 on the Brocken in Germany) is 'an enormously magnified shadow of an observer cast upon a bank of cloud when the sun is low in high mountain regions, reproducing every motion of the observer in the form of a gigantic but misty image of himself'.[43] In his footnote De Quincey is particularly interested in the effect which it has upon the observer:

> At first, from the distance and the colossal size, every spectator supposes the appearance to be quite independent of himself. But very soon he is surprised to observe his own motions and gestures mimicked: and wakens to the conviction that the phantom is but a dilated reflection of himself.[44]

In his 'Apparition of the Brocken' De Quincey transfers this experience of the observer to his reader. His article opens with an invitation 'Ascend with me on this dazzling Whitsunday the Brocken of North Germany'.[45] De Quincey deliberately makes the most of the obscurity and mystery surrounding his 'spectre'. Anticipating in his characteristic way the supposed questions of his reader, he promotes suspense by his evasive reply:

> On such a morning, and reaching the summits of the forest-mountain about sunrise, we shall have one chance the more for seeing the famous Spectre of the Brocken. Who and what is he? He is a solitary apparition, in the sense of loving solitude; else he is not always solitary in his personal manifestations, but, on proper occasions, has been known to unmask a strength quite sufficient to alarm those who had been insulting him.[46]

He continues to hold back the reader in this way at the same time as drawing him tantalisingly along. The reader is led ritualistically step by step through a number of motions until they culminate with the spectre, predictably, repeating the actions. The reader of the footnote would of course know this before, so that the suspense is really mock-suspense. There is, however, a real suspense since the outcome is known all along and we are conscious of being led along a false track. While De Quincey lingers over a known outcome he delays over the significance of the episode. It is for this that the reader is prepared to go along with him. Suddenly De Quincey reveals that this apparently mock serious ritual involvement of the reader is, in fact, a serious commemoration in religious terms of his and the reader's infant experiences. Eventually we find that childhood sorrow is the subject of our attention:

> If, then, once in childhood you suffered an affliction that was ineffable; if once, when powerless to face such an enemy, you were summoned to fight with the tiger that couches within the separations of the grave - in that case, after the example of Judea, sitting under her palm-tree to weep, but sitting with her head veiled, do you also veil your head. Many years are passed away since then; and perhaps you were a little ignorant thing at that time, hardly above six years old. But your heart was deeper than the Danube; and, as was your love, so was your grief. Many years are gone since that darkness settled on your head; many summers, many winters; yet still its shadows wheel round upon you at intervals, like these

> April showers upon this glory of bridal June. Therefore now, on this dovelike morning of Pentecost, do you veil your head like Judea in memory of that transcendant woe, and in testimony that, indeed, it surpassed all utterance of words. Immediately you see that the apparition of the Brocken veils *his* head, after the model of Judea weeping under her palm-tree, as if he also had a human heart; and as if *he* also, in childhood, having suffered an affliction which was ineffable, wished by these mute symbols to breathe a sigh towards heaven in memory of that transcendent woe, and by way of record, through many a year after, that it was indeed unutterable by words.[47]

By imploring his reader to make this recognition of childhood experience De Quincey speaks out directly from the autobiographer's isolated position, asking the reader to universalise his statement. His major concern at this point is to ask the reader to testify to the difficulty of communicating the experience from his isolated position. By involving the reader in this dramatic recognition De Quincey makes a short cut straight to the dilemma of this type of autobiographical writing: Suspiria de Profundis is an attempt, as the title suggests, to describe and analyse experiences which are difficult to communicate. In the episode we have been considering De Quincey's use of the reader reveals his awareness of these difficulties. Where analysis is impossible it becomes clear that one of the most important aspects of this autobiography is its commemorative, sacramental quality. By asking the reader to reflect upon past experience De Quincey asks for a finer awareness of his own task and, at the same time, attempts to define the degree to which it is valuably representative. In order to engage his reader in active participation De Quincey asserts his authority so that the reader is led childlike through all the particularities and is subject to tactics such as suspense. Although writer and reader ultimately do share this important recognition, it is possible only if the reader submits to the autobiographer's demands and accepts a passive position.

The following example of reader participation in De Quincey's work shows even more clearly how this passive position of the reader can be exploited. It shows more continuously than the last episode how the reader is forced to play an active part - how mere presence leads to involvement. In the first section of the paper On Murder Considered as One of the Fine Arts, entitled 'Advertisement of a man morbidly virtuous',[48] 'XYZ', as De Quincey characteristically calls himself, having informed his reader of a society 'For the Encouragement of Murder', joins with him in a challenge to the members of that society by quoting from Lactantius[49] an extract which cries out against the murders of the Roman amphitheatre. De Quincey fixes on the last sentence of the quotation:

> Let the Society of Gentlemen Amateurs consider this; and let me call their especial attention to the last sentence, which is so weighty, that I shall attempt to convey it in English: "Now, if merely to be present at a murder fastens on a man the character of an accomplice; if barely to be a spectator involves us in one common guilt with the perpetrator: it follows, of necessity, that, in these murders of the amphitheatre, the hand which inflicts the fatal blow is not more deeply imbrued in blood than his who passively looks on; neither can *he* be clear of blood who has countenanced its shedding; nor that man seem other than a participator in murder who gives his applause to the murderer and calls for prizes on his behalf".[50]

At first sight it would appear that the reader is distant from this predicament, having sided with 'XYZ' who is not himself involved in any such society, but who 'accidentally' has had the 'Monthly lecture' of the society fall into his hands. His aim, he tells us, is to alarm that society by publishing this lecture. Of course, De Quincey also alarms the reader who, having come to an article with the very title of the lecture, has inevitably become involved even if at one remove in the dilemma of the passive observer. De Quincey was particularly interested in the private side of public life and recognised the irony of the word 'publish'. He knew the extent to which an autobiographer could become public property, but he was also aware that the same public was composed of an aggregate of isolated individuals. Each reader must be involved in a private, hidden activity corresponding to some extent to the secret societies to which he refers in these papers on murder. Even in the opening notice, it is evident that the reader's own curiosity and position lead to an involvement in Lactantius' statement. When this notice closes and the text continues with the script of the lecture on murder, the reader is placed in a different position: 'Through this great gallery of murder, therefore, together let us wander hand in hand, in delighted admiration; while I endeavour to point your attention to the objects of profitable criticism.'[51] In a sense, the reader of Blackwood's is responsible for the degree of excess to which the lecture proceeds: the very force of the piece derives from the chilling correspondence made between a connoisseur of the arts and a murderer. That Blackwood's is specifically singled out for this treatment is more obvious to see in the original title to the opening notice which reads 'To the Editor of Blackwood's Magazine' and begins, 'Sir, We have all heard ...'; thereby focusing on the fact of a limited audience.

That De Quincey uses this particularised audience successfully reveals a characteristic tendency of his work. His use for the reader in the 'Murder Papers' is, in part, to make specific through an ironic inversion the secret, isolated horrors which are read with enthusiasm in the press by a public becoming more and more used to anaesthetising itself to the reality of this type of situation. De Quincey shows his awareness of this tendency in his society by citing the amphitheatre at the opening to Murder Considered. The amphitheatre accords with society cutting itself off from real reactions, while the secret society represents the other extreme which particularises and analyses so much that real concerns are lost. In his short story 'The Household Wreck', which reveals De Quincey's interest in the insularity of an individual's position in society, he prefaces his narrative with this very observation and uses the amphitheatre to illustrate his concern,

> The increasing grandeur and magnitude of the social system, the more it multiplies and extends its victims, the more it conceals them, and for the very same reason; just as in the Roman amphitheatres, when they grew to the magnitude of mighty cities (in some instances accommodating four hundred thousand spectators, in many a fifth part of that amount), births and deaths became ordinary events, which in a small modern theatre are rare and memorable; and, exactly as these prodigious accidents multiplied, *pari passu* they were disregarded and easily concealed; for curiosity was no longer excited; the sensation attached to them was

little or none.[52]

Having said that De Quincey the social observer is at work on these papers, satirising and expressing his concern at the tendency of the time to indulge in a morbid curiosity on the subject of murder, it is perplexing that the supplementary papers give full and particularised accounts of real murders. It would seem that De Quincey is supplying the demands of that morbid curiosity, especially when he joins with the reader in the following manner:

> It is really wonderful and most interesting to pursue the successive steps of this monster, and to notice the absolute certainty with which the silent hieroglyphics of the case betray to us the whole process and movements of the bloody drama, not less surely and fully than if we had been ourselves hidden in Marr's shop, or had looked down from the heavens of mercy upon this hell-kite that knew not what mercy meant.[53]

It becomes apparent that De Quincey joins with his reader as observer in these final murder papers. Just as we have seen this kind of participation involve authorial superiority, so again De Quincey's apparent equality with the reader is in fact a subtle means of increasing his authority:

> Meantime, at this point, let us leave the murderer alone with his victims. For fifty minutes let him work his pleasure ... Help there is none. Let us, therefore, in vision, attach ourselves to Mary; and, when all is over, let us come back with *her*, again raise the curtain, and read the dreadful record of all that has passed in her absence.[54]

This autobiographical involvement with the reader also finds a parallel in the nature of the subject matter. Just as with his own experiences De Quincey is in the privileged position of possessing all the details with the advantage of retrospect, so in this case he familiarised himself with all the daily newspaper accounts of the murders to build up a complete picture of what must have taken place: where evidence was lacking he deduced from the existing accounts. As a result, he could determine events which were taking place simultaneously. Although he seems to be making an appeal to join with the reader, he does so with regard to a subject in relation to which the reader is at a loss. Recreating from recollection, De Quincey presents murders which took place many years before and it is this distance of retrospect which is his defence against claims of morbid curiosity.

In his revised version of the murder papers De Quincey answers hostile reactions to his work by offering a defence which rests on two factors, both of which are defined against the example of Swift's A Modest Proposal.[55] De Quincey tries to defend himself by claiming 'an inevitable and perpetual ground in the spontaneous tendencies of the human mind'.[56] He gives examples, including Coleridge's reaction to a fire in which as soon as it became apparent that the fire did not endanger life Coleridge and his companions thought fit to value it as a spectacle. In a similar way, De Quincey claims, because 'forty-two years have elapsed since 1812, it cannot be supposed that either [of the murders] is known circumstantially to the men of the current generation'.[57] The basis of his 'bagatelle', as he calls it, which 'grazes the brink of horror'[58] is psychological truth; its safety mechanism is remoteness in time.

That De Quincey's defence incorporates these two arguments shows how congenial this kind of distance was to his best writing. In his truly autobiographical works, such as the Confessions and Suspiria de Profundis, he asks the reader to join him in his act of recreation, knowing that reader participation in the narrative does not impinge upon his actual experiences, since they are sheltered by distance of time. Because he directs and controls the participating reader he can obviate his own concern that his private and sacred recollections will be devalued by public curiosity. When he invites the reader to participate, both for his own comfort and his reader's, he regards 'that delicate and honourable reserve which ... restrains us from the public exposure of our own errors and infirmities'.[59]

By appealing to the real world of his public in both the Confessions and Murder Considered De Quincey is able to use his reader in two ways: in the first of these works this appeal allows him to substantiate his own experience; in the second he leads the reader through all the particularities of the murders knowing that he has implicated or at least involved the reader in the moral concern. Although these two uses are quite distinct, both point to a process of writing which maintains anonymity so that De Quincey reaches out to his reader through to his society and escapes from the painful process of self-revelation.

In this second section we have seen how De Quincey uses reader participation to reflect more obviously his own dilemma as autobiographer. In the 'Brocken' episode he cuts across the mannered social relationship between author and reader evident in the Confessions. The act of autobiographical revelation is made to confront the reader. In Murder Considered, freed from autobiographical writing, yet using its process, he manipulates the characteristic responses and demands of the autobiography reader. He attacks that reader in order to stress the sanctity which should be accorded to real events and private experience.

The conclusion to be drawn from this relationship as we have seen it in these two forms is that De Quincey ultimately shrinks back to the sanctuary of himself under cover of anonymity and by highlighting the reader's own involvement. Paradoxically, as we see ourselves enter more fully into his literary world, De Quincey himself disappears into the background. In such instances the autobiographer declares the privacy of his experience, cuts short his narrative and defines the reader's role simply as one of distanced spectator.

THE READER AS OUTSIDER

The reader is conscious of the difference between himself and the autobiographer when the autobiography is obscure or ends abruptly, and when the autobiographer appeals to him to analyse and reflect upon the text. The causes of this awareness in the reader may be split into two categories: those produced by the author's direct intercession, and those produced by the lack of authorial concession. Occasionally the two may be combined so that the author addresses the reader only to state that he is not going to provide more information, or to suggest that there is more material, and crucial material, which is being withheld.

When De Quincey attempts to excuse his tendency to digress in the Confessions, the effect of apologising is to make the reader peculiarly aware of the gulf which separates him from the autobiographer: 'I dally with my subject because to myself the remembrance of these times is profoundly interesting. But my reader shall not have any further cause to complain'.[60] A similar effect is produced when De Quincey would appear to be acknowledging his equality with the reader. To qualify that equality is to challenge it altogether: 'I now feel half inclined to join my reader in wondering that I should have overlooked it'.[61] In the chapter of the Autobiographic Sketches entitled 'Introduction to the World of Strife' De Quincey declares that his communication of this period of his childhood, seen in retrospect and with the aid of the reader in mind, does not correspond or do justice to the actual experience. He draws attention to the fact that his autobiographical process distorts. Looking back to his former self he is struck by disproportion, as it now seems, between the events and the importance he placed upon them. In this case, by viewing in retrospect De Quincey finds that he has more in common with his reader than with his childhood self. Realising this he attempts to correct the balance and do justice to that former self. In so doing he leaves his reader behind and has to announce,

> Oh, reader, do not laugh! I lived for ever under the terror of two separate wars in two separate worlds: one against the factory boys, in a real world of flesh and blood, of stones and brickbats, of flight and pursuit, that were anything but figurative; the other in a world purely aerial, where all the combats and the sufferings were absolute moonshine. And yet the simple truth is - that, for anxiety and distress of mind, the reality (which almost every morning's light brought round) was as nothing in comparison of that dream-kingdom which rose like a vapour from my own brain and which apparently by the *fiat* of my will could be forever dissolved.[62]

Up to this point the reader has joined with De Quincey in what appeared to be light-hearted amusement. Having entertained the reader as well as himself, De Quincey suddenly undermines the supposedly shared presentation of experience and leaves the reader on the outside of his narrative.

Recognition of the reader's point of view leads De Quincey to an explicit denial of his reader's participation, or infers that such a denial is taking place. When in the Confessions De Quincey considers his reader's propriety it is followed, quite against expectations, by a denial of the reader's point of view. He excuses himself by neglecting the reader altogether:

> You will think, perhaps, that I am too

> confidential and communicative of my own private history. It may be so. But my way of writing is rather to think aloud, and follow my own humours, than much to inquire who is listening to me; for, if once I stop to consider what is proper to be said, I shall soon come to doubt whether any part at all is proper. The fact is, I imagine myself writing at a distance of twenty - thirty - fifty years ahead of this present moment, either for the satisfaction of the few who may then retain any interest in myself, or of the many (a number that is sure to be continually growing) who will take an inextinguishable interest in the mysterious powers of opium.[63]

This passage opens with a consideration of the reader's point of view which might be thought to preface an apology, or at least a concession of some kind. In fact the immediate reader's interest is slighted as De Quincey asserts the future relevance of his work.

In this last example there seems to be an assumption on De Quincey's part that he cannot disentangle the permanent qualities of his work from their contemporary context. His denial of the reader is allied to his opposition of periodical magazine writing; he feels the need to justify himself against the temporary tastes and expectations of the audience which is before him. His confrontation with the reader is, in a sense, a denial of his own literary context. While the continuity of the autobiographical account can be delivered in spite of the reader, De Quincey can also blame the reader for digression or tedious explanation:

> if I have spent rather more words than should reasonably have been requisite in describing any obvious state of emotion, it is not because, in itself, it is either vague or doubtful, but because it is difficult, without calling upon a reader for a little reflection, to convince him that there is not something paradoxical in the assertion, that joy and festal pleasure, of the highest kind, are liable to *natural* combination with solemnity, or even with melancholy the most profound.[64]

De Quincey recognises that explanation is not simply a concession, but a means of defending himself: this last passage is perhaps more of a justification of the author than a conciliation of the reader. In the same way that De Quincey in Autobiographic Sketches pays due respect to his childhood self and thereby leaves the reader at a loss, so in the following explanation, the authorial importance of the statement seems to override its consideration for the reader:

> I assign the elements of what I did in reality feel at that time, which to the reader may seem extravagant, and by no means of what it was reasonable to feel. But, in order that full justice may be done to my childish self, I must point out to the reader another source of what strikes me as real grandeur.[65]

Although it may be desirable for explanation such as this to be distinguished from that sort which arises from De Quincey's position as learned scholar, or that which describes the particularities of a bygone era, in most cases the autobiographical concern includes such secondary approaches. When De Quincey says 'I must caution my readers specially against the brilliant author of "Anastasius"'[66] this too separates author from reader, and the distanced position of autobiographer is reinforced by the scholarly paternalism. Similarly - 'Now, reader, assure yourself, *meo periculo*, that no quantity of opium ever did, or could, intoxicate'[67] relies on the authoritarian voice of scholarship which dares rather than justifies its privileged position. In both these cases it is difficult to separate the opium-eater from the opium-scholar; the autobiographer is present in both. In the following quotation, for example, De Quincey's direct question to the reader makes what might otherwise have been simply the voice of the scholar, the earnest concern of the autobiographer:

> You have heard, reader, of pariahs. The pathos of that great idea possibly never reached you. Did it ever strike you how far that idea had extended? Do not fancy it peculiar to Hindostan. Before Delhi was, before Agra, or Lahore, might the pariah, say, I was.[68]

Significantly, De Quincey concentrates on the depth of feeling behind the idea and not the idea itself. Although undeniably there is arrogance in this, it is arrogance that has been summoned in order to make good the assertion: the confidence implicit in De

Quincey's situation is intended to authorise the very extravagance of his idea. It is another means of deflecting claims of eccentricity or charges of 'mysticism', both of which he periodically guards against.

When De Quincey reviews the question of morality in his Confessions some twenty years later in Suspiria de Profundis, he again maintains superiority over his reader, although this time he is more delicate and courteous in doing so:

> I could moralize, if I chose; and perhaps *he* will moralize, whether I choose or not. But in the meantime, neither of us is acquainted properly with the circumstances of the case; I, from natural bias of judgement, not altogether acquainted; and he (with his permission) not at all.[69]

Although he at least makes a concession on his own behalf in this instance the reader is denied altogether. De Quincey defends his own right to pass judgement upon himself and others at the same time as his reader is, of course, denied that opportunity.

In considering his exclusion of the reader from participation in the autobiographical commentary it is necessary to take into account De Quincey's position as a 'moralist' or assertive psychological observer. As we have already seen, distinction between his former self and his present writing self develops as a result of invoking the reader within the text. This affords some degree of objectivity to his task of self-analysis. When De Quincey makes observations on the psychology of dreams out of his own experience his position is not altogether defined as that of self-interested autobiographer: he is concerned with the combinations and principles that are present in psychological process. While he may be interested in the justification and the authenticity of his experience he is also interested in the psychological truth which extends beyond his own immediate concern. At times, the distanced position of the autobiographer, which is responsible for denying the reader ultimate participation, is sponsored by analytical inquiry as well as egotistical assertion.

In Suspiria de Profundis this spirit of inquiry is paramount. The autobiography here is relatively clear of moral justification - its aim is to communicate and interpret psychological process. It is concerned with making distinctions and connections, and vouching for the reality of the experiences. This is partly due to the distance of retrospect: De Quincey recognises the objectivity afforded to him simply by the act of writing about his childhood.

> Great convulsions, from whatever cause - from conscience, from fear, from grief, from struggles of the will, sometimes, in passing away themselves, do not carry off the changes which they have worked. *All* the agitations of this magnitude which a man may have threaded in his life, he neither ought to report, nor *could* report. But one which affected my childhood is a privileged exception. It is privileged as a proper communication for a stranger's ear; because, though relating to a man's proper self, it is a self so far removed from his present self as to wound no feelings of delicacy or just reserve. It is privileged also as a proper subject for the sympathy of the narrator. An adult sympathizes with himself in childhood because he *is* the same, and because (being the same) yet he is *not* the same. He acknowledges the deep, mysterious identity between himself, as adult and as infant, for the ground of his sympathy; and yet, with this general agreement, and necessity of agreement, he feels the differences between his two selves as the main quickeners of his sympathy. He pities the infirmities, as they arise to light in his young forerunner, which now perhaps he does not share ... and sometimes, also, he honours in the infant that rectitude of will which, under *some* temptations, he may since have felt it so difficult to maintain.[70]

De Quincey considers objectivity from two positions here. While he is primarily interested in self-objectivity (which allows him to write because it gives him the subject in toto, and because it guards against the self-destructive quality of autobiographical revelation) he consider's the reader's propriety as well. In doing the latter he is conscious of the reader's awareness of his objectivity. If he feels he has travestied himself due to a lack of that objectivity, he thinks the disgust would register equally with the reader. In a sense, De Quincey's reserve regards the reader's awareness of the private process of the autobiographer. It might thus be argued that when this process is inferred or spoken of in the text, although it distinguishes and separates author from reader, it is a distinction which is intended to be beneficial to both parties. When De Quincey refers to the _Confessions_ in _Suspiria de Profundis_ he indicates how selective his commentary was. The grounds of that selection may be more fully understood if the shared reluctance of both writer and his audience is considered:

> I have not mentioned, in the "Opium Confessions" a thousandth part of the sufferings I underwent in London and in Wales; partly because the misery was too monotonous, and, in that respect, unfitted for description; but still more because there is a mysterious sensibility connected with real suffering, which recoils from circumstantial rehearsal or delineation, as from violation offered to something sacred, and which is, or should be, dedicated to privacy. Grief does not parade its pangs, nor the anguish of despairing hunger willingly count again its groans or its humiliations.[71]

Here there would seem to be an assumption that the reader believes equally in that 'something sacred'. Because De Quincey recognises this shared reluctance, the reader often finds himself distanced from the autobiographer. When he suggests, 'that it is not for the mere facts that the case is reported, but because these facts move through a wilderness of natural thoughts or feelings: some in the child who suffers, some in the man who reports, but all so far interesting as they related to solemn objects'[72] he is removing or abstracting from his own experience. By declaring special significance for the thoughts and feelings he is separating the significant psychological phenomena from the actual man; he is celebrating the reality of the thoughts and feelings at the expense of his own identity. When he stresses the veracity, the authenticity of the feelings, he has cut them away from the particular man who experienced them. In a curious way we know more of the reporting than 'the man who reports' and more of the suffering than 'the child who suffers'. It is because of this that although De Quincey feels very strongly about reserve and propriety, as we have seen, he can also declare,

> Ah, reader, you will think this which I am going to say too near, too holy, for recital. But not so. The deeper a woe touches me in heart, so much the more am I urged to recite

> it. The world disappears: I see only the grand relics of a world - memorials of a love that has departed, has been - the record of a sorrow that is[73]

Precisely where we enter most deeply into the strongest emotions of the autobiographer we are most at a loss for factual details or other counters of realism. In the 'Brocken' episode De Quincey manoeuvres us into the heart of the autobiography, but we arrive there without the guidance of any familiar signs. Having gone so far we are then asked to return immediately to the outside. The opposite of this occurs in the London scenes in the Confessions where the reader is led by familiar signs and assumes that progress is being made towards the 'centre' of the autobiography, only to find that no progress has been made at all.

De Quincey's use of the reader includes two processes which operate simultaneously within the autobiography and which are an important part of its tactical presentation of experience. There is the process of recollection through which De Quincey highlights the distinction between his past identity and his present identity as writer, and there is the act of public explanation and significance. That which is self-justification may also serve as a plea for public acceptance. This is particularly true where De Quincey concentrates upon analysis, making distinctions between various threads of his past experience. He presents the reader with universal psychological truth: sincerity and veracity reinforce a concern for objectivity, rather than the usual function of creating an identity which asks for sympathy. Although he describes his own emotions and attempts to vouch for their reality it need not mean that De Quincey intends his reader to refer back, ultimately, to the man to whom they belong. In these analytical cases, the man's identity is given or assumed beforehand. The nature of the autobiography is to provide shared generalised truths rather than, as might have been expected, credible statements deliberately leading to and intended to consolidate the identity of the autobiographer.

The order of the three types of involvement outlined above occurs repeatedly in the short-term throughout De Quincey's autobiographical works. The autobiographer offers an involvement, then a reprimand and finally asserts the privacy of his subject. In the workings of this process, and most obvious in its final stage, is the characteristic movement of De Quincey between private meditation and public statement. Studying De Quincey's relationship with the reader leads to a finer understanding of the role he played in a transitional period. One can see in the autobiographical process how De Quincey's awareness and use of the reader made him: 'unlike Hazlitt, able to respond to the new energy of social thought and the revival of liberal hopes in the 1820's and 1830's'[74] and one can explain how he was a 'mixture of public educator and private dreamer'.[75] De Quincey delivers shared general truths in an intense, continuous process of self-examination which, at its best, is able to draw on his undoubted social awareness to effect a provocative movement between private experience and educational statement. When Alethea Hayter describes De Quincey in his Confessions as,

> a man who has just explored an almost unknown country and comes back to astound his own compatriots with his descriptions of it. Such a man does not at first pause to think whether the climate of this new country was healthy, or its political system just or humane; he is too much absorbed by the strangeness and novelty of it all, and comes home to boast about it with uncritical enthusiasm[76]

she seems (as well as ignoring his obvious reticence) to underplay his subtle use of social context which gives his work an entertaining and daring recognition of the interplay between acceptable contemporary values and the sometimes dubious workings of the individual mind.

In The English Mail-Coach De Quincey relates how, sitting on the front seat of the coach with the driver next to him asleep, he saw a carriage on the road ahead. In the seconds which occurred before the crash he reveals to us his horror at being in the position of the 'passive observer'. From this dramatic autobiographical re-enactment, he moves to the following commentary. In so doing he enacts the public/private movement we are considering, and at the same time describes its application to his technique of implicating the reader, evident in the 'Brocken' episode and in Murder Considered:

> The situation here contemplated exposes a dreadful ulcer, lurking far down in the depths of human nature. It is not that men generally

> are summoned to face such awful trials. But potentially, and in shadowy outline, such a trial is moving subterraneously in perhaps all men's natures. Upon the secret mirror of our dreams such a trial is darkly projected, perhaps, to every one of us. That dream, so familiar to childhood, of meeting a lion, and, through languishing prostration in hope and the energies of hope, that constant sequel of lying down before the lion, publishes the secret frailty of human nature - reveals its deep-seated falsehood to itself - records its abysmal treachery. Perhaps not one of us escapes that dream; perhaps, as by some sorrowful doom of man, that dream repeats for every one of us, through every generation, the original temptation in Eden. Every one of us, in this dream, has a bait offered to the infirm places of his own individual will[77]

The singular value of De Quincey's imaginative vision as shown in his relationship with the reader lies in his ability to 'publish' such 'secret frailty', to offer a bait to the infirm places of our will. By doing so he engages us in his own conscientious reassessment of past experience. The moral and imaginative implications of this process show how rich was the combination of dreamer and critic which he possessed. Instead of maintaining that De Quincey was, on the one hand, a bourgeois Romantic, and on the other, believing him to be a wandering pariah figure, we can see two such extremes necessary to and integrated in his autobiographical process. By assessing the depth of his involvement with the reader one can see how his reluctance to engage himself wholly in autobiographical revelation and to carry out the role of public commentator without his observations being grounded in, and validated by personal experience, defines a major characteristic of his autobiographical work.

De Quincey's involvement with the reader is fabricated by techniques which are related to both traditional forms of autobiography and the periodical magazine context. Both factors combine in the production of a text which is challenging and difficult because it offers no single and consistent foundation from one point of view. The tactics mentioned create a system of various authorities which can alternate or can be superimposed one upon another. Although these works cannot easily be characterised by any ultimate viewpoint, a description of their constructed involvement of the reader provides a central point of reference with which to evaluate the way they deliver a Romantic examination of experience. The relationship with the reader remains an important part of De Quincey's autobiographical writings even if within itself it reveals a process that consists of interruptions, disruptions and discontinuities.

NOTES

1. Thomas De Quincey, Confessions of an English Opium-Eater and Other Writings, Aileen Ward (ed.) (New York, 1966), p. 22.
2. Ibid., p. 24.
3. Ibid., p. 101.
4. Ibid., p. 83.
5. Ibid.
6. Ibid.
7. Ibid., pp. 22 and 72.
8. Ibid., p. 68.
9. Thomas De Quincey, The Collected Writings of Thomas De Quincey, David Masson (ed.) (14 vols, Edinburgh, 1889-90), vol. III, p. 221.
10. Ibid.
11. Ward, p. 22.
12. Ibid.
13. Henry Crabb Robinson, On Books and Their Writers, Edith J. Morley (ed.) (London, 1938), vol. II, entry for 1 March 1837, p. 513: 'Read an article, or chapter rather, of the opium-eater's autobiography *(Confessions of an English Opium-Eater)* which he makes valuable by the scattered moral reflections'.
14. Ward, p. 53.
15. Ibid., p. 61.
16. Ibid., p. 45.
17. Masson, vol. III, p. 226.
18. Ibid., p. 229.
19. Ibid., p. 278.
20. Ibid., pp. 271-272.
21. Ward, p. 21.
22. Thomas De Quincey, Recollections of the Lakes and the Lake Poets, David Wright (ed.) (Harmondsworth, 1970), p. 133.
23. Ibid., p. 145.
24. Ward, p. 74.
25. Ibid., p. 75.
26. Masson, vol. III, p. 442.
27. Ward, p. 68.

28. Ibid., p. 66.
29. Ibid.
30. Ibid.
31. Ibid., p. 40.
32. Ibid., p. 41.
33. Ibid., p. 72.
34. Ibid., pp. 73-74.
35. Masson, vol. III, p. 400.
36. Thomas De Quincey, _Blackwood's Edinburgh Magazine_ (March 1845), p. 277.
37. Masson, vol. III, p. 410.
38. Ibid., pp. 283-284.
39. Ward, p. 41.
40. _Blackwood's_ (April 1845), p. 501.
41. Ibid. (March 1845), p. 284.
42. Ibid., footnote.
43. _Encyclopaedia Brittanica_, 11th Edition, vol. IV, p. 624.
44. Masson, vol. I, p. 52 (first published in _Blackwood's Edinburgh Magazine_, June 1845, as a section of the _Suspiria_).
45. Ibid., p. 51.
46. Ibid.
47. Ibid., p. 54.
48. Masson, vol. XIII, p. 9.
49. Lactantius Firmianus c. 260 - c. 340, a Christian writer whose work _De Martibus Persecutorum_ attacks Diocletian.
50. Masson, vol. XIII, p. 11.
51. Ibid., p. 17.
52. Ibid., vol. XII, p. 160.
53. Ibid., vol. XIII, p. 85.
54. Ibid.
55. Ibid., p. 71.
56. Ibid.
57. Ibid., p. 74.
58. Ibid., p. 70.
59. Ward, p. 22.
60. Ibid., p. 52.
61. Ibid., p. 161.
62. Masson, vol. I, p. 91.
63. Ibid., vol. III, pp. 413-414.
64. Ibid., vol. I, p. 199.
65. Ibid., p. 126.
66. Ibid., vol. III, p. 384 n.
67. Ibid., p. 382.
68. Ibid., vol. I, p. 100.
69. _Blackwood's_ (March 1845), p. 270.
70. Ibid., p. 272.
71. Masson, vol. II, p. 55.
72. Ward, p. 119.

73. Ibid., p. 185.

74. Patrick Parrinder, _Authors and Authority_ (London, 1977), p. 101.

75. Ibid.

76. Alethea Hayter, _Opium and the Romantic Imagination_ (London, 1971), p. 104.

77. Masson, vol. XIII, p. 304.

Chapter 6

ROMANTIC PUBLIC COMMENTATOR

De Quincey's relationship with his reader moves beyond an exploitation of the traditional tactics of autobiographical writing such as justification and mediation. His works not only seek to remedy the split between the autobiographer and his reader, but deliberately exploit that gap. The same tactics which can defensively insulate the autobiographical statement can also serve to build out to other areas of interest. De Quincey's use of the reader is born out of a coincidence of periodical writer and autobiographer, and the tactic naturally leads to a mixed product. Mediation and justification can easily give way to explanation and persuasion not purely autobiographical. Though the reader may still find himself at the mercy of the autobiographer, both the terms of reference and the main impulse of this relationship may have changed sufficiently to justify his feeling that he is now at the mercy of a 'minor Victorian sage'.[1]

One of the most consistent registers of this side of De Quincey's work, though not specifically linked to his autobiographical writings, has been the appreciation of him as a learned scholar. Albert Goldman has both examined and successfully qualified the extent to which De Quincey is 'the Renaissance type of Polyhistor, or man of universal information'.[2] This scholarly pose is an integral part of De Quincey's autobiographical technique: it is an important facet of his position as magazine writer and public commentator. It is not in any way exorcised in the act of autobiography, but is deliberately exploited as a tactic.

In Confessions of an English Opium-Eater De Quincey fabricated a magazine personality of a particularly mixed sort which accommodated the role of scholar. Even though it is a natural product of its periodical context this role does not exist in a simple form: it is made to answer the demands of the particular text. The reader is confronted by the potentially disturbing combination of opium-eater and philosopher. Revelation and sermonising issue easily and subtly from this two-edged personality. Furthermore, the guise of philosopher in the Confessions also contains the two main impulses of De Quincey's method which seem problematical, and definitive, in relation to his being a Romantic autobiographer:

> the reader will find that the opium-eater boasteth himself to be a philosopher ... For amongst the conditions which he deems indispensable to the sustaining of any claim to the title of philosopher is not merely the possession of a superb intellect in its *analytic* functions ... but also such a constitution of the *moral* faculties as shall give him an inner eye and power of intuition for the vision and mysteries of human nature[3] .

It is claimed that a psychologically based visionary power rests on a moral basis, and operates in conjunction with a dissecting intellectual faculty. Of course, a combination of vision and analysis is not necessarily alien to a Romantic exploration of experience. In De Quincey's case, however, the harnessing of these two different approaches becomes problematical because the vision is often only suggested, and the analytic breakdown of an experience can also be the very presentation of an experience. It is not a simple question of experience first being adequately portrayed, and then rationalised.

Because vision and analysis are applied singly and unsystematically the reader - as we saw in the last chapter - may feel intimidated by a text which gestures towards the fullness of experience while operating partially. Robert Ready briefly suggests this effect of De Quincey's technique, although he locates it not in the text itself, but in the previous experience of the reader when he claims that, 'the Confessions is a calculated literary product meant to set going the reader's divisive experience of vision and analysis'.[4] This split does not represent the gap between De Quincey and his public: it is a component part of his work which is founded upon the fact of delivery to that public.

The potentially exciting and disturbing mixture of vision and analysis in De Quincey's work takes place in a public context where there is often an antagonistic gap between the public commentator and his audience. As we have seen in the case of his autobiographical works this gap can be self-consciously invoked for the opposite purposes of mediation and assertion. Rather than the extreme subject matter of the autobiographer isolating him from his reader, to a large extent the gap is inherited with the context and the roles which are available within it. If an emphasis on the act of delivery is maintained at the same time as viewing De Quincey with regard to a wider framework - to his being a late Romantic public commentator - then the mixture of so-called 'vision' and analysis in his work can be illuminated from a much more specific vantage point. This provocative mixture can then be seen to be rooted in the persuasive possibilities open to a writer engaged in a particular mode of public discourse. From this point of view Roy Park is able to suggest certain important similarities and differences, between Hazlitt's engagement with 'the spirit of his age' and Arnold's:

> Many of the essays deal in one way or another with the diverse contemporary manifestations of this exclusive spirit. One of the spheres in which Hazlitt was determined it should not flourish was in the field of literary criticism. His rejection of the exclusive mind - of sects, parties, creeds, systems, and dogmas - anticipates some of the major emphases in the writings of Matthew Arnold. But whereas Arnold sought to break down the opposition of the Victorian middle-classes to a free play of ideas by cultivating a style designed to charm and persuade, Hazlitt in advocating an affective openness could seldom conceal his irritation and sense of grievance. In some essays, "On People with One Idea", "On People of Sense", "On the Jealousy and Spleen of Party", "On Public Opinion" ... the overall impression is of an essayist writing against the grain of his audience.[5]

While this may be another way of describing Hazlitt's radicalism, it also provides an example in a more extreme form of De Quincey's own case. It is useful as a starting point from which to attempt to place De Quincey as a transitional figure between essayist and sage, because it includes, if briefly, an appreciation of method with an awareness of context.

Edgar Allan Poe's lampoon 'How to Write a Blackwood Article', even allowing for the exaggeration of its humour, reveals the extent to which De Quincey might not have been alone or unconstrained in writing against the grain of his audience. At least, there was a certain amount of conformity of address to the public which characterised Blackwood's. It is easy to see how well the Confessions would have suited the magazine it was originally intended for:

> Having determined upon your subject, you must next consider the tone, or manner, of your narration. There is the tone didactic, the tone enthusiastic, the tone natural - all common-place enough ... Then there is the tone elevated, diffusive, and interjectional. Some of our best novelists patronise this tone. The words must be all in a whirl, like a humming-top, and make a noise very similar, which answers remarkably well instead of meaning. This is the best of all possible styles where the writer is in too great a hurry to think.
>
> The tone metaphysical is also a good one. If you know any big words this is your chance for them. Talk of the Ionic and Eleatic schools of Archytus, Gorgias and Alcmaeon. Say something about objectivity and subjectivity. Be sure and abuse a man called Locke. Turn up your nose at things in general and when you let slip anything a little too absurd, you need not be at the trouble of scratching it out, but just add a footnote, and say that you are indebted for the above profound observation to the *"Kritik der reinen Vernunft"*.[6]

Poe's satire highlights the degree of expediency which could take place in this kind of journalism. This is the more pointed because the above statement supposedly issues from the mouth of Blackwood himself! The main thrust of the satire, however, is to suggest that journalistic expediency is achieved primarily at the expense of the reader through a mode of address which alienates him from the learned man of letters. Though Blackwood's sponsored this kind of elitism, it did not seem to antagonise its readers in the same way as it provoked Poe. Such a deliberate distinction between the public commentator and his audience was apparently a successful formula, capable of flattering and congratulating an old reading class at the same time as fulfilling, albeit in a patronising manner, the supposed educational needs of a new and expanding reading public.

Although the Autobiographic Sketches are perhaps the most conventionalised of De Quincey's autobiographical works in this respect, they too exhibit, on occasion, evidence of the public commentator at odds with and writing against the grain of his audience. In the following case the usually defensive qualifications eventually turn out to be aggressive. It is significant that this defence does not simply operate in order to support the individuality of De Quincey's own position, but the claim made from that position as a prescription for the rest of society. De Quincey has previously attempted to depict the ideal of a household, referring us to the 'morals of the gentry with the manners of the nobility' at the same time as defining his own familial situation:

> Books, literature, institutions of police, facts innumerable, within my own experience, and open to all the world, can be brought to bear with a world of evidence upon this subject. I am aware of the anger which I shall rouse in many minds by both doctrines; but I am not disposed to concede any point of what to me appears the truth, either to general misanthropy and cynicism, to political prejudices, or to anti-national feeling. Such notices as have occurred to me on these subjects, within my personal experience, I shall bring forward as they happen to arise. Let them be met and opposed as they shall deserve ... It is my infirmity, if the reader chooses so to consider it, that I cannot frame an ideal of society, happily constituted, without including, as a foremost element, and possibly in an undue balance, certain refinements in the spirit of manners, which, to many excellent people, hardly exist at all as objects of conscious regard ... With these feelings, and, if the reader chooses, these infirmities, I was placed in a singularly fortunate position.[7]

The dilemma for the autobiographer here does not derive so much from the embarrassing confessional as from the societal context which surrounds his statements. There is a blurring of the frequently separate categories of public and private in the opening sentence, to be followed by a false leniency which offers no possibility of choice. The outcome of this apparent 'defence' rests assertively on the word 'singularly'. Where the subject matter is extreme experience such a marked disparity between the writer and his reading public is to be expected. This fairly aggressive episode occurs where the subject matter is predominantly commonplace or, if extravagant at all, contained within the boundaries of a whimsical humour.

Such an extract is representative of De Quincey's work, however, because it draws attention to his position as a public commentator, rather than focusing on the provocative nature of what he has to say on any important public issue. When De Quincey cries out against government legislation in his essay on Charles Lloyd which forms part of the series on 'Lake Society', it is an exceptional act on his part.[8] In most of his work De Quincey is a public commentator, not a commentator on public affairs.

Any assessment of De Quincey's achievement in a line of genesis from Romantic journalist to Victorian sage is made particularly hazardous by this emphasis in his work. The opening promise of the Confessions, that they 'will prove not merely an interesting record, but, in a considerable degree, useful and instructive',[9] may, justifiably, be read as a tantalising ploy, ultimately perplexing. To claim that 'De Quincey consistently envisioned in his prose the ways in which the most irrational experience normal consciousness has, dreaming, challenged the sureties of a material and mechanical society',[10] suggests that his autobiographical writings have a more deliberate and coherent foundation than is actually the case. It also denies the marked ambivalence towards types of experience which could be both anarchic and restorative. Despite these difficulties, and a seeming preponderance of difference, De Quincey nevertheless shared with certain Victorian writers such as Carlyle, a common ground - the public platform of the periodical magazine. As a result of this background he also shared certain modes of address, persuasive techniques and tactics; even if they are applied with a different subject in mind, and with a different degree of consistency. An examination of such a contextual and strategic relationship replaces the tentative suggestions that have been made in this area from the point of view of the history of prose style. Among the most surprising of these is the connection Lewis E. Gates made between De Quincey and Newman.[11] It is, perhaps, less surprising that similarity should be claimed when the text concerned is a sermon, and is to be found in Newman's Discourses to Mixed Congregations.

Even though one of De Quincey's main concerns as an autobiographer might be to claim experiential superiority over his reader in an area which is his own property, there is an illuminating convergence of situation, interests and techniques between his work and the work of the Victorian sages which leads to a greater understanding of his own particular mixture of public commentary and autobiography. De Quincey's adoption of a scholarly pose well-suited to the magazines would seem to be related to a larger movement which was synchronised with the growth of the periodical press in the first few decades of the century. Roy Park in his study of Hazlitt values - at Bulwer-Lytton's suggestion - the possibility that there was a 'causal connection between the disappearance of the eighteenth century philosopher and the emergency of the nineteenth century periodical essayist and critic'.[12]

De Quincey certainly shared with Coleridge a learned manner based on philosophical and scholarly pretensions which was to become 'a characteristic pose in the journalism of the age'.[13] In his autobiographical writings this pose joins with personal revelation to form a combination of scholarship and sensationalism particularly characteristic of Blackwood's.[14] Poe's 'How to Write a Blackwood Article' suggests that De Quincey's Confessions is a good example of such a combination:

> Then we had the "Confessions of an Opium-eater" - fine, very fine! - - glorious imagination - deep philosophy - acute speculation - plenty of fire and fury, and a good spicing of the decidedly unintelligible. That was a nice bit of flummery, and went down the throats of the people delightfully. They would have it that Coleridge wrote the paper - but not so. It was composed by my pet baboon, Juniper, over a rummer of Hollands and water, "hot", without sugar.[15]

When considered from the point of view of a saleable commodity such a pose becomes an easy target for satire. When viewed from the point of view of the reader the tactics which claim authority for the autobiographer can be challenging and provocative. The experiential claim can easily change its function, moving from the statement of the isolated autobiographer to the assertive generalisation of the sage. In the Autobiographic Sketches there is the following curious construction: 'It is a fact, forced upon one by the whole experience of life, that almost all men are children, more or less, in their tastes and admirations'.[16] Such flexibility does not achieve its most interesting result in this compromised situation, but in the Confessions where the changes from one authority to another are at once more subtle and more aggressive.

Specifically public commentary in De Quincey's autobiographical works often has an introductory function, tending to stabilise the work as a whole as well as defining the initial mode of address, and protecting the main text. While providing this valuable protective role it can allow the autobiographical strain of the work access to parallel strategies usually based upon the difference between the writer and reader. Alternatively, such introductory public statements can actually accentuate, instead of smoothing over, the gap between the public commentator and his audience.

The introductory notice to Suspiria de Profundis contains a particularly severe and extended indictment of its contemporary society and its rapid rate of change. Although it is fairly obvious that such a change is threatening, the further possibility that this very attack is waged against the odds, only emerges gradually, to be encapsulated somewhat ironically in the word 'visionary' at the end of the passage:

> Already, in this year 1845, what by the procession through fifty years of mighty revolutions amongst the kingdoms of the earth, what by the continual development of vast physical agencies - steam in all its applications, light getting under harness as a slave for man, powers from heaven descending upon education and accelerations of the press, powers from hell (as it might seem, but these also celestial) coming round upon artillery and the forces of destruction - the eye of the calmest observer is troubled; the brain is haunted as if by some jealousy of ghostly beings moving amongst us; and it becomes too evident that, unless this colossal pace of advance can be retarded, (a thing not to be expected,) or, which is happily more probable, can be met by counterforces of corresponding magnitude, forces in the direction of religion or profound philosophy, that shall radiate centrifugally

> against this storm of life so perilously centripetal towards the vortex of the merely human, left to itself the natural tendency of so chaotic a tumult must be to evil; for some minds to lunacy, for others a reagency of fleshly torpor. How much this fierce condition of external hurry, upon an arena too exclusively human in its interests, is likely to defeat the grandeur which is latent in all men, may be seen in the ordinary effect from living too constantly in varied company. The word *dissipation*, in one of its uses, expresses that effect: the action of thought and feeling is too much dissipated and squandered. To reconcentrate them into meditative habits, a necessity is felt by all observing persons for sometimes retiring from crowds. No man ever will unfold the capacities of his own intellect who does not at least chequer his life with solitude. How much solitude, so much power ... Among the powers in man which suffer by this too intense life of the *social* instincts, none suffers more than the power of dreaming. Let no man think this a trifle. The machinery for dreaming planted in the human brain was not planted for nothing ... But if this faculty suffers from the decay of solitude, which is becoming a visionary idea in England[17]

The sense of urgency here is created melodramatically, the rapid rate of change being mimicked by the rhetorically prolonged first sentence. This reaches its first conclusion somewhat casually by means of a dash with the statement: 'the eye of the calmest observer is troubled'. This characteristic stance in De Quincey's work is reinforced later on by the appeal of 'all observing persons'. Though the appeal at this stage is to a familiar commonsense position it becomes easily identifiable with De Quincey's role as a commentator who happens himself to be a particularly gifted observer. His real status as a specialist is brought to the fore by singling out the word '*dissipation*', especially since it is followed by the phrase 'in one of its senses'. This display of a single word, often cleared of other associations or purified by reference to etymology, is a useful tactic to the public commentator, appearing to exist in its own right outside his assertive or fabricated argument. That his argument in this case is openly dictatorial is best measured by the archaic opening 'No man ever will', and by its counterpart which achieves much of its impact from its brevity - 'Let no man think this a trifle'. For the danger with this passage of alarmed social comment is that it tries to make a bridge between those larger social innovations and the private world of dreaming. After the extravagance of its opening it is difficult not to find some disproportion by the time we reach the word '*dissipation*' De Quincey's attempt to provide a wider public justification for Suspiria de Profundis is strained by a recognisable gap between those two areas, made evident by his use of tactics which suggest the vulnerability of his position.

While De Quincey may adopt certain roles and tactics which accrue a learned authority to his work, thereby distinguishing the autobiographer from the reader, and providing a requisite framework for his more public commentaries; there is a more negative aspect to his enterprise in that such commentaries are often accompanied by a curious condemnation of the public. Of course, it would be wrong simply to equate the public with the reader in this matter, and allowance must be made for the possibility of an enhanced relationship with the reader as a result of such general condemnation. The specific relationship fabricated by an individual text often seems to be an ideal, situated in a context which is in fact much more hostile. Indeed, the degree of intimacy or familiarity with the reader may even be considered to be in inverse proportion to the animosity directed towards a public which is unknowable and therefore potentially threatening.

Evidence of this situation is not restricted to De Quincey's autobiographical writings: it would appear to be characteristic of the dilemma facing other Romantic public commentators. When Hazlitt writes about The Tatler in 'On the Periodical Essayists' he delivers a commonplace frequently associated with his own achievement as a familiar essayist: 'The English journalist good-naturedly lets you into the secret both of his own affairs and those of others'.[18] This approaches the question from the other side, promoting the case for good relations based on a relaxed and easy geniality. But even here there is, perhaps, a suggestion that the essayist, and the reader to whom he makes his appeal, have joined together and become separate from the 'others' who make up the actual public. In his essay 'On Living to One's Self' Hazlitt outlines quite humourously how he might, given sufficient provocation, 'rail at the public'.[19] Behind his condemnation can be seen the vulnerability of that same public to any opportune commentator. Hazlitt's aggression here is curiously combined with an awareness of the potentialities of his own isolation. Whereas De Quincey used the Brocken phenomenon to involve the reader closely with his text, Hazlitt uses the same illustration as a means of attacking the characteristic reaction of the public:

> There is not a more mean, stupid, dastardly, pitiful, selfish, spiteful, envious, ungrateful animal than the Public. It is the greatest of cowards, for it is afraid of itself. From its unwieldy, overgrown dimensions, it dreads the least opposition of it, and shakes like isinglass at the touch of a finger. It starts at its own shadow like the man in the Hartz mountains, and trembles at the mention of its own name ... The idea of what the public will think prevents the public from ever thinking at all, and acts as a spell on the exercise of private judgement, so that in short the public ear is at the mercy of the first impudent pretender who chooses to fill it with noisy assertions, or false surmises, or secret whispers.[20]

The qualities which Hazlitt castigates are those which militate against the tactics of the familiar essayist. At the same time he clearly depicts a situation which is ripe for the commentator to save 'private judgement' from the anonymity produced by a blanketing consensus of opinion. The act of commentary is thus not without its risks; the commentator himself is not a spokesman for the public, but significantly at variance with his prospective audience. At least some of the venom here seems to belong to a specialist practitioner bemoaning the difficulty of his task. Such an attack may be said to reveal a markedly ambivalent response to its supposed enemy. This is not surprising given the other considerations which govern the context. Hazlitt's attack on the nature of the public is not contradicted, but really supported by the following awareness of more expedient concerns: 'We exist in the bustle of the world, and cannot escape from the notice of our contemporaries. We must please to live, and therefore live to please. We must look to the public for support'.[21] He shares a position common to other members of his profession: he freely admits to being a part of the periodical press. His depiction of the situation suggests unanimity among commentators with the real gap existing between them and the public.

Writing only about twenty years later at the beginning of his career, in the preface to On Modern Painters, Ruskin immediately dissociates himself from the press because he thinks that their professional involvement with the public necessitates a slavish adherence to general opinion rather than providing the freedom for outspoken criticism:

> I do not consider myself as in any way addressing or having to do with, the ordinary critics of the press. Their writings are not the guide, but the expression, of public opinion. A writer for a newspaper naturally and necessarily endeavours to meet, as nearly as he can, the feelings of the majority of his readers; his bread depends on his doing so.[22]

Later in the same preface the difference between Ruskin's emergent position as a sage and that of the periodical essayist is developed even further as emphasis is laid firmly on a long-term evolution of principles instead of the self-contained article,

> I am devoting years of labour to the development of the principles on which the great productions of recent art are based. I have a higher end in view, one which may, I think, justify me, not only in the sacrifice of my own time, but in calling on my readers to follow me through an investigation far more laborious than could be adequately rewarded by mere insight into the merits of a particular master, or the spirit of a particular age.[23]

Despite the significant difference between Ruskin and Hazlitt in this respect (including the particularly barbed language at the end of the last sentence) both seek to capitalise on the split that seems to exist between their idea of the public and the special role they assign to the reader in order to further their own interests. They both need to maintain a balance between a condemnation of the public world which justifies their argument, and a degree of equality conceded to the reader which will not undermine their own authority. The nature of this balance for these two writers clearly varies according to the scope which is available, and the pretensions that are made for the project in question. In De Quincey's case the alternation between the polarities involved in this balance is frequently abrupt, and as a result the reader may find that his position, though only recently established, is suddenly undermined.

Through their different statements of antagonism towards the public, or aspects of it, Hazlitt and Ruskin suggest the extent to which the act of public commentary can be defined by the fluctuation which takes place in the fortunes of the supposed reader. It would seem to be a compromise, a question of finding a technique through which the individual voice can be at once transmuted into a public or dictatorial one without the threat of alienating the speaker. Ironically, one of the main ways of consolidating the audience that he desires, is for the commentator to condemn another section of the public.

In De Quincey's case he already possesses a particular involvement with the reader which is integral to the basic forms of autobiography. Included within the traditional framework of the form is the underlying position of superiority adopted by the autobiographer which can usually be lessened by various acts of mediation. De Quincey's different autobiographical writings also take place in a context, and in a career, which includes other forms of literary activity such as the review essay, where the public authority attendant upon his position can be adopted more simply. Both the form and the context offer him strategies leading to accepted or established positions of authority and superiority. While G.B. Tennyson's statement about the development of Carlyle's Sartor Resartus significantly ignores the precarious balance involving the reader in the act of Romantic public commentary, it does at least emphasise that the genesis from reviewer to sage is determined according to the context. Carlyle, he writes,

> applied his experience in reviewing and essay writing to the task of the novel. The review essay offered a ready-made format that Carlyle was able to expand and adopt for imaginative purposes, a mode whereby he could speak to the age and speak for himself.[24]

It might also be added that as a result Sartor Resartus possesses a quasi-autobiographical form rather than a strictly novelistic one. Like De Quincey's autobiographical works one of its main processes is the act of revelation. The technique of revelation can be the justification and evidence for the superiority of the public commentator. Both the sage and the autobiographer make important disclosures which they claim can be verified by experience. Even though De Quincey as an autobiographer starts off from a different premise, rooting the text in the claim of his own experience, his acts of justification which develop from that premise ensure that his work possesses some form of social relevance. The nature of autobiography brings his work closer to that of a 'sage' than one might think: it determines parallel interests in the same context, even if its ultimate goals are different.

In his attempt to define the activities of the Victorian sages John Holloway offers, as a useful preliminary consideration, the following shared characteristic of their work:

> these authors insist on how acquiring wisdom is somehow an opening of the eyes, making us see in our experience what we have failed to see before ... This new perception, moreover, is usually allied to ordinary perception by the senses. It is not of some quite new reality: it is seeing old things in a new way. Wisdom in the sage's sense, that is, may not be wholly about experience, but it does find an adequate sanction in experience.[25]

Despite the fact that we are now dealing with 'wisdom' rather than experiential knowledge, the important role assigned to experience more generally is common to both autobiographer and sage. Another major difference, of course, is that the sage's interpretation of experience is paramount, whereas De Quincey more frequently offers his explanation or perception of experience. De Quincey is a specialist observer more than a specialist interpreter: he makes us see our experience more frequently than he makes us see in our experience. De Quincey shares in the description of the sage presented here in so far as his main concern is not the peculiarities of opium-eating, but the representative actions of the individual consciousness which can be found in that example.

De Quincey's ability to perceive experience provides him with the platform from which he can make his experiential revelations, impinging on public interest with a subject that is common to each of his readers. When De Quincey concentrates on the province of extraordinary experience he may startle and thrill his reader by briefly challenging the surety of his position. He develops and even sensationalises areas which the reader might have decided upon as mundane or everyday, or have passed over altogether. The impulse of many of his autobiographical explorations accords with Carlyle's admonishmen in Sartor Resartus: 'Shakespeare says, we are creatures that look before and after: the more surprising that we do not look round a little, and see what is passing under our very eyes'.[26] This common interest finds a technical outlet in the familiar practice of controlling the meaning of the single word. Writing about Carlyle John Holloway states that 'The earliest stage in coining a sense is apparently to suggest that the real meaning of a word is not properly known'.[27] A similar purpose is also served in De Quincey's work by a more oblique strategy which Michael Holstein refers to as an anapestic triad - a structural paradigm in De Quincey's prose. 'Each imaginative mode', he says, 'begins with the data of commonplace experience which it then elaborates and heightens'.[28]

According to De Quincey's own statement in his Autobiographic Sketches this development towards elaboration is not a deliberate complication of things essentially simple. He sees it almost as an inevitable result of probing further into the nature of experience:

> if I have spent rather more words than should reasonably have been requisite in describing any obvious state of emotion, it is not because, in itself, it is either vague or doubtful, but because it is difficult, without calling upon a reader for a little reflection, to convince him that there is not something paradoxical in the assertion, that joy and festal pleasure, of the highest kind, are liable to a *natural* combination with solemnity, or even with melancholy the most profound. Yet, to speak in the mere simplicity of truth, so mysterious is human nature, and so little to be read by him who runs, that almost every weighty aspect of truth upon that theme will be found at first sight to be startling, or sometimes paradoxical. And so little need is there for chasing or courting paradox, that, on the contrary, he who is faithful to his own experiences will find all his efforts little enough to keep down the paradoxical air beseiging much of what he *knows* to be the truth. No man needs to *search* for

> paradox in this world of ours. Let him simply confine himself to the truth, and he will find paradox growing everywhere under his hands as rank as weeds. For new truths of importance are rarely agreeable to any preconceived theories - that is, cannot be explained by these theories; which are insufficient, therefore, even where they are true. And universally it must be borne in mind - that not *that* is paradox which, seeming to be true, is upon examination false, but that which, seeming to be false, may upon examination be found true.[29]

Once again, a seemingly defensive autobiographical statement culminates in a gnomic declaration to the reader. As the text becomes more imperative it includes such a characteristic feature as the negative opening to the sentence - 'No man needs to *search*' - which was prominent in the introductory notice to Suspiria de Profundis. Gradually the ground is prepared for the conclusiveness of 'universally it must be borne in mind'. It is an assertive conclusion, a manifestation of support for the argument about the inadequacy of theory. So, too, the claim that paradox can be found 'growing everywhere ... as rank as weeds' provides further testimony to De Quincey's belief in the organic nature of experience, as well as suggesting once again the dangers resident in that same growth. It is this assumption about the nature of experience, and a humility in the face of its complexity and mystery, which rules out a coherent theoretical approach and necessitates an assertive approach. The assertions are delivered to a public which it is assumed, fails to pay due respect and reverence to experience.

In this way De Quincey can break down trite assumptions and pinpoint the limitations of accepted viewpoints. For the same purpose he is also willing to make a significant qualification to one of Wordsworth's poetic statements that has passed into popular currency as a dictum. Rather than resting solely on the authority of a quotation in the typical manner of the essayist, De Quincey draws attention to its partial truth with regard to his own interest in experience:

> *"The child"*, says Wordsworth, *"is father of the man"*; thus calling into conscious notice the fact, else faintly or not at all perceived, that whatsoever is seen in the maturest adult, blossoming and bearing fruit, must have pre-existed

> by way of germ in the infant. Yes; all that is now broadly emblazoned in the man, once was latent - seen or not seen - as a vernal bud in the child. But not, therefore, is it true inversely - that all which pre-exists in the child finds its development in the man. Rudiments and tendencies, which *might* have found, sometimes by accident, *do* not find, sometimes under the killing frost of counter forces *cannot* find, their natural evolution. Infancy, therefore, is to be viewed, not only as part of a larger world that waits for its final complement in old age, but also as a separate world itself; part of a continent, but also a distinct peninsula. Most of what he has, that grown-up man inherits from his infant self; but it does not follow that he always enters upon the whole of his natural inheritance.[30]

The complexity of experience for De Quincey resides not only in its organic expansion, but in its fragmentation; in loss that cannot adequately be accounted for. De Quincey's statements which offer an organic view of experience are to be found alongside others which point not to unity, but to separateness. In this last instance, for example, the word 'self', which might be thought to refer to coherency, when qualified by 'infant' refers us to the possibility of identity as something partial and temporary, not complete and fixed. The basis for these ideas is not theoretical: they are based on the act of perception or observation.

De Quincey's work as an autobiographer converges with the work of the Victorian sage, especially in the case of Sartor Resartus, due to a common interest in displaying to the public a new perception of an old or familiar subject. As a result of this common interest his work possesses a number of similar techniques. Most of these also derive from the shared context spoken of earlier, and from the precedency given to experience, whether it be used as a support for argument or appears as the main topic of inquiry.

Many of these techniques are, of course, centred on the special confrontation with the reader which is fabricated by the text itself. Describing the stylistic features which create involvement with the reader within Sartor Resartus G.B. Tennyson declares that, 'The imperative and interrogative moods are among Carlyle's favourites'. He notes that Teufelsdrockh 'uses ... almost three-fourths as many interrogative sentences as declarative ones', and then claims that this 'assault' on the reader is 'sustained by his use of tense'. He consolidates his description with reference to the context by informing us that 'Writing in the present tense is a feature Carlyle acquired from writing essays'.[31] Sartor provides ample evidence of a daring interplay between the Editor, Teufelsdrockh, and the invoked reader. The Editor pre-empts the response of his reader and profits by either conceding to or reprimanding the extreme Teufelsdrockh,

> Or, cries the courteous reader, has your Teufelsdrockh forgotten what he said lately about "Aboriginal Savages", and their "condition miserable indeed"? Would he have all this unsaid; and us betake ourselves again to the "matted cloak", and go sheeted in a "thick natural fell"?
>
> Nowise courteous reader! The Professor knows full well what he is saying; and both thou and we, in our haste, do him wrong[32]

It would seem that precisely such interplay owes its origin to the periodical magazine context exploited by De Quincey, when Gerry H. Brooks declares that,

> *Frazer's* and the magazines Carlyle associated with it offered him playful and varied rhetoric. They also offered him fictional voices. The use of fictional editors, commentators, and narrators to perform a variety of rhetorical functions was a highly developed convention in *Blackwood's*, the magazine on which *Frazer's* was modelled.[33]

Such a manipulation of the reader, as we saw in the last chapter, is an important and easily recognisable feature of De Quincey's autobiographical technique. It results from the various rhetorical forms of address and invocation that are employed. Less obvious, though not less stylised and rhetorical devices offer support to the autobiographer as they do to the sage, even if they achieve different results.

In De Quincey's mixture of autobiography and public commentary both polarities of his work - its public and 'private' facets - are equally served by an archaic feature of his style which is also to be found in the work of Carlyle who employs it more extensively.[34] This is the use of 'thou' and other accompanying archaic elements to create dramatic and lengthy apostrophes. These form distinct passages within the text, and frequently have the effect of producing significant transitions. In the following paragraph from the Autobiographic Sketches there is a marked change between two different sorts of language as a result of this feature:

> Grief! thou art classed among the depressing passions. And true it is that thou humblest to the dust, but also thou exaltest to the clouds. Thou shakest as with ague, but also thou steadiest like frost. Thou sickenest the heart, but also thou healest its infirmities. Among the very foremost of mine was morbid sensibility to shame.[35]

The archaic apostrophe here is a means of drawing the specific and personal autobiographical element out towards a principle, making it more abstract and even more universal in its application. As a result, a gap is produced with the introduction of the last sentence rather than a gradual transition. It feeds off the high-pitched opening provided by the apostrophe.

Passages of this sort interrupt the usual flow of the autobiography. When they obviously intrude and appear isolated in the text they can support the isolated role of the autobiographer. Their exclamations highlight emotion, rather than a public move towards abstraction. These archaic forms of language can easily support the sacramental or personally ritualistic aspect of the autobiography. However, the same solemnity and mystery which pertain to that aspect can also support its more mundane documentary tone. There is a Biblical authority in these archaisms which can be used to introduce assertive generalisations about experience. In the following extract from the Autobiographic Sketches there is an abrupt movement from the apostrophe to De Quincey's own case, to the declaration of the assured public commentator. This final declaration clearly profits from the preceding Biblical references:

> O Ahasuerus, everlasting Jew! fable or not a fable, thou, when first starting on thy endless pilgrimage of woe - thou, when first flying through the gates of Jerusalem, and vainly yearning to leave the pursuing curse behind thee - couldst not more certainly in the words of Christ have read thy doom of endless

> sorrow, than I when passing for ever from my sister's room. The worm was at my heart; and, I may say, the worm that could not die. Man is, doubtless *one* by some subtle *nexus*, some system of links, that we cannot perceive, extending from the new-born infant to the super-annuated dotard: but, as regards many affections and passions incident to his nature at different stages, he is *not* one, but an intermitting creature, ending and beginning anew; the unity of man, in this respect, is co-extensive only with the particular stage to which the passion belongs.[36]

Once again we are presented with a qualification to the usual view of experience, as De Quincey offers, after invoking a most fitting Romantic archetype, further complexity in keeping with his characteristic recognition of discontinuity and fragmentation. In this instance the declaration about experience, though related rhythmically and tonally to the archaic opening, still remains as a recognisable entity in its own right. On other occasions in his autobiographical writings these impassioned archaic passages actually contain rather than introduce a generalisation about experience. This can be delivered not as an apparently reasoned statement, but as a prayer-like celebration. In this way the reader is informed indirectly, sometimes obliquely, about the general features of the experience in question or the powers affecting that experience. The most widely known of these exclamatory passages is the glorification of opium in the Confessions:

> O just, subtle and mighty opium! That to the hearts of poor and rich alike, for the wounds that will never heal, and for "the pangs that tempt the spirit to rebel", bringest an assuaging balm - eloquent opium! That with thy potent rhetoric stealest away the purposes of wrath, and to the guilty man for one night givest back the hopes of his youth and hands washed pure from blood, and to the proud man a brief oblivion for
>
> Wrongs unredressed, and insults unavenged;
>
> that summonest to the chancery of dreams, for the triumphs of suffering innocence, false witnesses; and confoundest perjury; and dost reverse the sentences of unrighteous judges. Thou buildest upon the bosom of darkness, out

> of the fantastic imagery of the brain, cities and temples, beyond the art of Phidias and Praxiteles - beyond the splendour of Babylon and Hekatompylos; and "from the anarchy of dreaming sleep", callest into sunny light the faces of long-buried beauties, and the blessed household countenances, cleansed from the "dishonors of the grave". Thou only givest these gifts to man, and thou hast the keys of Paradise, O just, subtle and mighty opium![37]

From a simplistic autobiographical standpoint this might seem an emotional outburst - an interruption to the more sober act of definition which is taking place around it. However, it contains a persuasiveness which manipulates the reader's response to the shift between the text's public and private relevance. By eulogising the drug De Quincey is able to catalogue its effects without having to provide supporting evidence, and is able to switch the focus of attention from its effect on himself to the universal and social application of its properties. This archaic address provides another means of asserting significance at the same time as considering 'man' in general, instead of the autobiographer.

The use of archaisms is a technique which can be applied both to autobiography and public commentary. It involves drawing on resources from outside, using the authority of well-known forms of language. In contrast, the technique of placing special emphasis on single selected words highlights the intrinsic nature of the context. It draws its authority from the very fact of delivery. At its least elaborate this technique appears to be no more than a utilisation of the typographical possibilities afforded by the magazines. The single word can be starkly isolated by being printed in capitals or in italics. Even where no apparent explanation is available beyond the obvious one of emphasis, the reader is likely to feel that he is being dictated to, that meaning is having to be explained to him. In the following sentence from the Autobiographic Sketches, for example, the word 'representative' is singled out without being overtly explained. The sentence itself offers an explanation by pointing us to a particularly psychological or philosophical use of the word:[38] 'Henceforward the character of my thoughts changed greatly; for so *representative* are some acts, that one single case of the class is sufficient to throw open before you the whole theatre of possibilities in that direction'.[39] In this form the technique is relatively subdued. It is often much more flamboyant, making obvious the fact that the learned man of letters is displaying before his audience. When De Quincey describes the mental impact of approaching the metropolis of London, for example, the search for an appropriate word is accompanied by remote parallels. In conjunction with these other elements the highlighting of single words parades the process of articulation before the reader:

> you soon begin to feel yourself entering the stream as it were of a Norwegian *maelstrom*; and the stream at length becomes the rush of a cataract. What is meant by the Latin word *trepidatio*? Not anything peculiarly connected with panic; it belongs as much to the hurrying to and fro of a coming battle, as of a coming flight; to a marriage festival as much as to a massacre; *agitation* is the nearest English word. This *trepidation* increases both audibly and visibly at every half-mile, pretty much as one may suppose the roar of Niagara and the thrilling of the ground to grow upon the senses in the last ten miles of approach.[40]

While this public exhibition of knowledge furthers an attempt at explanation, the process could equally be seen as one of defamiliarisation. Rather than making another area of strange experience available for popular communication, this mystifies a relatively commonplace experience.

The same process also takes place on a linguistic level. This last example involves the difficulty of finding a suitable word. The word found is not entirely alien, but has a modern English equivalent. The case is characteristic in that a relatively familiar word - here both 'agitation' and 'trepidation' - is suddenly held back from its flexible, perhaps vague popular usage, and is made to adhere to a stricter, more circumscribed meaning, usually in accordance with its origins. The opening to one of the sections of the Autobiographic Sketches finds support in this historical authority of the single word:

> To teach is to learn: according to an old experience, it is the very best mode of learning - the surest, and the shortest. And hence, perhaps, it may be, that in the middle ages by the monkish word *scholaris* was meant indifferently

> he that learned and he that taught.[41]

Such a use of the technique occurs frequently in De Quincey's autobiographical texts, where it is a mannerism tending to maintain the pose of philosopher/scholar which pertains to the persona of the autobiographer. In the Confessions, for example, De Quincey finds he needs to justify his use of a word in the face of popular over-use. Referring to his separation from Ann he writes: 'During some years I hoped that she *did* live; and I suppose that, in the literal and unrhetorical use of the word *myriad*, I may say that on my different visits to London'.[42] Even here, of course, it is not only evidence of scholarship: it furthers the urgency of the autobiographical narrative and maintains the appearance of fidelity to past experience. It is certainly not unusual for this tactic of placing special emphasis on a single word to be harnessed to a more specifically autobiographical purpose. In the Confessions the larger process of justification which takes the form of a learned disputation and blends the roles of expert and opium-eater, is equally served by this tactic:

> though it was not possible to suppose a medical man unacquainted with the characteristic symptoms of vinous intoxication, yet it struck me that he might proceed on a logical error of using the word intoxication with too great latitude and extending it generically to all modes of nervous excitement, instead of restricting it as the expression of a specific sort of excitement connected with certain diagnostics.[43]

It is less surprising to find it being used in a logical debate of this sort in the Confessions, than to see it functioning in the more mysterious sections of Suspiria de Profundis.

In that section of the Suspiria entitled 'Levana and Our Ladies of Sorrow', De Quincey, in keeping with his belief in the power of suffering experienced in childhood, refers us to the figure of 'Levana', a personification of that power. Verbal definitions of different sorts play a key role in explaining the nature of experience which pertains to this figure. Some definitions are necessary to explain De Quincey's own peculiar alignment with Levana; others are no more than school-masterly declarations to a supposedly inferior reader who is making the wrong assumptions. The manipulation of the single key word in argument works in accordance here both with the aggressive autobiographer asserting the individuality of his own experience and the public commentator exploiting his scholarly function in a public context:

> And that mysterious lady, who never revealed her face, (except to me in dreams,) but always acted by delegation, had her name from the Latin verb (as still it is the Italian verb) *levare*, to raise aloft ... And hence it has arisen that some people have understood by Levana the tutelary power that controls the education of the nursery ... She therefore watches over human education. Now, the word *edŭco*, with the penultimate short, was derived (by a process often exemplified in the crystallisation of languages) from the word *edūco*, with the penultimate long. Whatsoever *educes* or develops - *educates*. By the education of Levana, therefore, is meant - not the poor machinery that moves by spelling-books and grammars, but that mighty system of central forces hidden in the deep bosom of human life, which by passion, by strife, by temptation, by the energies of resistance, works for ever upon children - resting not day or night, any more than the mighty wheel of day and night themselves ... If, then, *these* are the ministries by which Levana works, how profoundly must she reverence the agencies of grief! But you, reader! think - that children generally are not liable to grief such as mine. There are two senses in the word *generally* - the sense of Euclid where it means *universally*, (or in the whole extent of the *genus*,) and a foolish sense of this word where it means *usually*. Now I am far from saying that children universally are capable of grief like mine. But there are more than you ever heard of, who die of grief in this island of ours.[44]

The movement of this passage is not dictated by the subject, but by the delivery. It takes its rationale from its act of communication. It gradually becomes more concerned with the nature and the problems of language than with the esoteric nature of the subject. Assuming that a detailed description of Levana is required by author and reader, we might decide that the passage is evidence of De Quincey's characteristic habit of being led astray by qualifications. Another reading is available if we assume that the main interest of the text is the translation and communication of experience, in which the qualifications and the otherwise obsessive definitions become an understandable, though still provocative mode of development.

Once again, this sort of passage denotes a breach between the figure of the autobiographer and his audience, with his characteristic tactics drawing attention to this split rather than attempting to conceal it. De Quincey's use of the single highlighted word as an autobiographical tactic also involves an important public assumption about the nature of the readership. Like other tactics, this would seem to be sponsored by a belief in accordance with that expressed in *Sartor Resartus*: 'Gullible, however, by fit apparatus, all Publics are; and gulled, with the most surprising profit'.[45]

The main difference between De Quincey and other Romantic and Victorian sage figures lies in the final outcome of their relationship with the reader, even though similar tactics and techniques have been employed. Autobiographical use of a reader as a component part of De Quincey's texts can only loosely be described by the term 'profit', and where it may approximate to that term it inevitably moves away from any purely social relevance. The public sage-like declarations which emerge from the adoption of a common context and the use of similar techniques are ultimately controlled by the larger autobiographical framework of the texts concerned.

Many passages from De Quincey's autobiographical works which may be categorised as public commentary have frequently been used by critics who have, understandably, found it easy to divorce them from their immediate context. Such passages appear fairly self-contained. Nevertheless, such extractions undermine the mainly autobiographical impulse of the text by ignoring the transitions it makes as it alters its bias toward a more declamatory stance. For example, De Quincey's relatively famous declaration founded on his coinage of the noun 'involute', follows on from a much more specific concern, so that it might more easily be read as an explanation than as a conclusion. The present autobiographical narrative has to be supported: it is self-consciously interrupted before the reader is referred to the *Confessions* and then presented with the supposedly unplanned declaration:

> Let me pause for one instant in approaching a remembrance so affecting for my own mind,

> to mention that, in the "Opium Confessions", I endeavoured to explain the reason why death, other conditions remaining the same, is more profoundly affecting in summer than in other parts of the year - so far, at least, as it is liable to any modification at all from accidents of scenery or season. The reason, as I there suggested, lies in the antagonism between the tropical redundancy of life in summer, and the frozen sterilities of the grave. The summer we see, the grave we haunt with our thoughts; the glory is around us, the darkness is within us; and, the two coming into collision, each exalts the other into stronger relief. But, in my case, there was even a subtler reason why the summer had this intense power of vivifying the spectacle or the thoughts of death. And, recollecting it, I am struck with the truth, that far more of our deepest thoughts and feelings pass to us through perplexed combinations of *concrete* objects, pass to us as *involutes* (if I may coin that word) in compound experiences incapable of being disentangled, than ever reach us *directly*, and in their own abstract shapes.[46]

Even the whole of this passage could be said to be qualified though not subordinated by the claim that what follows is only in keeping with some form of emotional propriety, that the pause is insignificant compared with the impact the surrounding narrative is making on the autobiographer.

In this last extract we can see how an easily recognisable piece of public commentary, utilising the shared 'us' and employing the technique of the highlighted single word, takes its place alongside other forces operating in the text. It is evident that De Quincey's declaration concerning 'involutes' cannot simply be regarded as public commentary: its significance is altered according to those other concerns. In this way the overriding pressure of the autobiographical form cuts short any absolute correspondence between the work of De Quincey and that of other public commentators and sages.

This difference is also based on an intrinsically Romantic characteristic of De Quincey's autobiographical works. Although Ruskin refers in <u>Praeterita</u>, in quick succession to 'a new fact in existence'[47] and 'the real new fact in existence',[48] it can still be claimed when considering that work in relation to its autobiographical genre, that,

'Ruskin assumes and exercises an immense authority as Seer, Sage, or Prophet - not as an individual personality'.[49] In De Quincey's case, as we have seen, this last authority forms the basis of the work, even though it frequently blends with others to produce a more wide-ranging statement. If De Quincey's autobiographical works do not share, in a strictly poetical and Imaginative sense, with Wordsworth's Prelude the 'very high claim that the act of retrospection and composition is in itself the source of a knowledge higher than the particular truths of the experiences recorded';[50] they do, at least, consistently claim that they are part of a continuing revelatory process which celebrates the ability of an observer of experience. The accommodation of public commentary within the boundaries of autobiography is not an aberration, and not simply an inevitable result of the context, but consistent with their being Romantic texts. As Michael Cooke has written,

> Argument is at the bottom of the romantic adventure ... It must be kept in mind here that romanticism involves an argument *with*, using the double force of the preposition to suggest at once resistance and sharing. If the romantics resisted dogma as imposition, they shared with the dogmatist a feeling for truth, albeit an evolutionary one.[51]

In De Quincey's autobiographical works the act of self-justification moves out to confront the presumed social conventions of a magazine audience. It switches provocatively and tantalisingly, calling for the sympathetic involvement of the reader at one moment, preaching aggressively to that reader at the next.

NOTES

1. Patrick Parrinder, Authors and Authority (London, 1977), p. 101.
2. Albert Goldman, The Mine and the Mint (Carbondale and Edwardsville, 1965), p.1.
3. Thomas De Quincey, Confessions of an English Opium-Eater and Other Writings, Aileen Ward (ed.) (New York, 1966), pp. 26-27.
4. Robert Ready, 'De Quincey's Magnificent Apparatus', in Interspace and the Inward Sphere, Norman Anderson and Margene Weiss (eds.) (Illinois,

1978), p. 48.

5. Roy Park, Hazlitt and the Spirit of the Age (Oxford, 1971), pp. 192-193.

6. Edgar Allan Poe, The Complete Works of Edgar Allan Poe, James A. Harrison (ed.) (New York, 1965), vol. III, p. 275.

7. Thomas De Quincey, The Collected Writings of Thomas De Quincey, David Masson (ed.) (14 vols., Edinburgh, 1889-90), vol. I, pp. 20-21.

8. Thomas De Quincey, Recollections of the Lakes and the Lake Poets, David Wright (ed.) (Harmondsworth, 1970), p. 330.

9. Ward, p. 22.

10. Ready, 'De Quincey's Magnificent Apparatus', pp. 43-44.

11. Lewis E. Gates, Three Studies in Literature (London, 1899), pp. 94-96:

> In its freedom from artificiality and in its perfect sincerity, Newman's style contrasts noticeably with the style of a great rhetorician from whom he nevertheless took many hints - De Quincey. Of his careful study of De Quincey's style there can be no question. In the passage of the Deity, to which reference has just been made, there are unmistakable reminiscences of De Quincey in the iteration of emphasis on an important word, in the frequent use of inversions, in the rise and fall of the periods, and, indeed, in the subtle rhythmic effects throughout. The piece of writing, however, where the likeness to De Quincey and the imitation of his manner and music are most evident is the sermon on the *Fitness of the Glories of Mary*...[in Discourses to Mixed Congregations, ed. 1892, p. 373.]

12. Park, Hazlitt and the Spirit of the Age, p. 10.

13. Michael Allen, Poe and the British Magazine Tradition (New York, 1969), p. 60.

14. Ibid., pp. 22-23.

15. Poe, The Complete Works, vol. II, p. 273.

16. Masson, vol. I, p. 318.

17. Thomas De Quincey, Blackwood's Edinburgh Magazine, (March 1845), pp. 269-270.

18. William Hazlitt, The Complete Works of William Hazlitt, P.P. Howe (ed.) (London, 1932), vol. VI, p. 95.

19. Ibid., vol. VIII, p. 97.

20. Ibid., pp. 97-98.

21. Ibid., vol. XVI, p. 220.

22. John Ruskin, On Modern Painters, The Works of John Ruskin, E.T. Cook and Alexander Wedderburn (eds.), vol. i, vol. III, p. 16.

23. Ibid., p. 20.

24. G.B. Tennyson, Sartor Called Resartus (Princeton, 1965), p. 284.

25. John Holloway, The Victorian Sage (New York, 1965, first published London, 1953), p. 9.

26. Thomas Carlyle, Sartor Resartus, Collected Works, vol. I, Library Edition (London, 1869), p. 2.

27. Holloway, The Victorian Sage, p. 42.

28. Michael Holstein, 'The Anapestic Triad: A Structural Paradigm in De Quincey's Imaginative Prose', Etudes Anglaises, vol. 28 (1975), p. 407.

29. Masson, vol. I, p. 199.

30. Ibid., p. 121.

31. Tennyson, Sartor Called Resartus, p. 256.

32. Carlyle, Sartor Resartus, p. 40.

33. Gerry H. Brooks, The Rhetorical Form of Carlyle's Sartor (Berkeley and Los Angeles and London, 1972), p. 22.

34. Holloway, The Victorian Sage, pp. 23-24:

> It was therefore a powerful weapon for Carlyle, to write in a language which is influenced, through and through by that of the Authorized Version. This revived a whole world of associations that were deeply rooted in his readers' minds.

and Tennyson, Sartor Called Resartus, pp. 257-258:

> Simultaneous with the use of the present tense appears an archaising feature of the style - the extensive use of the second person singular form *thou*. Surely the least justification for the frequent *thou's* and the corresponding archaic verb is the illusion of translation ... More pertinent, I think, is the Biblical association.

35. Masson, vol. I, p. 44.

36. Ibid., p. 43.

37. Ward, p. 71.

38. OED 'representative'; l.c. De Quincey's use of the word points to its use as a metaphysical term, rather than referring us to Representationism.

39. Masson, vol. I, p. 35.

40. Ibid., p. 181.

41. Ibid., p. 378.
42. Ward, p. 56.
43. Ibid., p. 65.
44. *Blackwood's* (June 1845), p. 744.
45. Carlyle, *Sartor Resartus*, p. 76.
46. Masson, vol. I, pp. 38-39.
47. Ruskin, *The Works*, vol. XXXV, p. 493.
48. Ibid.
49. Clinton Machann, 'Ruskin's *Praeterita* and Nineteenth Century Autobiographical Genre', *ELN*, vol. XVI (December 1978), p. 167.
50. John M. Morris, *Versions of the Self* (London/New York, 1966), p. 16.
51. Michael G. Cooke, *Acts of Inclusion* (New Haven and London, 1979), p. xix.

CONCLUSION

To consider De Quincey's autobiographical writings from the point of view of his situation as a journalist, not by exhaustively cataloguing the details of that situation, but by outlining the significant relationships which take place within it, is not to isolate them from the more celebrated works of his era. Such important Romantic concerns as the difficulty of translating experience, belief in literature as revelation, and the claims of spontaneity and process, can be more fully appreciated as a result of considering how the context informs the work. We can see De Quincey share with the poets of the period an interest in art as enactment, seeking a sympathetic involvement of the reader which mirrors the act of imagination. We can see how he also makes moral conclusions from experience despite the parallel and partly conflicting claims of process, spontaneity, and experiential complexity.

More particularly, it is easier, given his act of public commentary, to place De Quincey's work as it develops from the Romantic era to the Victorian era. His work provides an example which makes it easier to see continuity between periods supposedly fostering two different literary movements. It is not the example of a long career, but an example of similar techniques and a similar tactical position. Writers in both areas worked extensively in De Quincey's field of public commentary.

The analogies to be found in De Quincey's own record of writing to publishers and friends, when consolidated by the parallel notion of resistance and power resident in his critical terminology and his definitions of different types of literature, provide a suitable foundation for an analysis of the characteristic method of his autobiographical works. This method is composed of techniques which have arisen from, and now take place in, a particular context. Although it might be thought, initially, that this context is remote from the major issues confronting Romantic poets and essayists, it can be seen to be conducive to a successful handling of some of these issues. In particular, De Quincey's depiction of the high points of experience, his fabrication of 'suspended moments' within the framework of autobiography, can, on occasion, use the periodical context to good effect. Techniques and tactics which have arisen from a magazine setting can be the means of achieving the 'power' or sublime effects traditionally accepted as the most important and most characteristic achievement of Romantic literature.

By understanding the tactical foundation of De Quincey's example we can begin to see how a vision of Romantic unity is achieved by a method of fragmentation, or at least a method of abrupt transition. There is a discontinuity between process and assessment which creates rather than thwarts meaning. In De Quincey's case this characteristic Romantic situation is further complicated by the fact that the vision he has to offer is also frequently one of severance rather than synthesis, despite his being celebrated for the coinages 'involute' and 'subconscious', and his insistence on describing the human mind in terms of memory as a palimpsest. This last analogy is, perhaps, the one which most readily reveals that for De Quincey perceptions of unity are rare events. Most perceptions of experience would seem to capriciously obscure if not deny the existence of that background synthesis. While the technique may shock, startle or surprise because it disregards continuity, it may do so in order to enact the sudden perception of unity.

Autobiography highlights De Quincey's contribution to Romanticism because it provides him with an exercise which does not simply refer to experience, but incorporates a split between the importance of past experience and the present process of public articulation. Articulating past life as an autobiographer is an act where words themselves are offered as the very substance of experience. As a result, De Quincey's autobiographical texts are structured around a gap between evaluation and enactment. Autobiographical forms offered De Quincey an opportunity to contribute to the Romantic debate not by reporting or translating from German literature, or by expressing characteristic preferences in literary criticism, but by giving him the opportunity of creating works which actually realised, at least in part, those ideas and preferences. Simply by adopting a retrospective vision a discrepancy is produced when evaluating experience which mirrors the disequilibrium Robert Langbaum sees as the distinguishing feature of post-Enlightenment poetry when he refers to, 'a poetry founded upon the deliberate disequilibrium of experience and idea'.[1] The revelatory nature of autobiography as practised by De Quincey, though frequently the source of difficulty and contradiction, also offers relativity instead of fixity.

The very nature of autobiography seems to reinforce some of the most important tenets of Romantic and post-Romantic literature. Because autobiography constantly draws attention to itself as an act and refuses to attain conclusiveness, it might seem to refute a basic Romantic belief in individuality. James Olney, in his collection of theoretical and critical essays on the genre, reiterates the widely-held and commonplace view that 'no autobiography as conceived in a traditional, common-sense way can possess wholeness because by definition the end of the story cannot be told, the *bios* must remain incomplete'.[2] This would seem to work against a belief that literature offers a way of knowing that individuality. If individuality is assumed before-hand then literature can only play a subordinate role. If this is not assumed then the relationship between the two is of greater significance. Olney highlights the particularly Romantic nature of the genre when he offers the alternative viewpoint that 'the self is (like autobiography that records and creates it) open-ended and incomplete: it is always in process, more precisely, is itself a process'.[3] In this possibility of not simply recording but creating, the act of autobiography moves to the centre of the Romantic predicament. It suggests the primacy of language in relation to experience, and thereby explains why certain forms of language, notably poetic ones, received such reverence.

This parallelism of autobiography and Romanticism can easily be seen in Georges Gusdorf's forthright statement that 'the original sin of autobiography is first one of logical coherence and rationalism'.[4] He recognises how the Romantic era offers a new version of autobiography (with Rousseau as an example), in which 'complexities, contradictions, and aberrations do not cause hesitation or repugnance, but a kind of wonderment'.[5]

The description of tactics and techniques in De

Quincey's autobiographical works outlined here is not intended to wilfully celebrate such aberrations and discontinuities for their own sake; or to hypothesise on the extent to which disequilibrium within them is a deliberate construction. Indeed, a more continuous reading of De Quincey's work is offered as a result of considering the various strategies which have been described. As we have seen, the autobiographer, in the case of De Quincey's works, is more likely to marvel at complexity rather than contradiction, or when primarily concerned with the latter to refer the reader to his retrospective resolution of the problem. Such straightforward contradiction would rule out the dictatorial aspect of his task which was examined in the final chapter. A more fundamental and important contradiction results from the different aspects of the tactical method: it is to be found in the conjunction of assertive generalisations with counter claims stressing the difficulty of 'translating' experience.

By drawing attention to the difficulty of translating experience, by highlighting the 'resistance' or 'reluctance' offered in the task, the focus of attention can be shifted in order to emphasise the change or difference to be found in the translation. An awareness of the difficulty in this case need not promote mystery: it does not have to emphasise the strange nature of experience that lies behind the literary works. Too frequently De Quincey's place in the Romantic movement has been dictated by the nature of his experience, especially his 'opium experience'. He has been viewed as a man who had significant experiences, rather than as an autobiographer. His autobiographical writings have often been referred to as if they were the raw material or simple evidence of experience.

An analysis of the autobiographical paradigms and fundamental positions of De Quincey's prose as its exists in its magazine setting, not only provides an opportunity for checking the way in which these key Romantic experiences are delivered, but also leads to the conclusion that the autobiographical method is itself Romantic. Not only De Quincey's assumptions about the nature of experience, but his ways of handling it may be described by that term. A reading of De Quincey's autobiographical works which is based on technique can accommodate them to a view of Romanticism interested in contradiction and gaps rather than myth-making. It offers a useful alternative to those views of De Quincey which are primarily interested in apocalypse and vision.

NOTES

1. Robert Langbaum, *The Poetry of Experience* (London, 1957), p. 28.

2. James Olney, 'Autobiography and the Cultural Moment: A Thematic, Historical, and Bibliographical Introduction', in *Autobiography: Essays Theoretical and Critical*, James Olney (ed.) (Princeton, 1980), p. 25.

3. Ibid.

4. Georges Gusdorf, 'Conditions and Limits of Autobiography' in *Autobiography: Essays Theoretical and Critical*, James Olney (ed.) (Princeton, 1980), p. 4.

5. Ibid.

SELECT BIBLIOGRAPHY

BIBLIOGRAPHY

Axon, W.E.A., 'The Canon of De Quincey's Writings with some references to his unidentified articles', _Transactions of the Royal Society of Literature_, XXXII (1912)

Dendurant, H.O., _Thomas De Quincey: A Reference Guide_ (Boston, 1978)

Green, J.A., _Thomas De Quincey: A Bibliography Based Upon the De Quincey Collection in the Moss Side Library_ (Manchester, 1908)

Houtchens, C.W. and Houtchens, L.H., _The English Romantic Poets and Essayists: A Review of Research and Criticism_ (New York, 1966)

DE QUINCEY'S WORKS

Selections Grave and Gay from Writings Published and Unpublished of Thomas De Quincey, Revised and Arranged by Himself (14 vols., Edinburgh, 1853-60)

The Collected Writings of Thomas De Quincey, David Masson (ed.) (14 vols., Edinburgh, 1889-90)

Uncollected Writings of Thomas De Quincey, James Hogg (ed.) (2 vols., London, 1890)

De Quincey Memorials, A.H. Japp (ed.) (2 vols., New York, 1891)

The Posthumous Works of Thomas De Quincey, A.H. Japp (ed.) (2 vols., London, 1893)

Confessions of an English Opium-Eater and Other Writings, Aileen Ward (ed.) (New York, 1966)

New Essays by De Quincey, Stuart M. Tave (ed.) (Princeton, 1966)

Recollections of the Lakes and the Lake Poets, David Wright (ed.) (Harmondsworth, 1970)

Select Bibliography

Tait's Edinburgh Magazine
Blackwood's Edinburgh Magazine

SECONDARY SOURCES

Abrams, Meyer Howard, _The Milk of Paradise_ (Cambridge Mass., 1934)
——— _The Mirror and the Lamp_ (New York, 1953)
Allen, Michael, _Poe and the British Magazine Tradition_ (New York, 1969)
Ball, Patricia, _The Central Self_ (London, 1968)
Bauer, Josephine, 'The London Magazine 1820-29', _Anglistica_ (Copenhagen, 1953)
Bilsland, John W., 'De Quincey on Poetic Genius', _Dalhousie Review_, vol. 48 (1968-69)
——— 'De Quincey's Opium Experience', _Dalhousie Review_, vol. 55 (1975)
Bishop, Jonathan, 'Wordsworth and the Spots of Time', _ELH_, vol. 26 (1959)
Blake, Kathleen, 'The Whispering Gallery and Structural Coherence in De Quincey's Revised _Confessions of an English Opium-Eater_', _Studies in English Literature 1500-1900_, vol. 13 (1973)
Bonner, Willard Hallam, 'De Quincey at Work', _University of Buffalo Studies_, vol. XI, (1936)
Brooks, Gerry H., _The Rhetorical Form of Carlyle's Sartor_ (Berkeley and Los Angeles and London, 1972)
Brown, Calvin S., 'The Musical Structure of De Quincey's _Dream-Fugue_', _Musical Quarterly_ (1938)
Bruss, Elizabeth, _Autobiographical Acts_ (Baltimore and London, 1976)
Burke, Edmund, _The Works of the Right Honourable Edmund Burke_ (London, 1801)
Burwick, Frederick (ed.), _Selected Essays on Rhetoric by Thomas De Quincey_ (Carbondale and Edwardsville, 1967)
——— 'The Dream-Visions of Jean-Paul and Thomas De Quincey', _Comparative Literature_, vol. XX (1968)
Byrns, Richard H., 'An Analytical Study of the Prose Style of Thomas De Quincey', unpublished dissertation, University of Edinburgh, 1955
——— 'De Quincey's Revisions of the _Dream-Fugue_' _PMLA_, vol. 77 (1962)
Carlyle, Thomas, _Sartor Resartus_, _Collected Works_, vol. I, Library Edition (London, 1869)
Carnall, Geoffrey, 'De Quincey on "The Knocking at the Gate"', _Review of English Literature_, vol. II (1960)
Chilcott, Tim, 'De Quincey and The London Magazine',

Charles Lamb Bulletin, vol. 1 (1973)
Clapton, G.T., Baudelaire et De Quincey (Paris, 1931)
Clarke, David F., 'On the Incompleteness of the Confessions of an English Opium-Eater', Wordsworth Circle, vol. 8 (1977)
Coleridge, S.T., Anima Poetae, E.H. Coleridge (ed.) (London, 1895)
——Biographia Literaria, J. Shawcross (ed.) (Oxford, 1967, first published 1907)
——Coleridge's Shakespearean Criticism, Thomas Middleton Raysor (ed.) (London, 1930)
——Table Talk, T. Ashe (ed.) (London, 1909)
Cooke, Michael G., Acts of Inclusion (New Haven and London, 1979)
Cooper, Lane, Prose and Poetry of Thomas De Quincey (Leipzig, 1902)
Davie, Donald, Purity of Diction in English Verse (London, 1952)
——Articulate Energy (London, 1955)
De Luca, Vincent A., 'Satanic Fall and Hebraic Exodus: An Interpretation of De Quincey's "Revolt of the Tartars"', Studies in Romanticism, vol. 8 (1969)
——'"The Type of a Mighty Mind": Mutual Influence in Wordsworth and De Quincey', Texas Studies in Literature and Language, vol. 13 (1971)
——'De Quincey's "Knocking at the Gate in Macbeth": Dream and Prose Art', ELN, vol. 13 (1976)
——'Motifs of Convergence in De Quincey's Imaginative Prose', English Studies in Canada, vol. III (1977)
——Thomas De Quincey: The Prose of Vision (Toronto, 1980)
Dunn, W.A., Thomas De Quincey's Relation to German Literature and Philosophy (Strasbourg, 1900)
Durham, Weldon B., 'The Elements of De Quincey's Rhetoric', Speech Monographs, vol. 37 (1970)
Eaton, Horace A., 'De Quincey's Love of Music', JEGP (1914)
——(ed.), A Diary of Thomas De Quincey (New York, 1927)
——Thomas De Quincey: A Biography (Oxford, 1936)
Elwin, Malcolm, De Quincey (London, 1935)
Findlay, John Ritchie, Personal Recollections of Thomas De Quincey (Edinburgh, 1886)
Gates, Lewis E., Three Studies in Literature (London, 1899)
Goldman, Albert, The Mine and the Mint (Carbondale and Edwardsville, 1965)
Grantham, Evelyn, 'De Quincey to His Publisher', More Books (1945)

Gusdorf, Georges, 'Conditions and Limits of Autobiography' in Autobiography: Essays Theoretical and Critical, James Olney (ed.) (Princeton, 1980)
Haltrecht, Michael, 'The Meaning of De Quincey's "Dream-Fugue on Sudden Death"', Literature and Psychology, vol. 26 (1976)
Hart, Francis R., 'Notes for An Anatomy of Modern Autobiography', New Literary History (1970)
Hartman, Geoffrey, Wordsworth's Poetry 1787-1814 (New Haven and Yale, 1964)
Hawthorn, J.M., 'The Strange Deaths of Sally, Ann, Lucy, and Others', Trivium, vol. 6 (1971)
Hayden, John O., 'De Quincey's Confessions and the Reviewers', Wordsworth Circle, vol. 6 (1975)
Hayter, Alethea, Opium and the Romantic Imagination (London, 1971)
Hazlitt, William, The Complete Works of William Hazlitt, P.P. Howe (ed.) (London, 1932)
Herbert, Christopher, 'De Quincey and Dickens', Victorian Studies, vol. 17 (1974)
Hill, Geoffrey, 'Poetry as Menace and Atonement', University of Leeds Review, vol. 21 (1978)
Hogg, James (ed.), De Quincey and His Friends (Edinburgh, 1895)
Holloway, John, The Victorian Sage (New York, 1965, first published London, 1953)
Holstein, Michael E., '"The Anapestic Triad": a Structural Paradigm in De Quincey's Imaginative Prose', Etudes Anglaises (1975)
Hopkins, Robert, 'De Quincey on War and the Pastoral Design of The English Mail-Coach', Studies in Romanticism, vol. VI (1967)
Howarth, William, 'Some Principles of Autobiography', New Literary History, vol. 5 (1974)
Jack, Ian, 'De Quincey Revises His Confessions, PMLA, vol. 72 (1957)
Japp, A.H., see Page, H.A.
Jordan, John E., 'De Quincey's Dramaturgic Criticism', ELH (1951)
——— Thomas De Quincey, Literary Critic (Berkeley and Los Angeles, 1952)
——— 'De Quincey on Wordsworth's Theory of Diction', PMLA (1953)
——— (ed.), Confessions of an English Opium-Eater (London, 1960)
——— De Quincey to Wordsworth: the Biography of a Relationship (Berkeley and Los Angeles, 1962)
——— De Quincey as Critic (London, 1973)
Kant, Immanuel, Observations on the Feeling of the Beautiful and Sublime, translated by

J.T. Goldthwait (Berkeley and Los Angeles, 1965)
Langbaum, Robert, The Poetry of Experience (London, 1957)
Law, Marie Hamilton, The English Familiar Essay in the Early Nineteenth Century (Philadelphia, 1934)
Leech, Clifford, 'De Quincey as Literary Critic', Review of English Literature, vol. II (1961)
Levin, Susan Michelle, 'The Art of Confession: A Study of Romantic Confessional Writing in France and England', unpublished dissertation, Columbia, 1974
Levine, George, and Madden, William (eds.), The Art of Victorian Prose (London, 1968)
Lindenberger, Herbert, On Wordsworth's Prelude (Princeton, 1963)
Lindop, Grevel, The Opium-Eater: A Life of Thomas De Quincey (London, 1981)
Lyon, Judson S., Thomas De Quincey (New York, 1969)
Machann, Clinton, 'Ruskin's Praeterita and Nineteenth Century Autobiographical Genre', ELN, vol. XVI (1978)
Mallinson, Paul, 'De Quincey's Ann in Judea', Notes and Queries (December 1980)
Maniquis, Robert M., 'Lonely Empires: Personal and Public Visions of Thomas De Quincey' in Literary Monographs, Eric Rothstein and Anthony Wittrech (eds.), vol. 8 (Wisconsin, 1976)
Miller, J. Hillis, The Disappearance of God (London, 1963)
More, E.H., 'Some Unpublished Letters of Thomas De Quincey', RES (1953)
Moreux, F., Thomas De Quincey: La vie - l'homme - l'oeuvre (Paris, 1964)
Morris, John M., Versions of the Self (London/New York, 1966)
McConnell, Frank D., The Confessional Imagination: A Reading of Wordsworth's Prelude (Baltimore and London, 1974)
McGarran, James Holt, 'The "Creative Soul" of The Prelude and the "Sad Incompetence of Human Speech"', Studies in Romanticism (1977)
Oliphant, Mrs, Annals of a Publishing House: William Blackwood and His Sons (Edinburgh and London, 1897)
Olney, James, Metaphors of Self (Princeton, 1972)
——(ed.), Autobiography: Essays Theoretical and Critical (Princeton, 1980)
Owen, W.J.B., 'The Sublime and the Beautiful in The Prelude', Wordsworth Circle, vol. 4 (1973)
Page, H.A. [A.H. Japp], Thomas De Quincey: His Life

and Writings (London, 1897, first published 1877)
Park, Roy, Hazlitt and the Spirit of the Age (Oxford, 1971)
Parrinder, Patrick, Authors and Authority (London, 1977)
Parsons, Coleman O., 'The Woes of Thomas De Quincey', Review of English Studies, vol. X (1934)
Pascal, Roy, Design and Truth in Autobiography (London, 1960)
Poe, Edgar Allan, The Complete Works, James A. Harrison (ed.) (New York, 1965)
Porter, Roger Jeffrey, 'The Double Self: Autobiography and Literary Form in Gibbon, De Quincey Gosse, and Edwin Muir', unpublished dissertation, Yale, 1967
——'The Demon Past: De Quincey and the Autobiographer's Dilemma', Studies in English Literature 1800-1900, vol. XX (1980)
Poulet, Georges, 'Timelessness and Romanticism', Journal of the History of Ideas, vol. XV, no. 1 (1954)
Praz, Mario, The Hero in Eclipse in Victorian Fiction (Oxford, 1956)
Procter, Sigmund K., Thomas De Quincey's Theory of Literature (London, 1943)
Ready, Robert, 'De Quincey's Magnificent Apparatus' in Interspace and the Inward Sphere, Norman Anderson and Margene Weiss (eds.) (Illinois, 1978)
Reed, Arden, 'Abysmal Influence: Baudelaire, Coleridge, De Quincey, Prianesi, Wordsworth', Glyph, vol. 4 (1978)
Robinson, Henry Crabb, On Books and Their Writers, Edith J. Morley (ed.) (London, 1938)
Ruskin, John, The Works of John Ruskin, E.T. Cook and Alexander Wedderburn (eds.) (London, 1908)
Sackville-West, Edward, A Flame in Sunlight (London, 1936)
Salamann, Esther, The Great Confession: from Aksakov and De Quincey to Tolstoy and Proust (London, 1973)
Salt, H.S., 'The Depreciation of De Quincey', National Review, p. 399 (1928)
Schiller, Fredrich, On the Aesthetic Education of Man, E.M. Wilkinson and L.A. Willoughby (eds.) (Oxford, 1967)
Schneider, Elisabeth, Coleridge, Opium and Kubla Khan (Chicago, 1953)
Sheats, Paul P., 'Wordsworth's "Retrogrades" and the Shaping of The Prelude', JEGP, vol. 71

(1972)
Shelley, P.B., _Poetical Works_, Thomas Hutchinson (ed.) (Oxford, 1970)
Shumaker, Wayne, _English Autobiography: Its Emergence, Materials, and Forms_ (Berkeley and Los Angeles, 1954)
Spector, Stephen J., 'Thomas De Quincey: Self-Effacing Autobiographer', _Studies in Romanticism_, vol. 18 (1979)
Spender, Stephen, 'Confessions and Autobiography', in _The Making of a Poem_ (London, 1955)
Spengemann, William C., _The Forms of Autobiography_ (New Haven and London, 1980)
Stapleton, Laurence, _The Elected Circle_ (Princeton, 1973)
Stephen, Leslie, _Hours in a Library_ (London, 1874)
Stonier, G.W., review, _Statesman and Nation_, vol. XXXV, no. 893, p. 316 (1948)
Swinnerton, Frank, 'Thomas De Quincey: Forgotten Highbrow', _Saturday Review_ (17 September 1960)
Symonds, Arthur, 'A Word on De Quincey', in _Studies in Prose and Verse_ (London, 1910)
Tennyson, G.B., _Sartor Called Resartus_ (Princeton, 1965)
TLS, 'Autobiographical Fantasies' (27 March 1948)
——'De Quincey's Retreat' (10 June 1939)
Tredrey, F.D., _The House of Blackwood 1804-1954_ (Edinburgh and London, 1954)
Tulley, Paul M., 'De Quincey on Persuasion, Invention and Style', _Central States Speech Journal_, vol. XVI (1965)
Ward, William S., 'Periodical Literature', in _Some British Romantics_, James V. Logan, John E. Jordan and Northrop Frye (eds.) (Ohio, 1966)
Warren, Leland E., 'A Sudden Vision of De Quincey's "The English Mail-Coach"' _Studies in the Humanities_, vol. 2 (1971)
Wellek, Rene, 'De Quincey's Status in the History of Ideas', _Philological Quarterly_, vol. XXIII, no. III (1944)
Wolfe, Ralph Haven, 'De Quincey, Wordsworth, and Hamlet', _Notes and Queries_ (January 1961)
——'Some Affinities Between De Quincey and Wordsworth', _Ball State University Forum_, vol. VI, no. 3 (1965)
Woolf, Virginia, 'On Being Ill', in _The Moment and Other Essays_ (London, 1947)
——'Impassioned Prose', in _Granite and Rainbow_ (London, 1958)
——'De Quincey's Autobiography', in _The Common Reader_ (London, 1965)

Wordsworth, Jonathan, 'Fructifying Spots of Time', _TLS_, (11 November 1977)

Wordsworth, William, _The Prelude_, Ernest De Selincourt (ed.), revised by Helen Darbishire (London, 1959)

——— _Preface to the Lyrical Ballads_, R.L. Brett and A.R. Jones (eds.) (London, 1963)

——— _The Prose Works of William Wordsworth_, W.J.B. Owen and Jane Worthington Smyser (eds.) (Oxford, 1974)

Wright, Brooks, 'The Cave of Trophonius: Myth and Reality in De Quincey', _Nineteenth-Century Fiction_, vol. 8 (1954)

INDEX